Conversations with James Baldwin

Edited by
Fred L. Standley and Louis H. Pratt

University Press of Mississippi
Jackson and London

Books by James Baldwin

Go Tell It on the Mountain (New York: Knopf, 1953).
Notes of a Native Son (Boston: Beacon, 1955).
Giovanni's Room (New York: Dial, 1956).
Nobody Knows My Name (New York: Dial, 1961).
Another Country (New York: Dial, 1962).
The Fire Next Time (New York: Dial, 1963).
Nothing Personal. With Photographs by Richard Avedon (New York: Atheneum, 1964).
Blues for Mister Charlie (New York: Dial, 1964).
Going to Meet the Man (New York: Dial, 1965).
The Amen Corner (New York: Dial, 1968).
Tell Me How Long the Train's Been Gone (New York: Dial, 1968).
A Rap on Race. With Margaret Mead (Philadelphia: Lippincott, 1971).
One Day When I Was Lost: A Scenario Based on 'The Autobiography of Malcolm X' (New York: Dial, 1972).
No Name in the Street (New York: Dial, 1972).
A Dialogue. With Nikki Giovanni (Philadelphia: Lippincott, 1973).
If Beale Street Could Talk (New York: Dial, 1973).
The Devil Finds Work (New York: Dial, 1976).
Little Man, Little Man: A Story of Childhood. With Yoran Cazac. (New York: Dial, 1976).
Just Above My Head (New York: Dial, 1979).
The Evidence of Things Not Seen (New York: Holt, Rinehart and Winston, 1985).
Jimmy's Blues: Selected Poems (New York: St. Martin's Press, 1985).
The Price of the Ticket: Collected Non-Fiction 1948-1985 (New York: St. Martin's Press, 1985).

Copyright © 1989 by the University Press of Mississippi
All rights reserved
Manufactured in the United States of America
99 98 97 96   6 5 4 3

Library of Congress Cataloging-in-Publication Data

Baldwin, James, 1924-
   Conversations with James Baldwin / edited by Fred L. Standley
and Louis H. Pratt
      p. cm. — (Literary conversations series)
   Includes bibliographical references and index.
   ISBN 0-87805-388-3 (alk. paper). — ISBN 0-87805-389-1 (pbk. :
alk. paper)
   1. Baldwin, James, 1924- —Interviews. 2. Authors,
American—20th century—Interviews. 3. Civil rights workers—United
States—Interviews. 4. Afro-Americans—Civilization. 5. Race
relations. 6. Authorship. I. Standley, Fred L. II. Pratt, Louis
H. III. Title. IV. Series.
PS3552.A45Z464   1989
818.5409—dc19

88-36560
CIP

British Library Cataloguing in Publication data is available.

Conversations with James Baldwin

Literary Conversations Series

Peggy Whitman Prenshaw
General Editor

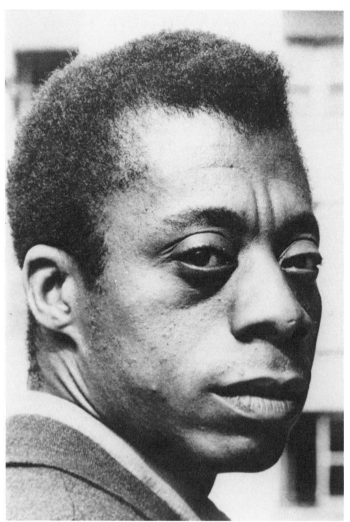

Photograph courtesy of Wide World Photos

Contents

Introduction

James Baldwin died on Monday 1 December 1987 at the age of sixty-three, and by virtue of his accomplishments "this author retains a place in an extremely select group: that comprised of the few genuinely indispensable American writers."[1] For nearly four decades—from November 1948 to his death—Baldwin lived abroad in a mode of self-imposed exile, primarily in France; however, he refused to consider himself an expatriate, retained his United States citizenship, and referred to himself when questioned as "a kind of trans-Atlantic commuter." As he stated so emphatically to Studs Terkel: "I am an American writer. This country is my subject."[2]

While remaining a controversial figure to the end, Baldwin nevertheless sustained a clear perception of his own literary mission and described it variously as being a "witness" ("I am a witness. That's my responsibility. I write it all down.") and "a disturber of the peace" ("Artists are here to disturb the peace. Otherwise chaos"). Sometimes commenting on the work of others and at other times on his own, Baldwin never waivered from the basic conviction that "real writers question their age. They demand yes and no answers. Typers collaborate. You collaborate or you question."[3] To witness, to disturb the peace, and to question meant for him that a writer was constantly having to confront the dilemma "to be immoral and uphold the status quo or to be moral and try to change the world."[4]

During the sixties, seventies, and eighties, Baldwin participated in more than fifty situations having the format of interview, conversation, discussion or dialogue, with the results appearing in print in such

---

[1]Benjamin DeMott, "James Baldwin and the Sixties: Acts and Revelations," *Saturday Review*, 55 (27 May 1972), p. 66.

[2]Interview with Studs Terkel, reprinted in this collection. Hereafter, all quotations in the text without footnotes are from the interviews collected here.

[3]Dan Georgkas, "James Baldwin . . . in Conversation," in Abraham Chapman, ed. (New York: New American Library, 1968), p. 665.

[4]Hoyt Fuller, "Reverberations from a Writer's Conference," *African Forum*, 1, Fall 1965, p. 79.

places as France, England, Italy, Kenya, Puerto Rico, Turkey and the
United States. The twenty-seven pieces selected for this collection
range from 1961 after his fourth book, *Nobody Knows My Name,* to
just prior to his death in a last formal conversation with poet Quincy
Troupe; and the selections included here are drawn from a variety of
sources—newspapers, radio, journals, and reviews. None of the items
have been edited; and, therefore, some overlapping is evident.
However, the collection also demonstrates the latitude and consisten-
cy of the author's concerns over the years.

As a man of letters Baldwin worked prodigiously during his forty-
year career to explore a broad spectrum of topics and themes in his
fiction, drama, essays, and poetry. Among those especially germane
to that vocation were the following: the responsibility of the writer to
promote the evolution of the individual and society; the indivisibility
of the private life and the public life; the essential need to develop
sexual and psychological consciousness and identity; the past historical significance and the current potential explosiveness of color
consciousness and the racial crisis; the need for demythologizing the
prevailing ethos of American history, religion, and culture; and the
intertwining of love and power in the universal scheme of existence as
well as in society's structures.

This volume of "conversations" candidly attests to the diversity of
attitudes, ideas, and opinions held by the author and expressed in
various settings. From the advantage of a centrally focused moral
stance developed on the basis of his status as a black American,
Baldwin's thinking evolved into a vortex of expanding significances
that were increasingly related to the larger context of cultural,
economic, political, and social circumstances. The fascination of that
movement from the personal to the national and the international is
easily discernible in the numerous subjects covered in the interviews:
the critical need for love, the racial climate in America, the influence
of Christianity on blacks and whites, the Watergate affair, American
foreign policy, the exploitation of blacks in South Africa, the political
imprisonment of Angela Davis and Eldridge Cleaver, the Vietnam
War, colonialism, American foreign policy, the Black Muslims, Third
World countries, the images presented in Hollywood, to cite only a
few. To chart the course of his concerns is to see at first hand the
operation of an imagination and mind devoted to the fundamental

tenet of raising questions of a moral nature and offering observations based on the necessity of changing current situations. Alternating between a voice at times stridently angry and hostile and on occasion a voice consolingly compassionate and hopeful, Baldwin remained "an active observer," in the words of *The Black Scholar,* fulfilling his own dictum that "an artist is here not to give you answers but to ask questions" in order to show "that what is happening now is that a new vision of the world is beginning to be born."

Scattered throughout this volume are myriad accounts of and allusions to Baldwin's relations with a host of notable individuals: Martin Luther King, Jr., Robert Kennedy, Richard Wright, Kenneth Clark, Norman Mailer, Malcolm X, Ralph Ellison, Lorraine Hansberry, William Styron, Eldridge Cleaver, Maya Angelou, Chinua Achebe, Toni Morrison, Amiri Baraka, Sidney Poitier, and others. Regretfully, other interviews, also indicating his relations with other figures, especially from the sixties, could not be included. "The Negro in American Culture" (*Cross Currents,* Spring 1961), a discussion held on the occasion of the Civil War Centennial, featured Langston Hughes, Alfred Kazin, Lorraine Hansberry, Emile Copouya, Nat Hentoff and Baldwin, in a joint commentary on the depiction of blacks in literature, white values, and the question of social versus artistic responsibility. "Liberalism and the Negro" (*Commentary,* March 1964) was a roundtable discussion on contemporary issues among Sidney Hook, Norman Podhoretz, Nathan Glazer, Gunnar Myrdal and Baldwin; it focused on the necessity for a radical transformation of society to bring blacks into the mainstream of American life. Baldwin's conversation with Budd Schulberg, entitled "Dialog in Black and White" (*Playboy,* December 1966), considered the problem of how blacks and white liberals might form a coalition to save America by working toward the goals of freedom and justice for all. "How Can We Get the Black People to Cool It" (*Esquire,* July 1968), was recorded in the aftermath of the funeral of Dr. Martin Luther King, Jr. and called for a national policy to transform the labor market, schools, government, and housing into vehicles of opportunities for all citizens.

The purpose, then, for this volume has been the collecting of those interviews and conversations which contribute substantially to an understanding and clarification of James Baldwin's personality and perspective, his interests and achievements. The collection also represents a kind of companion piece to the earlier dialogues, *A Rap on Race* with Margaret Mead and *A Dialogue* with Nikki Giovanni. Therefore, we think that those with an interest in Baldwin will find this volume useful in examining and reexamining the life and legacy of an American author who affirmed unequivocally in 1986 to David Estes that "every writer has only one tale to tell, and he has to find a way of telling it until the meaning becomes clearer and clearer, until the story becomes at once more narrow and larger, more and more precise and more and more reverberating."

FLS
LHP
November 1988

Chronology

1924	James Arthur Baldwin born on 2 August in New York City
1927	Marriage of mother to minister David Baldwin, who becomes stepfather
1936-38	Influenced by Countee Cullen, advisor to the literary club at Frederick Douglass Junior High School. Receives letter of congratulations from Mayor La Guardia for a poem.
1938	Begins to preach at the Fireside Pentecostal Assembly
1938-42	Attends DeWitt Clinton High School; edits the school literary magazine
1942	Graduates from high school and renounces ministry
1943	David Baldwin dies on 29 July.
1944	Introduced to Richard Wright by a mutual friend. Begins to write a novel, *In My Father's House.*
1945	Awarded a Eugene Saxton Fellowship on the recommendation of Richard Wright
1947	Beginning of career as writer with publication of "Maxim Gorky as Artist," a review in *The Nation*
1948	Receives a Rosenwald Fellowship. Publication of first essay, "The Harlem Ghetto: Winter, 1948," and short story, "Previous Condition," in *Commentary.* Leaves for Paris on 11 November.
1949	"Everybody's Protest Novel" published; Richard Wright alienated by essay

1953   Publication of *Go Tell It on the Mountain,* his first novel
        which was nominated for the National Book Award

1954   Appearance of his first drama, *The Amen Corner.*
        Receives a Guggenheim Fellowship

1955   Publication of *Notes of a Native Son.* Baldwin praised as
        essayist by Langston Hughes. *The Amen Corner* per-
        formed at Howard University.

1956   *Giovanni's Room* published. Receives Partisan Review
        Fellowship and a National Institute of Arts and Letters
        Grant. Establishes friendship with Norman Mailer.

1957   Returns to the United States to visit the South for the first
        time; records his impressions in *Harper's* and *Partisan
        Review.*

1959   Selected for Ford Foundation Grant; returns to Paris

1960   Beginning of friendship with William Styron

1960s   Active in the civil rights movement in the South

1961   Publication of *Nobody Knows My Name,* a collection of
        essays chosen as one of the outstanding books of the year
        by the Notable Books Council of the American Library
        Association

1962   *Another Country* published. Baldwin selected for Broth-
        erhood Award by the National Conference of Christians
        and Jews. Travels to Africa

1963   Publication of best-seller, *The Fire Next Time.* Baldwin
        selected for the George Polk Memorial Award for out-
        standing magazine reporting

1964   *Blues for Mister Charlie* and *Nothing Personal* (with
        photographs by Richard Avedon) published. *Blues* opens
        at the ANTA Theater on 23 April under direction of
        Burgess Meredith. Receives the Foreign Drama Critics
        Award, and an honorary Doctor of Letters from the

University of British Columbia. Elected to the National
Institute of Arts and Letters.

1965   Publication of *Going to Meet the Man*. *The Amen Corner*
        opens on Broadway at the Ethel Barrymore Theater on 5
        April. Debates William F. Buckley, Jr. before 1200 stu-
        dents at Cambridge University

1968   *The Amen Corner* and *Tell Me How Long the Train's
        Been Gone* published

1971   Publication of *A Rap on Race* (with Margaret Mead)

1972   *No Name in the Street* and *One Day, When I was Lost: A
        Scenario Based on 'The Autobiography of Malcolm X'*
        published

1973   *A Dialogue* (with Nikki Giovanni) published

1974   Publication of *If Beale Street Could Talk,* chosen for the
        Best Young Adult Book List by the American Library
        Association

1976   *The Devil Finds Work* and *Little Man, Little Man: A Story
        of Childhood* (with Yoran Cazac) published. Baldwin
        receives honorary doctor of letters from Morehouse
        College.

1979   Publication of *Just Above My Head,* his last novel

1982   Awarded honorary degree by City University of New York

1985   Publication of *The Evidence of Things Unseen,* based on
        child murders in Atlanta; *Collected Nonfiction, 1948-
        1985;* and *Jimmy's Blues: Selected Poems.* Television
        adaptation of *Go Tell It on the Mountain* presented on
        Public Broadcasting System in January.

1986   Receives citation as Commander of the French Legion of
        Honor from President François Mitterand

1987   Death at age 63 on 1 December in St. Paul de Vence,
        southern France. Eulogized at funeral service on 8
        December at the Cathedral of St. John the Divine in New
        York by Toni Morrison, Maya Angelou, and Amiri Baraka.

Conversations with James Baldwin

An Interview with James Baldwin
Studs Terkel/1961

This interview was taped in the WFMT studios in Chicago on 15 July 1961, and it was broadcast by the station on the Studs Terkel program "Almanac" on 29 December 1961. This transcript was prepared by permission.

When it thunders and lightning and the wind begins to blow,
When it thunders and lightning and the wind begins to blow,
There's thousands of people
They ain't got no place to go.

My house fell down
And I can't live there no more.

Bessie Smith: *Back Water Blues* (1927)

Interviewer: Sitting with me hearing Bessie Smith singing of disaster, a flood, is James Baldwin, the young American novelist. But perhaps a more specific description of Mr. Baldwin, since he is one of the rare men in the world who seems to know who he is today, would be: James Baldwin, brilliant young Negro American writer. As you listen to this record of Bessie Smith, Jim, what is your feeling?

Baldwin: It is very hard to describe that feeling. The first time I heard this record was in Europe, and under very different circumstances than I had ever listened to Bessie in New York. What struck me was the fact that she was singing, as you say, about a disaster, which had almost killed her, and she accepted it and was going beyond it. The *fantastic* understatement in it. It is the way I want to write, you know. When she says, "My house fell down, and I can't live there no mo' "—it is a great . . . a great sentence. A great achievement.

Interviewer: I'm looking at a passage in your new book, a remarkable one, *Nobody Knows My Name,* a series of essays, articles, opinions. You say here that when you went to live in the mountains of Switzerland you arrived armed with two Bessie Smith records and a typewriter:

3

"I began to try to re-create the life I had first known as a child and from which I had spent so many years in flight," you wrote. "It was Bessie Smith, through her tone and her cadence, who helped me to dig back to the way I myself must have spoken when I was a pickaninny, and to remember the things I had heard and seen and felt. I had buried them very deep." Now, here's the part, Jim: "I had never listened to Bessie Smith in America (in the same way that, for years, I never touched watermelon), but in Europe she helped me to reconcile myself to being a "nigger.' "

Baldwin: Well, that winter in Switzerland, I was working on my first novel—I thought I would never be able to finish it—and I finally realized that one of the reasons that I couldn't finish this novel was that I was ashamed of where I came from and where I had been. I was ashamed of the life in the Negro church, ashamed of my father, ashamed of the Blues, ashamed of Jazz, and, of course, ashamed of watermelon: all of these stereotypes that the country inflicts on Negroes, that we all eat watermelon or we all do nothing but sing the Blues. Well, I was afraid of all that; and I ran from it.

When I say I was trying to *dig back* to the way I myself must have spoken when I was little, I realized that I had acquired so many affectations, had told myself so many lies, that I really had buried myself beneath a whole fantastic image of myself which wasn't mine, but white people's image of me.

I realized that I had not always talked—obviously I hadn't always talked—the way I had forced myself to learn how to talk. I had to find out what I had been like in the beginning, in order, just technically as a writer, to re-create Negro speech. I realized it was a cadence; it was not a question of dropping s's or n's or g's, but a question of the *beat*. Bessie had the beat. In that icy wilderness, as far removed from Harlem as anything you can imagine, with Bessie Smith and me. . . . I began. . . .

Interviewer: And white snow. . . .

Baldwin: And *white* snow, white mountains, and white faces. Those Swiss people really thought I had been sent by the devil; it was a very strange . . . they had never seen a Negro before. In this isolation I managed to finish the book. And I played Bessie every day. A lot of the book is in dialogue, you know, and I corrected things according to what I was able to hear when Bessie sang, and when James P. Johnson plays. It's that *tone*, that sound, which is in me.

Interviewer: This "tone" is in your forthcoming novel?

Baldwin: Yes, yes, in a forthcoming novel.

Interviewer: Did you feel a sense of shame about a heritage that is really so *rich*, when you accepted the white man's stereotype of yourself?

Baldwin: I'm afraid that is one of the great dilemmas, one of the *great* psychological hazards, of being an American Negro. In fact, it is much more than that. I've seen a great many people go under because of this dilemma. Every Negro in America is in one way or another menaced by it. One is born in a white country, a white Protestant Puritan country, where one was once a slave, where all the standards and all the images . . . when you open your eyes on the world, everything you see: none of it applies to you.

You go to white movies and, like everybody else, you fall in love with Joan Crawford, and you root for the Good Guys who are killing off the Indians. It comes as a great psychological collision when you realize all of these things are really metaphors for your oppression, and will lead into a kind of psychological warfare in which you may perish. I was born in the church, for example, and my father was a very rigid, righteous man. But we were in Harlem—you lived, you know, in a terrible house. Downstairs from us there were what my father called "good-time" people: a prostitute and all of her paramours, and all that jazz. I remember I loved this woman; she was very nice to us; but we were not allowed to go to her house, and if we went there, we were beaten for it.

When I was older, that whole odor of home-made gin, pigs' feet, chitlin', and poverty, and the basement: all this got terribly mixed together in my mind with the Holy Roller, White God business. I really began to go a little out of my mind. Obviously I wasn't white— it wasn't so much a question of wanting to be white—but I didn't quite know anymore what being *black* meant. I couldn't accept what I had been told.

All you are ever told in this country about being black is that it is a terrible, terrible thing to be. Now, in order to survive this, you have to really dig down into yourself and re-create yourself, really, according to no image which yet exists in America. You have to impose, in fact—this may sound very strange—you have to *decide* who you are, and force the world to deal with you, not with its *idea* of you.

Interviewer: You have to decide who you are—whether you are black or white—who you are. . . .

Baldwin: Yes, who you are. Then the pressure of being black or white is robbed of its power. You can, of course, still be beaten up on the South Side by anybody; I mean, the social menace does not lessen. The world perhaps can destroy you physically. The danger of your destroying yourself does not vanish, but it *is* minimized.

Interviewer: The name of your book—this is directly connected—*Nobody Knows My Name.* For years you have been known as James but never as James Baldwin—"Home, James"; sometimes called George; in the old days, Sam; sometimes, Boy.

Baldwin: Sometimes. . . .

Interviewer: *Nobody Knows My Name.* Why did you choose that title?

Baldwin: Well, at the risk of sounding pontifical—I suppose it is a fairly bitter title—it is meant as a kind of warning to my country. In the days when people . . . well, in the days when people called me Boy. . . . Those days haven't passed except that I didn't answer then and I don't answer now. To be a Negro in this country is really—Ralph Ellison has said it very well—never to be *looked at*. What white people see when they look at you is not visible. What they *do* see when they *do* look at you is what they have invested you with. What they have invested you with is all the agony, and pain, and the danger, and the passion, and the torment—you know, sin, death, and hell—of which everyone in this country is terrified.

As a Negro, you represent a level of experience which Americans deny. This may sound mystical, but I think it is proven in great relief in the South. Consider the extraordinary price, the absolutely prohibitive price, the South has paid to keep the Negro in his place; and it has not succeeded in doing that, but has succeeded in having what is almost certainly the most bewildered, demoralized white population in the Western world.

On another level, you can see in the life of the country, not only in the South, what a terrible price the country has paid for this effort to keep a distance between themselves and black people. In the same way, for example, it is very difficult—it is hazardous, psychologically personally hazardous—for a Negro in the country really to hate white people. He is too involved with them: not only socially but historically.

No matter who says what, in fact, Negroes and whites in this country are related to each other. Half of the black families in the South are related, you know, to the judges and the lawyers and the white families of the South. They are cousins, and kissing cousins at that—at least kissing cousins. Now, this is a terrible depth of involvement.

It is easy for an African to hate the invader and drive him out of Africa, but it is very difficult for an American Negro to do this. He obviously can't do this to white people; there's no place to drive them. This is a country that belongs equally to us both. One has got to live together here or else there won't be any country.

Interviewer: This matter of living together, this ambivalent attitude that the South has towards the Negro perhaps is most eloquently, perhaps tragically, expressed in the life, the sayings, of William Faulkner. His remarkable story *Dry September* seems to analyze the malaise, but, at the same time, he himself makes comments that are shocking. You have a chapter in your book dealing with Faulkner and desegregation. Is it this ambivalence, too?

Baldwin: It's his Love-Hatred . . . Love-Hatred. I hate to think of what the spiritual state of the South would be if all the Negroes moved out of it. The white people there don't want them . . . they want them in their place. But they would be terrified if the Negroes left. I really think the bottom of their world would have fallen out.

Faulkner in *Dry September*—or *Light in August,* or even in *The Sound and the Fury*—can really get at (as you put it, "to the bone") the truth of what the black-white relationship is in the South, and how what a dark force it is in the Southern personality. At the same time, Faulkner, as a man, as a citizen of Mississippi, is committed to what in Mississippi seems to be their past. It is one thing for Faulkner to deal with the Negro in his imagination, where he can control him; and quite another thing to deal with him in life, where he can't control him. In life, obviously the Negro, the uncontrollable Negro, simply is determined to overthrow everything in which Faulkner imagines himself to believe. It is one thing to demand justice in literature, and another thing to face the price that one has got to pay for it in life.

No matter how Southerners, and whites in the rest of the nation, too, deny it, or what kind of rationalizations they cover it up with, they know the crimes they have committed against black people. And they are terrified that these crimes will be committed against them.

Interviewer: The amount of guilt here is a point you make very beautifully somewhere in *Nobody Knows My Name.* In the South, the white man is continuously bringing up the matter of the Negro; in the North, *never.* So obsessed in one case, so ignored in the other.

Baldwin: It's very funny. It is very funny especially because the results have gotten to be, in the case of the Negro's lot in the world, so very much the same in both South and North. It must be absolute torment to be a Southerner, when you imagine that these people . . . even Faulkner himself was raised by a black woman (probably a model for Dilsey in *The Sound and the Fury*) . . . and one fine day, the child of three or four or five, who has been involved with black people on the most intense level, and at the most important time in anybody's life, suddenly it breaks on him like a thundercloud that it is all taboo.

And since we know that nobody ever recovers, really, from his earliest impressions, the torment that goes on in a Southerner, who is absolutely forbidden, you know, to excavate his beginnings: it seems to me this is a key to those terrifying mobs. It isn't hatred that drives those people in the streets. It is pure terror.

Interviewer: And perhaps a bit of schizophrenia here, too?

Baldwin: Yes, of course, schizophrenia. And not only in the South. But the South is a very useful example, on a personal and social level, of what is occurring really in the country. And the sexual paranoia. It is very important to remember what it means to be born in a Protestant Puritan country, with all the taboos placed on the flesh, and have at the same time in this country such a vivid example of a decent pagan imagination and the sexual liberty with which white people invest Negroes—and then penalize them for.

Interviewer: The very nature of the American heritage: the combination of Puritanism and Paganism. The conflict.

Baldwin: The terrible tension.

Interviewer: The terrible tension that comes as a result.

Baldwin: It's a guilt about flesh. In this country the Negro pays for that guilt which white people have about the flesh.

Interviewer: Since you bring up this point, I think, too, of the position of Negro women and the Negro man. In the beautiful article you wrote for *Tone* magazine, you were saying something about the white mistress of the house, who admires her maid very much, but speaks of the no-account husband. What does it mean to be a Negro male?

Baldwin: The old, old phrase: "Negroes are the last to be hired and the first to be fired." This doesn't apply to the Negro maid particularly, though it can. It actually applies, without exception, and with great rigor, to Negro men. One has got to consider, especially when you talk about this whole tension between violence and non-violence, the dilemma and the rage and the anguish of a Negro man, who, in the first place, is forced to accept all kinds of humiliation in his working day, whose power in the world is so slight he can not really protect his home, his wife, his children, when he finds himself out of work. And then he watches his children growing up, menaced in exactly the same way he has been menaced.

When a Negro child is fourteen, he knows the score already. There is nothing you can do. And all you can do about it is try . . . is pray *really* that this will not destroy him. But the tension this creates within the best of the Negro men is absolutely unimaginable, and something this country refuses to imagine, and very, very dangerous.

It complicates the sexuality of the country, and of the Negro, in a hideous way, because all Negroes are raised in a kind of matriarchy, since, after all, the wife can go out and wash the white ladies' clothes and steal from the kitchen. And this is the way we have all grown up. This creates another social and psychological problem, in what we like to refer to as a sub-culture, which is part of a bill the country is going to have to pay. Bills always do come in.

Interviewer: A phrase Sandburg used: "Slums always seek their revenge."

Baldwin: Yes, they do, indeed.

Interviewer: Thinking about the matriarchal set-up of the Negro family and Negro life—even back in slave days the underground railway leaders were women, like Harriet Tubman.

Baldwin: Yeah. It is a terrible thing: Negro women for generations have raised white children, who sometimes lynched *their* children, and they have tried to raise their own child, like a man; and yet in the full knowledge that if he really walks around like a man he is going to be cut down. A terrible kind of dilemma. A terrible price to ask anybody to pay. In this country, Negro women have been paying it for 300 years; and for 100 of those years when they were legally and technically free. When people talk about *time*, therefore, I can't help but be absolutely not only impatient but bewildered. *Why* should I wait any longer? In any case, even if I were willing to—which I am not—*how*?

Interviewer: You mean the point about "Go slow."

Baldwin: "Go slow," yes.

Interviewer: The final sentences in your essay on Faulkner: "There is never time in the future in which we will work out our salvation. The challenge is in the moment, the time is always now."

Baldwin: Now.

Interviewer: The world we are living in . . . we have to make it over. We made the world we live in. You speak of *now*. It is always *now*.

Baldwin: Time is always now. Everybody who has *ever* thought about his own life knows this. You don't make resolutions about something you are going to do next year. No! You decide to write a book: the book may be finished twenty years from now, but you've got to start it now.

Interviewer: I'm thinking of the sub-title of your book—and of the position of the Negro woman and Negro man—*More Notes of a Native Son*. Naturally, I immediately think of Richard Wright, who has meant so much to you as an artist and a man. . . .

Baldwin: Yes.

Interviewer: . . . his short story, which you refer to beautifully here in the chapter "Alas, Poor Richard," the story *Man of All Work,* in which the husband, in order to get a job, dresses himself up in his wife's clothes and hires out as a cook.

Baldwin: A beautiful, terrifying story. It really gets something which has been hidden for all these generations, which is the ways in which . . . it really suggests, more forceably than anything I've ever read, the humiliation the Negro male endures. And it is this that our country doesn't want to know. And, therefore, when people talk about the Noble Savage, and the greater sexuality of Negroes, and all that *jazz* . . . I could name six men with whom I grew up, who are on the needle just because there is really no . . . the demoralization is so complete. In order to make the act of love, there has got to be a certain confidence, a certain trust. Otherwise it degenerates into nothing but desperate and futureless brutality.

Interviewer: You've mentioned the needle; and we think of course of junkies and narcotics. For some, perhaps, it is the only means of escape from the brutal reality.

Baldwin: Yes, that's right. I knew a boy very well once who told me, in almost just that many words, that he wasn't trying to get "high," he was just trying to hold himself together. He talked about himself walking through one of our cities one morning, and the way people looked at him, and he said to himself, he told me, "You ought to be able to bear me if I can bear you." What is most important about it is that all these things might not be so terrible if, when facing well-meaning white people, one didn't realize that they don't know anything about this at all. They don't want to know.

Somehow this is really the last drop in a very bitter cup. If they don't know and don't want to know, then, what hope is there? People talk to me about the strides that have been made—and all these dreary movies Hollywood keeps showing about "Be kind to Negroes today" and "Isn't this a good sign?" Well, of course, they've never seen these movies with a Negro audience watching them.

Interviewer: What is the reaction?

Baldwin: Well, for example, in *The Defiant Ones*, a movie which I. . . . I really cannot say.

Interviewer: That's O.K. Go ahead. Please do.

Baldwin: At the end of that movie, when Sidney [Poitier] . . . and he was very brilliant in that movie; he does his best with a rather dreary role; he does something with it which I wouldn't believe could have been done. Anyway, at the end of that movie when Sidney jumps off the train to rescue Tony Curtis. . . . I saw it twice, deliberately, in New York. I saw it Downtown with a white liberal audience. There was a great sigh of relief and clapping: they felt that this was a very noble gesture on the part of a very noble black man. And I suppose, in a way, it was.

Then I saw it Uptown. When Sidney jumped off the train, there was a tremendous roar of *fury* from the audience, with which, I must say, I agreed. They told Sidney to "Get back on the train, you fool." In any case, why in the world should he go back to the chain gang, when they were obviously going to be separated again: it's still a Jim Crow chain gang.

What's the movie supposed to prove? What the movie is designed to prove, really, to white people, is that Negroes are going to forgive them for their crimes, and that somehow they are going to escape scot-free. Now, I am not being vengeful at all when I say this . . . because I'd hate to see the nightmare begin all over again, with shoes on the other foot. But I'm talking about a human fact. The human fact is this: that one cannot escape anything one has done. One has got to pay for it. You either pay for it willingly or pay for it unwillingly.

Interviewer: That Negro audience shouting, "Get back on the train, you fool" . . . we think of two movements happening simultaneously with the Negro in America today: the Black Muslim movement and Martin Luther King. Isn't there a direct connection here, Jim?

Baldwin: Yes, yes, precisely. And I must admit that there is a great ambivalence in myself. For example, I'm devoted to King and I worked with CORE and tried to raise money for the Freedom Riders. I adore those children. I have a tremendous respect for them. Yet, at the same time, in talking to very different people, somewhat older, and also talking to ex-sit-in students who said, "No, I simply can't take it anymore . . .": I don't know.

Let me put it in another way: King's influence in the South is tremendous, but his influence in the North is slight, and the North doesn't talk about the South. Chicagoans talk about Mississippi as though they had no South Side. White people in New York talk about Alabama as though they had no Harlem. To ignore what is happening in their own back yard is a great device on the part of the white people. Whether I were for or against violence is absolutely irrelevant. The question that really obsesses me today is not whether or not I like violence, or whether or not you like it—unless the situation is ameliorated, and very, very quickly, there *will* be violence. There will be violence (and of this I am as convinced as I am that I am sitting in this chair) one day in Birmingham. And it won't be the fault of the Negroes in Birmingham. It is the fault of the administration of Birmingham, and the apathy of Washington. An intolerable situation. It has been intolerable for 100 years.

I can't . . . I really cannot tell my nephew or my brother—my nephew is fourteen, my brother is a grown man—I can't tell my nephew that if someone hits him he shouldn't hit back. I really cannot tell him that. And I can still less tell my brother that, if someone comes to his house with a gun, he should let him in, and allow him to do what he wants with his children and his wife. But the point is: even if I were able to tell my brother he should, there is absolutely no guarantee that my brother will, and I can't blame him.

It is too easy, in another way, for the country to sit in admiration before the sit-in students, because it doesn't cost them anything. They have no idea what it costs those kids to go through that picketed building, for example, where people upstairs are spitting down on your head or trying to vomit down on you. This is a tremendous amount to demand of people who are technically free, in a free country, which is supposed to be the leader of the West.

It seems to me a great cowardice on the part of the public to expect that it is going to be saved by a handful of children, for whom they refuse to be responsible.

Interviewer: It's so much more easy, say, for a Black Muslim speaker to win followers than a Martin Luther King. . . .

Baldwin: It is always much easier, obviously, to—how can I put this?—to . . . well, in Harlem, those Black Muslim meetings every Saturday night, and people there listening to those speeches, and all kinds of other speeches, because they *are* in despair. They don't believe—and this is the most dangerous thing that has happened—they don't believe . . . they've been betrayed so often and by so many people, not all of them white, that they don't believe the country really means what it says, and there is nothing in the record to indicate that the country means what it says.

Now, when they are told that they are better than white people, it is a perfectly inevitable development. Through all of these hundreds of years, white people going around saying they are better than anybody else, sooner or later they were bound to create a counterweight (especially with Africa on the stage of the world now): which is simply to take the whole legend of Western history—and its entire theology, changing one or two pronouns, and transferring it

from Jerusalem to Islam, just this small change—and turn it all
against the white world. The white world can't do anything about
this, can't call down the Muslim leaders, or anybody else on this, until
they are willing to face their own history.

Interviewer: How does all this, then, connect with being a Negro
artist? Coming back to a man who meant so much to you, Richard
Wright: he escaped. He spoke of Paris as a refuge. You looked upon
it as a sort of way-station.

Baldwin: In the beginning, I must admit, I looked on Paris as a
refuge, too. I never intended to come back to this country. I lived
there so long, I got to know a great deal about Paris.

Several things happened to me: one of them was watching
American Negroes there, who, so to speak, dragged Mississippi
across the ocean with them and were operating now in a vacuum. I
myself carried all my social habits to Paris with me, where they were
not needed. It took me a long time to learn how to do without them.
And this complex frightened me very much.

But more important than that, perhaps, was the relationship
between American Negroes and Africans and Algerians in Paris, who
belonged to France. It didn't demand any spectacular degree of
perception to realize that I was treated, insofar as I was noticed at all,
differently from them because I had an American passport. I may not
have liked this fact: but it was a fact. And I could see very well that if I
were an Algerian, I would not have been living in the same city in
which I imagined myself to be living as Jimmy Baldwin; or if I were
an African, it would have been a very different city to me.

And also I began to see that the West—the entire West—is
changing, is breaking up; and that its power over *me*, and over
Africans, was gone. And would never come again. So then it seemed
that exile was another way of being in Limbo.

I suppose finally the most important thing was that I am a writer.
That sounds grandiloquent, but the truth is that I don't think that,
seriously speaking, anybody in his right mind would want to be a
writer. But you do discover that you are a writer and then you
haven't got any choice. You live that life or you won't live any. And I
am an American writer. This country is my subject. And in working
out my forthcoming novel, I began to realize that the New York I was
trying to describe was the New York which, by this time, was nearly

twenty years old. I had to come back to check my impressions, and, as it turned out, to be stung again, to look at it again, bear it again, and to be reconciled to it again.

Now, I imagine, I will have to spend the rest of my life as a kind of trans-Atlantic commuter. At some point when I'm in this country, I always get to the place where I realize that I don't see it very clearly, because it is very exhausting—after all, you do spend 24 hours a day resisting and resenting it, trying to keep a kind of equilibrium in it—so that I suppose I'll keep going away and coming back.

Interviewer: You feel your years in Europe afforded you more of a perspective?

Baldwin: I began to see this country for the first time. If I hadn't gone away, I would never have been able to see it; and if I was unable to see it, I would never have been able to forgive it.

I'm not mad at this country anymore: I am very worried about it. I'm not worried about the Negroes in the country even, so much as I am about the country. The country doesn't know what it has done to Negroes. And the country has no notion whatever—and this is disastrous—of what it has done to itself. North and South have yet to assess the price they pay for keeping the Negro in his place; and, to my point of view, it shows in every single level of our lives, from the most public to the most private.

Interviewer: Can we expand a bit on this, Jim—what the country has done to itself?

Baldwin: One of the reasons, for example, I think that our youth is so badly educated—and it is inconceivably badly educated—is because education demands a certain daring, a certain independence of mind. You have to teach some people to think; and in order to teach some people to think, you have to teach them to think about everything. There mustn't be something they can not think about. If there is one thing they can not think about, very shortly they can't think about anything.

Now, there is always something in this country, of course, one can not think about—the Negro. This may seem like a very subtle argument, but I don't think so. Time will prove the connection between the level of the lives we lead and the extraordinary endeavor to avoid black men. It shows in our public life.

When I was living in Europe, it occurred to me that what

Americans in Europe did not know about Europeans is precisely what they did not know about me; and what Americans today don't know about the rest of the world, like Cuba or Africa, is what they don't know about me. The incoherent, totally incoherent, foreign policy of this country is a reflection of the incoherence of the private lives here.

Interviewer: So we don't even know our own names?

Baldwin: No, we don't. This is the whole point. And I suggest this: that in order to learn your name, you are going to have to learn mine. In a way, the American Negro is *the* key figure in this country; and if you don't face him, you will never face anything.

Interviewer: If I don't know your name, I, a white man, will never know mine. I'm thinking of Africa, and of how you have come home again by returning to your work here. Even though I have said that *Nobody Knows My Name* is a collection of essays, it isn't that; it is a novel; it is an autobiography, in a way. In it you wrote a journalistic report, very accurate and astute, "Princes and Powers." You were covering a meeting of Negro writers of the world. African writers, too, were speaking. . . .

Baldwin: It was really an African conference. Predominantly African. The Negroes were there as Africans, or, well, as the black people of the world, let's put it that way.

Interviewer: What of the African writer? Isn't there a problem here: the uncovering of this rich heritage, so long buried by kidnappers and colonial people, while at the same time technological advances are taking place, slums are being cleared.

Baldwin: The 20th century, in fact.

Interviewer: Yes. Isn't there loss as well as gain here? It is a question of things happening at the same time.

Baldwin: It is a very great question. It is almost impossible to assess what was lost, which makes it impossible to assess what is gained. How can I put this? In a way, I almost envy African writers because there is so much to excavate, and because their relationship to the world—at least from my vantage point, I may be wrong—seems much more *direct* than mine can ever be. But, God knows, the colonial experience destroyed so much, blasted so much, and, of course, changed forever the African personality. One doesn't know what there really was on the other side of the Flood. It will take generations before that past can be reestablished and, in fact, used.

At the same time, of course, all of the African nations are under the obligation, the necessity, of moving into the 20th century, and really, sometimes, at a fantastic rate of speed. This is the only way they can survive. And, of course, all Africans, whether they know it or not, have endured the European experience, and have been stained and changed by the European standards; and in a curious way the unification of Africans, as far as it can be said to exist, is a white invention.

The only thing that really unites all black men everywhere is, as far as I can tell, the fact that white men are on their necks. What I'm curious about is what will happen when this is no longer true. For the first time in the memory of anybody living, black men have their destinies in their own hands. What will come out then, what the problems and tensions and terrors will be then, is a very great, a very loaded question.

I think that if we were more honest here, we could do a great deal to aid in this transition, because we have an advantage, which we seem to consider to be a disadvantage, over all the other Western nations. We have created—no other nation has—a black man who belongs, who is a part of the West. In distinction to Belgium or any other European power, we had our slaves on the mainland. No matter how we deny it, we couldn't avoid a human involvement with them, which we have almost perished in denying, but which is nevertheless there.

Now, if we could turn about and face this, we would have a tremendous advantage in the world today. As long as we don't, there isn't much hope for the West. How can I put this? If one could accept the fact that it is no longer important to be white, it would begin to cease to be important to be black. If we could accept the fact that no nation with 20 million black people in it for so long and with such a depth of involvement, that no nation under these circumstances can be called a white nation, this would be a great achievement, and it would change a great many things.

Interviewer: Assuming that sanity . . . assuming that humanity itself, the humanity in all of us, will triumph, there will be, as you say, no white nation and no black nation but nations of people. Now we come to the question of this long-buried Negro heritage. At the beginning of this interview, a Bessie Smith record was played. Once upon a time, you were ashamed of it. Now you realize that there is a great pride here—and artistry. Thinking now of the young African: if a certain identity, imposed from the outside, is lost, will he reject that which was uniquely his in the beginning for a greyness, even though it be more materially advanced?

Baldwin: I have a tendency to doubt it; but, of course, there is no way of knowing. Judging only from my very limited experience in Paris with a few Africans, my tendency is to doubt it. I think the real impulse is to excavate that heritage at no matter what cost, and bring it into the present. This is a very sound idea. It is needed. In all the things that were destroyed by Europe, which will never really be put in place again, still, in that rubble, there is something of very, very great value, not only for Africans, but for all of us.

We are living at a moment like that moment when Constantine became a Christian. All of the standards for which the Western world has lived so long are in the process of break-down and revision; and a kind of passion, and beauty, and joy, which was in the world before and has been buried so long, has got to come back.

Interviewer: Now we come to the matter of dehumanization, don't we: the impersonality of our time?

Baldwin: Yes, yes. Obviously this cannot—I would hate to see it—continue. I don't ever intend to make my peace with such a world; there is so much that's more important than Cadillacs, Frigidaires, and IBM machines. No. And precisely one of the things wrong with this country is this notion that IBM machines and Cadillacs *prove* something.

People always tell me how many Negroes bought Cadillacs last year. This *terrifies* me. I always wonder: Do you think this is what the country is for? Do you really think this is why I came here, this is why I suffered, this is what I would die for? A lousy Cadillac?

Interviewer: That holds for white or black, doesn't it?

Baldwin: For white or black, yes, exactly. I think the country has to find out what it means by freedom. Freedom is a very dangerous thing. Anything else is disastrous. But freedom is dangerous. You've got to make choices. You've got to make very dangerous choices. You've got to be taught that your life is in your hands.

Interviewer: The matter of freedom leads to another chapter in your book, in which you discuss a meeting with Ingmar Bergman, whom you described as a free, a relatively free, artist. Would you mind telling us about that?

Baldwin: Well, part of Bergman's freedom, of course, is purely economical. It is based on the social and economic structure of Sweden. He hasn't got to worry about money for his films, which is a very healthy thing for him. But on another level, he impressed me as being free because—and this is a great paradox about freedom—he'd accepted his limitations: limitations within himself, limitations within his society. I don't mean that he necessarily accepted *all* these limitations, or that he was passive in the face of them. But he recognized that he was Ingmar Bergman, could do some things and could not do some others, and was not going to live forever; he recognized something that people in this country have a great deal of trouble recognizing: that life is very difficult, very difficult for anybody, anybody born.

People cannot be free until they recognize this. Bessie Smith was much freer—onerous and terrible as this may sound—much freer than the people who murdered her or let her die. Big Bill Broonzy, too—a much freer man than the success-ridden people running around on Madison Avenue today. If you can accept the worst, as someone once said to me, then you can see the best; but if you think life is a great, big, glorious plum pudding, you know, you'll end up in the madhouse.

Interviewer: To perhaps even extend the example you just offered: the little girl who walked into the Little Rock School House and was spat on was much freer than the white child who sat there with a misconceived notion.

Baldwin: Well, I think the proof that Negroes are much stronger in the South today is simply . . . you know. . . .

Interviewer: She knew who she was. . . .

Baldwin: She knew who she was. She *knew* who she was. After all, that child has been coming for a very long time. She didn't come out of nothing. Negro families are able to produce such children; whereas the fact that the good white people of the South have yet to make an appearance proves something awful about the moral state of the South. Those people in Tallahassee who are never in the streets when the mobs are there: why aren't they? It's their town, too!

Interviewer: What about someone like Lillian Smith?

Baldwin: Lillian Smith is a very great, and heroic, and very lonely figure. Obviously. She has very few friends in that little hamlet in Georgia where she carries on so gallantly. She has paid a tremendous price for trying to do what she thinks is right. And the price is terribly, terribly high. The only way the price can become a little bit less is for more people to do it.

Interviewer: This leads to what you wrote in your chapter, "In Search of a Majority," about the question of majority and minority.

Baldwin: The majority is usually—I hate to say this—wrong. There is a great confusion in this country about that.

Interviewer: Ibsen's *An Enemy of the People . . . ?*

Baldwin: Yes. I really think, seriously, that there is a division of labor in the world. Let me put it this way: there are so many things I am not good at—I can't drive a truck; I can't run a bank. Well, all right—other people have to do that. In a way, they are responsible for me; and I am responsible to them.

My responsibility to them is to try to tell the truth as I see it—not so much about my private life, as about *their* private lives. So that there is in the world a standard, you know, for *all* of us, which will get you through your troubles. Your troubles are always coming. And Cadillacs don't get you through. And neither do psychiatrists, incidentally. All that gets you through it, really, is some faith in life, which is not so *easy* to achieve.

Now, when we talk about majorities and minorities, I always have the feeling that this country is talking about a popularity contest in which everybody works together, you know, towards some absolutely hideously material end. But in truth, I think that all the Southern politicians have failed their responsibility to the white people of the South. *Somebody* in the South must know that obviously the status quo cannot exist another 100 years. The politicians' real responsibility is to prepare the people who are now forming those mobs, prepare those people for their day: to minimize the damage to *them*.

The majority rule in the South is not a majority rule at all. It's a mob rule. And what these mobs fill is a moral vacuum, which is created by the lack of a leader. This is the way the world is, and I am not talking about dictatorships.

Interviewer: Statesmen?

Baldwin: Statesmen, exactly. People who are sitting in government are supposed to know more about government than people who are driving trucks, and digging potatoes, and trying to raise their children. That's what you are in office for.

Interviewer: Someone, then, with a sense of history?

Baldwin: That is precisely what we don't have here. If you don't know what happened behind you, you've no idea of what is happening around you.

Interviewer: Earlier, Jim, you mentioned that for a national policy to be straightened out, the private policies, these private, individual lives must be, too. You spoke of your job as a writer, and of how you've got to write. In that chapter on Bergman, "The Northern Protestant," is a beautiful comment:

"All art is a kind of confession, more or less oblique. All artists, if they are to survive, are forced, at last, to tell the whole story, to vomit the anguish up."

Baldwin: Art has to be a kind of confession. I don't mean a true confession in the sense of that dreary magazine. The effort, it seems to me, is: if you can examine and face your life, you can discover the terms with which you are connected to other lives, and they can discover, too, the terms with which they are connected to other people.

This has happened to everyone of us, I'm sure. You read something which you thought only happened to you, and you discovered it happened 100 years ago to Dostoyevsky. This is a very great liberation for the suffering, struggling person, who always thinks that he is alone. This is why art is important. Art would not be important if life were not important, and life *is* important.

Most of us, no matter what we say, are walking in the dark, whistling in the dark. Nobody knows what is going to happen to him from one moment to the next, or how one will bear it. This is irreducible. And it's true for everybody. Now, it is true that the nature of society is to create, among its citizens, an illusion of safety; but it is also absolutely true that the safety is always necessarily an illusion. Artists are here to disturb the peace.

Interviewer: Artists are here to disturb the peace?

Baldwin: Yes, they have to disturb the peace. Otherwise, chaos.

Interviewer: Life is risk.

Baldwin: It is, indeed. It always is. People have to know this. In some way they will have to know it in order to get through their risks.

Interviewer: So the safety itself is wholly illusory?

Baldwin: There's no such thing as safety on this planet. No one *knows* that much. No one ever will. Not only about the world but about himself. That's why it's unsafe.

This is what the whole sense of tragedy is really about. People think that a sense of tragedy is kind of . . . embroidery, something irrelevant, that you can take or leave. But, in fact, it is a necessity. That's what the Blues and Spirituals are all about. It is the ability to look on things as they are and survive your losses, or even not survive them—to know that your losses are coming. To know they are coming is the only possible insurance you have, a faint insurance, that you will survive them.

Interviewer: Again, in your book, you mention that Americans, although we have tremendous potentialities, are lacking in that which non-Americans may have: a sense of tragedy.

Baldwin: It's incredible to me that—and I'm not trying to over-simplify anything—in this country where, after all, one is for the most part better off materially than anywhere else in the world: it is incredible that one should know so many people who are in a state of the most absolute insecurity about themselves. They literally can't get through a morning without going to see the psychiatrist. I find it very difficult to take this really seriously.

Other people who have really terrifying and unimaginable troubles, from the American point of view, don't dream of going anywhere near a psychiatrist, and wouldn't do it even if they were mad enough to dream of it. This seems a very great, well, not illness, exactly, but fear. Frenchmen and Frenchwomen whom I knew spent much less time in this dreadful and internal warfare, tearing themselves and each other to pieces, than Americans do.

Why this is so is probably a question for someone else; but it *is* so, and I think it says something serious about the real aim and the real standards of our society. People don't live by the standards they say they live by, and the gap between their profession and the actuality is what creates this despair, and this uncertainty, which is very, very dangerous.

Interviewer: In your essay, "The Black Boy Looks at the White Boy," you explore your relationship with Norman Mailer. You infer that the White Boy, if he can deal as truthfully as he knows how with our present fortunes, these present days, these "sad and stormy events," and if he has understood them, "then he is richer and we are richer, too; if he has not understood them, we are all much poorer. For, though it clearly needs to be brought into focus, he has a real vision of ourselves as we are, and it cannot be too often repeated in this country now, that, where there is no vision, the people perish."

Baldwin: I mean that.

Interviewer: During this hour, which has passed so ludicrously fast, we have only scratched the surface in getting to know James Baldwin, who has confessed in a very beautiful way. Besides *Nobody Knows My Name,* he has written two earlier novels, *Giovanni's Room* and *Go Tell It On the Mountain,* and now, the forthcoming novel. . . .

Baldwin: *Another Country.* It is about this country.

Interviewer: One last question. James Baldwin: who are you, now?

Baldwin: [long pause] Who, indeed. Well, I may be able to tell you who I am, but I am also discovering who I am not. I want to be an honest man. And I want to be a good writer. I don't know if one ever gets to be what one wants to be. You just have to play it by ear, and . . . pray for rain.

The Image: Three Views—Ben Shahn, Darius Milhaud and James Baldwin Debate the Real Meaning of a Fashionable Term

Malcolm Preston/1962

From the *Opera News*, 27 (8 December 1962), pp. 9-12. Reprinted by permission.

These Comments were drawn from a symposium at Hofstra College, Hempstead, Long Island, in May 1961. Moderator was Malcolm Preston, chairman of the humanities department, who posed questions to the three creative artists.

Moderator Malcolm Preston: We are here to discuss man's images in the arts of today. Let us begin with a tentative definition: "An image is made up of those sounds, forms or words which, singly or together, elicit meaning in a work of art." I should like to ask Mr. Shahn if he finds this definition reasonable and, if so, whether today's images are distinct from those of previous periods.

Painter Ben Shahn: I can speak only for the kind of image I have been involved with. There seems to be trouble about the image today, particularly the visual image. I often feel that one man's image may be another's icon, or something for the iconoclast in him. Speaking, for example, of the image of man: do we mean the figures of primitive fertility idols? Do we mean the Greek image of man, or the Byzantine, or that created during the Renaissance? Do we mean the image that the X-ray machine takes?

Occasionally I am forced to explain my own subjective definition of an image. I believe that the image I create must contain within it everything man concerns himself with: his hopes, his fears, his tears. And I find that a great deal of the imagery in use today precludes most of these concerns.

Question from a Student Panelist: Mr. Shahn, you indicated that each civilization, each period in history, leaves its own kind of image of man. What kind do you think we will leave?

Shahn: There is a cliché that the artist is the person who best reflects his time. I am not ready to accept that definition of the artist, nor the idea that the art is best which best reflects its time. The function of the artist is a little more than to reflect; he has to refract, to set things off in another direction. As for the reflection of our own time, a great deal has been written about that. Several broad categories of art have emerged today, and I cannot answer you directly as to which—or in what way all of them together—may reflect our time.

Question: Would you say we have found a certain affinity with primitive forms?

Shahn: This adulation of primitivism is comparable to "cook-outs." We have had it so good that we cannot stand the six-thermostatic-control oven, so we go and burn the food outdoors. The images Grandma Moses created were of a period that never existed, and it gets to be embarrassing. I think it is charming when a child says "I dood it," but if he grew to be about four years old and still said "I dood it," I would take him to a doctor.

Question: The conditions under which Renaissance artists worked are similar to those today: an awareness of almost unlimited space, breaking out, reaching into the unknown. And the cities, like ours, were terrifying places to live. Is there today, in terms of the artist and his image of man, a concern for the same things that concerned the Renaissance artist?

Writer James Baldwin: There is a major difference between the Renaissance and our time; it has to do with a certain body of belief, things that are taken for granted. In the Renaissance, God was in his heaven and hell was beneath, and this was a current definition of the world, therefore of oneself. This is no longer true. There is nothing now that can be said to be taken for granted, and the image of man in the arts suffers from this fact. What has gone out of the world for us, what must be brought back one way or another, is this notion of the universe as ordered, the notion of a life that has standards to which one can aspire, certain penalties, hopes, achievements.

It is difficult for a young person today to know what to do. You cannot take advertising seriously; you cannot be truly involved with selling, or respect yourself, if the product you make is meant to become obsolete in a year or two. There is very little real, important work to do. And where there is no work, something goes, because we discover through working what we cannot discover any other way. As Faulkner says, you cannot make love eight hours a day, or drink or walk eight hours a day. You have to do something with your life, and you have to find out what it is. If the time has no standards—and ours hasn't—then you have to make them up in order to discover what you really believe.

The order I am talking about is a very private order. When I am writing a novel, I am writing about me and all of you, and the great difficulty is to discover what connects us. Something does connect us, and what it is is hidden. It is not science or prosperity; it is not to be found in any church, so far as I know.

The foundations of society are shifting and have been broken. There will be no more English gunboats down a Chinese river; this means that the English are different and the Chinese are different, and whatever is going to unite us from here on cannot be what has united us until now. Some other basis will have to be established if we are all going to remain alive, human, free. What one needs is a way of making one's life really endurable. This calls for testimony by people who have witnessed life, who put it on canvas or write it or put it in sound. What you see then is something that tells the truth about you. To define ourselves means defining a great many other things.

So we cannot speak of ourselves, I think, as belonging to a golden age or even a Renaissance. But if we can deal with the conundrums that face us now, people later may think of us as having begun a Renaissance or even a golden age. Because I believe there is something sleeping beneath the chaos that is of extraordinary value, if only we have the courage to go down and bring it up. To destroy, for example, the myth of the Far West and find out what really happened there, to destroy the myth of the founding fathers and discover who they really were, why they came here and what they did. Because we are the issue of those beginnings, and until we excavate our history, we will never know who we are.

The problem of the American identity has everything to do with all the things that happened in this country but never have been admitted or dealt with. We are facing problems so grave that we may not survive them; if we don't deal with the facts, the truth, then obviously we are doomed. The importance of an image is that this country has never really been described, never discovered. It is not up to politicians to do this, it is up to the people who really care about it, who in one way or another are always the poets. The truth about America is much worse and much better than you will ever discover by reading the newspaper or most of the intellectuals. It is somewhere contained in all of us, in something we have not accepted about ourselves that is of utmost importance.

Question: Mr. Milhaud, in finding new values or reshaping old ones, do you feel that new electronic techniques may help in music?

Composer Darius Malhaud: There has always been a constant evolution in music, like a river that flows. Every period has brought new possibilities. It is the same with electronic music: there are new possibilities. What I find absurd is the idea that it will replace anything. I do not think we are going to burn the libraries, tear down the concert halls and replace them with a roomful of loudspeakers where we can listen to little noises all day long. Some young extremists seem to think music will disappear; I doubt it, because you can still listen to Machaut or some Renaissance music and be moved.

These new materials are an addition, not a replacement. Suppose you have a field of expression of a certain size. If the new methods make it bigger, then bravo, we are delighted. There is a lot of fuss about the "new" electronic music today, but I remember hearing a concert in 1910 by the Futurist group of Marinetti. There was a composer there who said he was replacing music for the era of Futurism with noises. He did not use electricity, because at that time there were no engineers clever enough; he used some kind of mechanical device, and after two hours you would cry to hear perhaps a flute coming out of all that.

To make electronic music is not easy, because it adds to the techniques a composer must master if he wants to use it. He must become a sound engineer, study electricity, understand all those charts and figures. What will come of this new branch of our technique? I am not a fortuneteller; it will develop, but I cannot tell you how. It offers very important and powerful possibilities, for example, in dramatic music and the movies. We shall just have to deal with it as we ought to try to deal with everything else in our field, which means honestly.

Shahn: I think we are being shilled for a lot of scientific terminology. In painting there has been a remarkable invention, the airbrush, but there has to be someone to use it. Once, when I was visiting M.I.T., there was a physicist working with great dedication to bring art and science together. He felt that Leonardo da Vinci's self-portrait, say, was a work of art, whereas a photograph from a model agency was not. One was made mechanically, the other was made by an artist who everybody would agree was a great artist. How do you integrate these? He scanned the Da Vinci with an apparatus, the way you do with a photograph for transmission over the radio. He arrived at a kind of negative, a tonal rhythm, for that drawing. Then he superimposed that on the photograph and felt he was bringing art to science.

During that same visit, I heard they had perfected a timekeeping device that was supposed to be so accurate it would lose only one-tenth of a second in 10,000 years, or something like that. I expected it to be a sort of clock, but it turned out to fill a large room. Half-facetiously I took out my watch to set it by this thing—and they told me it wasn't working.

Question: Artists in all fields seem to feel that modern man is incapable of really communicating. Why does the artist find this more true now than during other periods?

Shahn: Every artist would like to communicate, but often he fails to ask himself with whom he is trying to do it. If I want to paint for *Art News,* it would be silly to paint Norman Rockwell covers; I would get no approval there. On the other hand, if I want approval from *The Saturday Evening Post,* it would be silly to work along the lines of Picasso's "Guernica." If I am temperamentally the kind who wants approval from *The Saturday Evening Post* but am painting for *Art News,* then I am making a lie of my life, of my very being.

Artists want approval, but sometimes they have nothing to say. Under our system an automobile, a television set, a refrigerator is available to almost everybody; now we feel that we must distribute the things of the spirit to everybody, too. That is not quite possible; there are not enough "spiritual" people around who really care. But we force it on them. If we cannot make it possible for every artist to make a painting for everybody, we are going to teach people to do it themselves. There's a book out that promises "Abstract Painting in Six Weeks."

Question: Why do we need images?

Shahn: The question seems odd, because you need images to ask it. We need images in order to communicate. I use visual images. Written words, musical notations are images, and they communicate to a person who looks at them. Today we have entered a period in our art where we are afraid of communicating. Is it because we have very little to communicate? Is it because we have created a certain elite so we can feel that our communication is only for those few? Is it because what we're communicating is so unimportant that we surround it with a kind of mystique so it will seem to have more importance because it is less understood?

I had occasion to meet with a group of young Princeton physicists who organized art classes as an extracurricular hobby. I asked each one why he wanted to do this, and he indicated that his area of work was not quite enough; he needed something else. An area of his feeling, of his being, needed a medium other than what his chosen field of communication already was.

One of the group exemplified the attitude of many when he started off by saying, rather defiantly, "Look, I don't want to know anything about this cubistic, modernistic art." And I said, "Well, if you are interested in communicating, as you suggested, then you'll have to learn a series of words, maybe even begin with an alphabet." To this he said, "But my language—scientific language—is universal." I asked him, "Is it really?" I drew on the blackboard the image of the square root; then I drew three similar lines, the profile of a chair, about which I said, "This is an image. It communicates. I'll wager, even though it's in the area of this mystical art you're so afraid of, that this image communicates to more people than the image of the square root." It didn't have much effect on him.

Then I picked up some colored chalk and drew what seemed to him—and began to irritate him immediately—an abstraction. He kept interrupting me to demand what it was. I explained, "This is the directions for getting from the Art Center to the Institute for Advanced Studies. You see, this line is Spring Street, and these three circles—red, yellow and green—are the traffic lights at Mercer and

Nassau Streets. This crenelated shape is a building, these triangles are the trees that surround the Institute." He said, " Why didn't you tell me?" And I said, "I cannot begin to tell you until I have begun to teach you something about images."

Milhaud: We musicians live in a completely different world, where there are no words or images to convey our sentiments. It is the world of sound, a very mysterious world to which we are adjusted. Of course we often collaborate with words—when we write a song, a dramatic work or an opera. There have been periods when composers took literary or even physical images as a basis; the symphonic poems of Richard Strauss, for example, follow stories, describe events and characters. If you think of the impressionistic period, you find Debussy using titles of descriptive imagery: "Clouds," "Festivals," "Sirens."

But if the piece were not called "Clouds," it would still be a beautiful piece of music. You could listen to it and dream of anything you like without thinking that clouds were concerned. After the first few bars of music, you forget the title. That is why I don't feel terribly competent to speak about images.

Question: Mr. Milhaud, don't you feel that anything you compose is actually a projection of your own image?

Milhaud: I don't know what you call "image." If you meant heart, sensitivity, or if you mean what I need to compose—which is a fountain pen—that is up to you. The composer constructs a piece, and it has to express something: mood, sentiment, excitement or whatever. As for the rest—well, a cook doesn't give away his recipes.

Baldwin: The cook *can't* give them. Mr. Milhaud needs a fountain pen; so do I. Beyond that, there is no formula. You're on your own.

Shahn: I think the term "self-expression" ought to be forbidden. It's finished. A person, if he has a gram of honesty, naturally does nothing but express himself. Self-expression is as much part of the artist as teeth are to the dentist; it is part of his life, his work.

I look upon my work as a craftsman. I am one of many who practice a craft. I am one of many who have beliefs and fears and hopes, and I want to incorporate those, with all the tools I have learned to use over many years, into what I will call a piece of work. But not a masterpiece—I'd be terrified of that. There is a tendency for the artist to take himself seriously. But if I ever sat down before a canvas with the feeling that I was now creating a masterpiece, I'd lay an egg.

Baldwin: It is easy to think of the artist as a glamorous person, one who projects his own feelings—his image—with ease and a certain grandeur. But the truth is that nobody in his right mind should ever want to be an artist. You don't decide to be an artist, you discover that you are one; it is a very great difference. What you do, you do because you must. The way fish breathe water, writers write; if they don't, they'll die.

One needs an image in order to see oneself and be released from oneself. One has an image of oneself that is always at variance with the facts; the great effort is somehow to see that I in my mind and I in life are not the same. Something connects them, but the effort is to bring these two things together, to fuse the reality and the image.

Art has this advantage: that you can see yourself in it, if you will bring yourself to it. The trouble with art in our time, it seems to me, is that most artists are not involved with that. They are involved with creating a fantasy that corroborates my fantasy of myself and yours of you and imprisons all of us in it. People love *Peyton Place* not because it says anything about their own experience but because it corroborates them in a kind of fantasy. There is no way out of *Peyton Place,* there is no way out of most of the bad painting with which we are afflicted, because there is nothing in it, nothing to which you can go. There is nothing new. And what is new is always very, very old; it is always you.

'It's Terrifying,' James Baldwin: The Price of Fame

Nat Hentoff/1963

From the *New York Herald Tribune Books,* 16 June 1963, pp. 1-2. I.H.T. Corporation. Reprinted by permission.

In the past year, as racial tensions have tugged increasingly at the nation's unity, one writer has vaulted to prominence with two controversial and best-selling works on the Negro-white conflict. In this remarkably candid interview, the writer himself tells what it's like now to be James Baldwin.

At the end of May, James Baldwin flew to Puerto Rico in order to become a writer again. He had been hurled through the country in his other role—preaching in public of "the fire next time"—since returning to America at the beginning of that month. Exhausted by weeks of lectures, he found no surcease at home in New York where, in addition to television and radio appearances, he had been involved in an opaque confrontation with Attorney General Robert Kennedy and its aftermath of interviews.

One of the last of those interviews was at Downey's, an Eighth Avenue refuge for theater people. As he neared the door, Baldwin was stopped twice for autographs. Inside, he ordered a double Scotch and shook his head in unabated wonder at the whirlpool his life had become.

"I'm like a jazz musician," Baldwin said. "It's terrifying. The one-nighters seemed never to have an end. Yet I can't blame anybody for being where I am. This all happened because I'm a writer, but it didn't happen because people read that much. The country is going through a crisis and I've been thrown up as this kind of public figure because I'm the top Negro writer in the country—whatever that means." His eyes intent on his questioner, Baldwin broke into a

32

characteristic smile compounded of irony and challenge. "It's like Sidney Poitier being America's only Negro movie star. That's the country's fault, not ours. But I'm still trying to speak just for me, not for twenty million people."

For Baldwin, the act of writing continues to be an obsessive need as well as the most meaningful way in which he can speak for himself. Accordingly, as he has done in the past, he had to leave the country again. "It's always been difficult for me to write in New York," he explained. "Now it's impossible. I've always hated this city, and yet it's where I was born and where my family is. So, in another way, when the chips are down, I love it. I can't entirely escape it, but I can't work in it. Since I can't ever become an expatriate again, I'm going to continue spending half my time abroad doing what I should be doing and the other half here—doing what I have to do."

The immediate work in progress, to be completed in Puerto Rico, is a play, *Blues for Mr. Charlie,* which will probably be produced on Broadway this fall. The action of the play is in a small town in the deep South. Before it begins, a 20-year-old Negro, who has been living in the North since he was 14 and who has become a drug addict, comes home to die. He is killed, and the play pivots on his murder. Built on the testimony service of the Negro church, "Blues for Mr. Charlie" reconstructs the crime and examines the ways in which both the whites and the Negroes in the town had, without knowing it, made the death inevitable.

This is Baldwin's third play. *The Amen Corner,* about a Negro woman pastor in the North, had been produced in 1953 at Howard University. Baldwin had also dramatized his novel "Giovanni's Room" for an Actors Studio workshop production in 1958. Both had been intermittently optioned for Broadway, but the options had never led to a production.

"I have come back to writing a play," Baldwin emphasized, "for the same reason I wrote my first one. After *Go Tell It on the Mountain,* everybody expected me to write another book just like it. I wasn't about to do that. I wanted, for one thing, to see if I could write a play; and I also knew that if I could, I'd be a better novelist.

"For example," Baldwin continued, "I think *Another Country* is my best novel so far. Not because I achieved everything I wanted to in it—in that respect, I'm only at the beginning of my life as a writer.

But *Another Country* was harder and more challenging than
anything I'd ever attempted, and I didn't cheat in it. I didn't tell any
lies; at least I wasn't aware of telling any. I know some critics said the
characters were cardboard and that I had become more of a
polemicist than a novelist. I deny it. I'm much too good a pro to have
let that happen. That book saved my life as a writer—in my own
eyes.

"Yet," Baldwin went on, "Ossie Davis told me he did feel the
essayist had intruded somewhat into the novel, and he may have a
point. By writing a play, therefore, I can work at being more laconic,
more economical. I can work at letting the story tell itself. Economy is
the problem of nearly every writer in this country. We're all too self-
indulgent, too explanatory. We all tip our hand too much. Now, in
Blues for Mr. Charlie, there are no stage directions at all. If I've done
it right, no stage directions will be needed."

Baldwin clearly continues to consider himself primarily a novelist,
and he is also working on a long novel. The new work, "Tomorrow
Brought Us Rain," starts when the slaves began to realize they were
free, and it examines the impact of that event on both Negroes and
whites. The narrative follows two families North and ends roughly
about the time Baldwin himself was born 38 years ago. Baldwin calls
it "my first political novel." One of the protagonists is a charismatic
Negro leader and the other is a painter. "Both," says Baldwin, "are
betrayed in different ways."

Another project is a book of essays, "The Beast in the Playground." "On one of my trips," Baldwin explains, "I was walking up
a residential street. I don't remember exactly where, but it could just
as easily have been in New England as in Florida. There was a very
tranquil lawn in front of a very tranquil house. Walking by on the
sidewalk, saw a white cat pushing his daughter in a swing. The sun
was shining, the grass was green, and it looked like heaven on earth.
Except that I was there. America is the playground, and I'm the
beast." The book will include investigations of housing, education
and American conceptions of sex as well as profiles of a few key
Negro figures such as Martin Luther King.

Baldwin, who has already traveled in Africa, also intends to return
for a longer stay after he has done more preparation. ("I have a
whole file of my Africa homework.") The only writing on Africa he

may do before he goes back is an article on Sierra Leone which he calls "The Price of Diamonds." There will not, however, be a book on Africa for a long time. "When I was there," Baldwin says, "people I met asked me not to go back and write a book after only a six-week trip. And I'm not going to."

Inevitably, Baldwin will also return from time to time to the sounding of alarms in America. Whether this activity will involve any further seminars with the Kennedys depends, says Baldwin, on the Attorney General. "I want to leave the door open. If it's slammed shut, Robert Kennedy will have done it—not me." Although reluctant to detail fully his acute disappointment with what he regarded as the Attorney General's lack of moral urgency—so that the door can be kept open—Baldwin did nod affirmatively when a friend, who had been at the meeting, said, "It's frightening to see power in the flesh and then realize how empty it is of almost everything but a concern with strategy for keeping itself in power."

In a Herald Tribune interview on May 26, Baldwin had said of the Attorney General, "There's a tremendous gap between the bulk of the Negro people and his office. And something he doesn't realize— there's an increasing gap between the bulk of the Negro people and me."

Shortly before he left for Puerto Rico, Baldwin elaborated on that double-edged warning. "When a Negro becomes famous, he's assumed by the bulk of those he helplessly represents to have become a whore. You can see this happening with some Negro politicians. Many Negroes will say of them. 'Those politicians couldn't have made it unless they're just as corrupt as the whites are.' And with a Negro writer, they'll also feel I must have made some kind of deal to have 'made it.'

"So, what I can get through to Negroes," Baldwin knocked on the wood paneling of the restaurant wall, "depends on what I get through as *me* when I actually talk to them. Some of the young people do trust me, including some of those who have been jailed and beaten in the South. I'd rather be eaten by dogs or put in a concentration camp than betray them in any way. You know, the real point is that people like me and Harry Belafonte and even Martin Luther King are not Negro *leaders*. We're doing our best to find out where the people are and to follow them."

Some, especially among the Northern young, are becoming
disaffiliated in the manner—if not with the particular philosophy—of
the Black Muslims. "When a young Negro," Baldwin emphasizes,
"tells me he has no country and no flag, I can't answer him. The
country has to. Many of those I deal with are considerably younger
than I, and what I *am* trying to show them is that, in addition to not
yielding on equality, we should also be proud of what we have been,
of what we have endured. It's a betrayal of those kids to advocate
either that they imitate a white image or, as the Muslims do, that they
fantasize their beginnings in some regal Egyptian setting. When the
chips are down, I've got to remember my mother carried white
women's washing on her head and that my grandmother was a slave.
For me to say that I come from a long line of African kings, which
may or may not be true, is absolutely irrelevant.

"Some whites," Baldwin continued, "talk of total miscegenation as
the only real final answer. The idea of my vanishing as the simplest
way out for whites is absurd. I am not about to vanish. There is no
reason why I should get to be like you or that you should get to be
like me. On the other hand, the Muslims' goals are also impossible. I
can't drive all white men into the sea and you can't send me back to
Africa. We're going to make this revolution here—together—or not at
all."

Asked how much time he thought remained before the fire,
Baldwin somberly shook his head from side to side. Finally, he said,
"The press has been deliberately suppressing many incidents of flash
violence in nearly every Northern city, incidents which have
particularly increased since Birmingham. It's much worse in the North
than in the South. Every Northern city is at the edge of conflagration."

Baldwin, therefore, feels he has to keep taking time from his
writing to preach, to do as much as one writer can to help prevent
whites and Negroes from slipping over that edge. "One thing about
traveling," he adds, "is that it enables me to meet a lot of beautiful
people—black and white—I couldn't have known otherwise. The kids
especially. They ask real questions, something the grownups seldom
do. At a junior high school in Oakland, Calif., a few weeks ago, the
kids were mostly black. One of them asked how it was possible to tell

the innocent from the guilty. I said I couldn't answer that question but I'd think about it and I hoped he would too."

Baldwin paused and this time his smile was undiluted. "After another lecture, I was signing autographs and a white cat, wearing blue jeans, came up. He said, 'I don't need your autograph because I heard what you said.' That redeems a lot."

A Conversation with James Baldwin

Kenneth B. Clark/1963

From *Freedomways*, 3 (Summer 1963), 361-68. Reprinted by permission.

Taped by WGBH-TV Friday May 24 immediately following Mr. Baldwin's now celebrated meeting with Attorney
General Robert Kennedy and with other Negro leaders on
the strategy of integration. Interviewed by Kenneth Clark,
Professor of Psychology at the City College of New York.

Clark: One of the significant things of the present revolution of the
Negro people in America is maybe the fact, that for the first time,
there's genuine communication between Negroes and whites.
Negroes are saying out loud now things which they have long said
only to themselves. Probably one of the most articulate, passionate
and clear communicators to the American conscience is my guest,
James Baldwin. James Baldwin's name is known throughout America
for saying so passionately and so clearly and with such grace and
style what every Negro has long known and has long felt. Welcome
James—it's good to have this opportunity to talk with you and have
you share with us some of your present feelings about our country,
America, but before we get into the issues of the day, I'd like to know
a little more about you. I've read practically everything that you have
written, but I still would like to know something about you, the young
man growing up in Harlem, what schools you went to, maybe a little
about some of the teachers that you might have come in contact with
in Harlem.

    Baldwin: What a funny question! My mind is some place else,
really, but to think back on it—I was born in Harlem, Harlem
Hospital, and we grew up—first house I remember was on Park
Avenue—not the American Park Avenue, or maybe it is the American
uptown Park Avenue where the railroad tracks are. We used to play

on the roof and in the—I can't call it an alley—but near the river—it was a kind of garbage dump. Those were the first scenes I remember. My father had trouble keeping us alive—there were nine of us. I was the oldest so I took care of the kids and dealt with Daddy. I understand him much better now. Part of his problem was he couldn't feed his kids, but I was a kid and I didn't know that. He was very religious and very rigid. He kept us together, I must say, and when I look back on it—that was over 40 years ago that I was born—when I think back on my growing up and walk that same block today because it's still there, and think of the kids on that block now, I'm aware that something terrible has happened which is very hard to describe. I am, in all but in technical legal fact, a Southerner. My father was born in the South—my mother was born in the South, and if they had waited two more seconds I might have been born in the South. But that means I was raised by families whose roots were essentially southern rural and whose relationship to the church was very direct because it was the only means they had of expressing their pain and their despair. But 20 years later the moral authority which was present in the Negro northern community when I was growing up has vanished, and people talk about progress, and I look at Harlem which I really know—I know it like I know my hand—and it is much worse there today than it was when I was growing up.

Clark: Would you say this is true of the schools too?

Baldwin: It is much worse in the schools.

Clark: What school did you go to?

Baldwin: I went to P.S. 24 and I went to P.S. 139.

Clark: We are fellow alumni. I went to 139.

Baldwin: I didn't like a lot of my teachers, but I had a couple of teachers who were very nice to me—one was a Negro teacher. You ask me these questions and I'm trying to answer you. I remember coming home from school—you can guess how young I must have been—and my mother asked me if my teacher was colored or white, and I said she was a little bit colored and a little bit white, but she was about your color. As a matter of fact I was right. That's part of the dilemma of being an American Negro: that one is a little bit colored and a little bit white, and not only in physical terms but in the head and in the heart, and there are days when you wonder what your role is in this country and what your future is in it. How precisely are you going to reconcile yourself to your situation here and how are you going to communicate to the vast headless, unthinking, cruel white majority; that you are here, and to be here means that you can't be anywhere else. I could, my own person, leave this country and go to Africa, I could go to China, I could go to Russia, I could go to Cuba, but I'm an American and that is a fact.

Clark: Yes, Jim.

Baldwin: Am I going ahead?

Clark: These are certainly some of the things that we are after, but as I read your writings and know that you came out of P.S. 24 and my alma mater—Junior High School 139—I see that no one could write with the feeling and with the skill with which you write if you did not get—in P.S. 24 and 139—a certain type of education. Now I'd like to go back to the point that you made that the Harlem you knew when you were growing up is not the Harlem now and see if we can relate this also even to the school.

Baldwin: Let's see if we can. It was probably very important for me—I haven't thought of it this way for a long time—at the point I was going to P.S. 24 the only Negro school principal as far as I know in the entire history of New York was a principal named Mrs. Ayer, and she liked me. In a way I guess she proved to me that I didn't have to be entirely defined by my circumstances, because you know that every Negro child knows what his circumstances are but he cannot articulate them, because he is born into a republic which assures him in as many ways as it knows how, and has got great force, that he has a certain place and he can never rise above it. What has happened in Harlem since is that that generation has passed away.

Clark: Mrs. Ayer was a sort of a model in a sense.

Baldwin: Proof. She was a living proof that I was not necessarily what the country said I was.

Clark: Then it is significant Jim, that we do not have a single Negro principle in the New York public school system today.

Baldwin: The great victims in this country of the institution called segregation, which is not solely a southern custom but has been for a hundred years a national way of life—the great victims are the white people, and the white man's children. Lorraine Hansberry said this afternoon when we were talking about the problem of being a Negro male in this society. Lorraine said that she wasn't too concerned really about Negro manhood since they had managed to endure and to even transcend fantastic things, but she was very worried about a civilization which could produce those 5 policemen standing on the Negro woman's neck in Birmingham or wherever it was, and I am too. I'm terrified at the moral apathy—the death of the heart which is happening in my country. These people have deluded themselves so long, that they really don't think I'm human. I base this on their conduct and not on what they say, and this means that they have become in themselves moral monsters. It's a terrible indictment—I mean every word I say.

Clark: Yes, well, we are confronted with the racial confrontation in America today. I think the pictures of dogs in the hands of human beings attacking other human beings—

Baldwin: In a free country—in the middle of the 20th century.

Clark: In a free country. This Birmingham is clearly not restricted to Birmingham as you so eloquently pointed out. What do you think can be done to change—to use your term—the moral fibre of America?

Baldwin: I think that one has got to find some way of putting the present administration of this country on the spot. One has got to force somehow, from Washington, a moral commitment, not to the Negro people, but to the life of this country. It doesn't matter any longer, and I'm speaking for myself, James Baldwin, and I think I'm speaking for a great many other Negroes too. It doesn't matter any longer what you do to me; you can put me in jail, you can kill me. By the time I was 17, you had done everything that you can to me. The problem now is, how are you going to save yourselves. It was a great shock to me—I want to say this on the air—that the Attorney General did not know—

Clark: You mean the Attorney General of the U.S.?

Baldwin: Mr. Robert Kennedy—that I would have trouble convincing my nephew to go to Cuba, for example, to liberate the Cubans in the name of a government which now says it is doing everything it can do but cannot liberate me. Now, there are 20 million Negro people in this country, and you can't put them all in jail. I know how my nephew feels, I know how I feel. I know how the cats in the barbershop feel. A boy last week, he was sixteen, in San

Francisco, told me on television—thank God we got him to talk, maybe somebody thought to listen. He said, "I got no country. I got no flag." Now, he's only 16 years old, and I couldn't say, "you do." I don't have any evidence to prove that he does. They were tearing down his house, because San Francisco is engaging . . . most cities are engaged in . . . something called urban renewal, which means moving Negroes out: it means Negro removal, that is what it means. The federal government is an accomplice to this fact. Now, we are talking about human beings, there's no such a thing as a monolithic wall or some abstraction called the Negro problem. These are Negro boys and girls, who at 16 and 17 don't believe the country means anything it says and don't feel they have any place here on the basis of the performance of the entire country. Am I exaggerating?

Clark: No, I certainly cannot say that you are exaggerating, but there is this picture of a group of young Negro college students in the south coming from colleges where the whole system seems to conspire to keep them from having courage, integrity, clarity and the willingness to take the risks which they have been taking for these last three or four years. Could you react to the student non-violent movement which has made such an impact on America, which has affected both Negroes and whites, and seems to have jolted them out of the lethargy of tokenism and moderation. How do you account for this?

Baldwin: Well, one of the things I think has happened, Ken, is that the Negro has never been as docile as white Americans wanted to believe. That was a myth. We were not singing and dancing down on the levee—we were trying to keep alive; we were trying to survive. It was a very brutal system. The Negro has never been happy in his place. What those kids first of all proved—first of all they proved that—they come from a long line of fighters and what they also prove is not that the Negro has changed but that the country has arrived at a place where he can no longer contain the revolt. Let's say I was a Negro college president, and I needed a new chemistry lab, I was a Negro leader, I was a Negro leader because the white man said I was, and I came to get a new chemistry lab, please, suh, and the tacit price I paid for the chemistry lab was to control the people I represented. And now I can't do that. We were talking to a Negro student this afternoon who had been through it all, who's half dead and only about 25, Jerome Smith. That's an awful lot to ask a person to bear. The country sat back in admiration of all those kids for three or four or five years and has not lifted a finger to help them. Now, we all knew. I know, you knew and I knew that a moment was coming when we couldn't guarantee, that no one can guarantee, that he won't reach the breaking point. You can only survive so many beatings, so much humiliation, so much despair, so many broken promises, before something gives. Human beings are not by nature non-violent. Those children had to pay a terrible price in discipline, moral discipline, an interior effort of courage which the country cannot imagine.

Clark: You said something—that you cannot expect them to remain constantly non-violent.

Baldwin: No, you can't! And, furthermore, they were always, these students that we are talking about, a minority. The students we are talking about were not in Tallahassee. They were some students protesting, but there were many, many, many, many more students who had given up, who were desperate and who Malcolm X can reach, for example, much more easily than I can.

Clark: What do you mean?

Baldwin: What Malcolm tells them in effect, is that they should be proud of being black, and God knows that they should be. That is a very important thing to hear in a country which assures you that you should be ashamed of it. Of course, in order to do this, what he does is destroy a truth and invent a history. What he does is say "you're better because you're black." Well, of course that isn't true. That's the trouble.

Clark: Do you think this is an appealing approach and that the Black Muslims in preaching black supremacy seek to exploit the frustration of the Negro?

Baldwin: When Malcolm talks or one of the Muslims talks, they articulate for all the Negro people who hear them; who listen to them. They articulate their suffering, the suffering which has been in this country so long denied. That's Malcolm's great authority over any of his audiences. He corroborates their reality; he tells them that they really exist.

Clark: Jim, do you think that this is a more effective appeal than the appeal of Martin Luther King?

Baldwin: It is much more sinister because it is much more effective. It is much more effective, because it is, after all, comparatively easy to invest a population with false morale by giving them a false sense of superiority, and it will always break down in a crisis. That is the history of Europe simply—it's one of the reasons that we are in this terrible place. It is one of the reasons that we have five cops standing on the back of a woman's neck in Birmingham, because at some point they were taught and they believed that they were better than other people because they were white. It leads to moral bankruptcy. It is inevitable, it cannot but lead there. But my point here is, that the country is for the first time worried about the Muslim movement. It shouldn't be worried about the Muslim movement, that's not the problem. The problem is to eliminate the conditions which breed the Muslim movement.

Clark: I'd like to come back to—get some of your thoughts about the relationship between Martin Luther King's appeal—that is, the effect of non-violence and his philosophy of disciplined love for the oppressor. What is the relationship between this and the reality of the Negro masses?

Baldwin: Well, to leave Martin out of it for a moment. Martin's a very rare, a very great man; Martin's rare for two reasons; probably just because he is and because he's a real Christian. He really believes in non-violence. He has arrived at something in himself which allows him to do it, and he still has great moral authority in the south. He has none whatever in the north. Poor Martin has gone through God knows what kind of hell to awaken the American conscience, but Martin has reached the end of his rope. There are some things Martin can't do—Martin's only one man. Martin can't solve the nation's central problem by himself. There are lots of people, lots of black people I mean, now, who don't go to church no more and don't listen to Martin, you know, and who are themselves produced by a civilization which has always glorified violence unless the Negro had the gun, so that Martin is undercut by the performance of the country. The country is only concerned about non-violence if it seems as if I'm going to get violent, because I worry about non-violence if it's some Alabama sheriff.

Clark: Jim, what do you see deep in the recesses of your own mind as the future of our nation, and I ask that question in that way because I think that the future of the Negro and the future of the nation are linked.

Baldwin: They're insoluble.

Clark: What do you see? Are you essentially optimistic or pessimistic, and I don't really want to put words in your mouth, because I want to find out what you really believe.

Baldwin: I'm both glad and sorry you asked me that question, but I'll do my best to answer it. I can't be a pessimist because I'm alive. To be a pessimist means that you have agreed that human life is an academic matter, so I'm forced to be an optimist; I'm forced to believe that we can survive whatever we must survive, but the future of the Negro in this country is precisely as bright or as dark as the future of the country. It is entirely up to the American people and our representatives, it is entirely up to the American people whether or not they are going to face and deal with and embrace the stranger whom they maligned so long. What white people have to do, is to try to find out in their own hearts why it was necessary to have a nigger in the first place, because I'm not a nigger, I'm a man, but if you think I'm a nigger, it means you need it. Why? That's the question you have got to ask yourself—the white population has got to ask itself—north and south, because it's one country for a Negro. There's no difference between the north and south. There's just a difference in the way they castrate you, but the fact of the castration is the American fact. If I'm not a nigger here and you, the white people invented him, then you've got to find out why. And the future of the country depends on that. Whether or not it's able to ask that question.

Clark: As a Negro and an American, I can only hope that America has the strength and the capacity to ask and answer that question in an affirmative and constructive way. Thank you very much.

Race, Hate, Sex, and Colour: A Conversation with James Baldwin and Colin MacInnes

James Mossman/1965

From *Encounter*, 25 (July 1965), 55-60. Reprinted by permission.

This conversation was recorded and televised recently by the B.B.C. in its Encounter series. *James Baldwin's* novels, *Go Tell It on the Mountain* and *Another Country* have just been released as Corgi paperbacks. *Colin MacInnes'* trilogy on London life, *City of Spades, Absolute Beginners,* and *Mr. Love and Justice* (MacGibbon & Kee and Penguin), also deals with aspects of Negro life. *James Mossman,* is a foreign correspondent and the author of *Rebels in Paradise.*

Mossman: James Baldwin, can I start by reminding you that somewhere in your work you said that when you were young you hated white people. When did you stop hating them—and assuming you have, what made you?

Baldwin: When I was young, I don't remember exactly what I said, but I remember the moment—I hated white people because I was afraid of them, because they made me suffer: and, as far as I could tell, tended to continue making me suffer, and people around me, because of our colour. I was in Paris when I was talking to a girl-friend of mine—this is the moment I remember. We were having a fight, and I forget what we were fighting about exactly, but something I said made her say: "Why do you hate them?" I forget why I hated them according to what I said. But she said: "That isn't why you hate them."

Mossman: She was coloured?

Baldwin: She was white, Norwegian. She said: "That isn't why you hate them, you hate them because they're white." I can't describe this exactly, but the moment she said it I realised it was true.

It was as though I was looking at some pit at my feet, and the moment I realised that it was true, if you see what I mean, it ceased to be true. Once I realised, and could accept in myself, in fact, it was true I hated white people, then I didn't hate them any more.

Mossman: Was your family, when you were brought up in Harlem, white-hating naturally, and did they take it for granted that you would be?

Baldwin: No, it's more subtle than that. It's something which seeps into you before you know it. For example, I'm sure my father hated white people. He never said he did—or didn't say so till I was much older—but he must have, because of what he had endured during all his working days. And he must have because of what he watched happening to his children.

MacInnes: Do you think a hatred is sometimes necessary and creative in certain contexts of life?

Baldwin: Well it depends, I would think, Colin, on some kind of fusion of energy in the person, which can be a useful hatred, certainly. But the hatred I'm speaking of is mainly useless; it's mainly self-destructive. It turns against the person, it turns against yourself.

MacInnes: Can I ask you, James, when you find people of your own race who have hatred still for white people what your reaction is?

Baldwin: Well . . . I can't . . . To tell you the truth, I have two reactions or at least two. . . . I can't blame any black boy or girl for what they feel about white people. I really can't from the bottom of my heart blame them for it. The evidence is all too clear. On the other hand, for their sakes, for the sake of their souls, having nothing whatever to do with the white world, or anybody else except this one person, this girl and this boy, one would like to make vivid to them, make real to them, that this hatred is a poison which is killing them.

Mossman: Well, take a man like Malcolm X, for example, and his creed of violence, or the use of violence as justified in pursuing equality for Negroes in America—now would you say that Malcolm X in the end was destroying the people he promoted to use violence? Destroying, therefore, in a sense, the Negro cause?

Baldwin: I'm not sure I know exactly what the Negro cause is. . . .

Mossman: The search for equality as individual persons in America.

MacInnes: Search for identity and freedom, isn't it?

Baldwin: Which is much closer to my intention certainly than the word "equality" which always leaves me wondering equal to whom and to what, and why, what for? But I would never have sent any child of mine to school to Malcolm, and I would—for myself—much rather die than become that kind of theologian.

Mossman: Your father was a preacher, wasn't he? And wanted you to become one, and you refused, or you didn't like it and you. . . .

Baldwin: No, I became a preacher for three years, and I quit.

Mossman: You were about 18 when you quit. Does that mean you rejected his sort of holy and passive attitude to the subject?

MacInnes: To add a rider to that question—you spoke just now of the soul, the soul of the black man, the soul of the white man. I never have been able to make out, Jimmy, whether you are or are not a religious writer. Are you? Does the concept of God mean something to you? Are you a believer in any sense, or not?

Baldwin: I'm not a believer in any sense which would make sense to any church, and any church would obviously throw me out. I believe—what do I believe? I believe in . . . I believe in love—that sounds very corny, you . . .

MacInnes: Not to me, it doesn't.

Baldwin: I believe we can save each other. In fact I think we must save each other. I don't depend on anyone else to do it.

Mossman: But—getting back to the politics of Negro activists who are fighting for these legal and social rights—how far does your concept of love force them to behave in the utmost passive way, and just wait for the sun to rise?

MacInnes: This is nonsense. Love is not passive, is it? Love is active.

Mossman: Well, I don't know what he means by love.

Baldwin: I don't mean anything passive. I mean something active, something more like a fire, like the wind, something which can change you. I mean energy. I mean a passionate belief, a passionate knowledge of what a human being can do, and become, what a human being can do to change the world in which he finds himself.

MacInnes: I know it's maddening when people quote single sentences of yours back at you, but I remember you writing that in New York there are no lovers and nobody ever sings. How come that three months ago I saw everybody singing in Washington Square, and hundreds of lovers, of both races, walking around together?

Baldwin: Of course, your Washington Square, if I may say so, Colin, is not mine. And you may call that singing in Washington Square, and you may think they're lovers, but I spent years in Washington Square, with those singers and those lovers: they're not singing and that's not love.

MacInnes: Develop that a bit, please. Is it just sex?

Baldwin: It's not even sex; I wish it were. It is a kind of desperate—according to me—a kind of desperate advertising. It's a wistful kind of uniform, so that to sing in Washington Square Park, or to walk around, if you're white, with a black girl, or vice-versa, is a kind of badge of your emancipation.

MacInnes: Is that not a step in the right direction, or is it worse than . . . ?

Baldwin: It seems to me that it would be much better for them to be home with each other, than parading around in public to prove to everyone else, not themselves, how free they are.

Mossman: How can you rebel, then, if that is what they're doing, against the process of dehumanisation in society and the loss of freedom?

Baldwin: Unluckily, of course, no matter how you rebel it's got to be awkward, and the people you're speaking about are not middle-aged; they're young. And perhaps the peculiar ways that they go about trying to integrate themselves are the only ways they can find. But in my experience, it seems to me that the gesture, the gesture of revolt, becomes all, a substitute for the revolt itself.

MacInnes: You're a very urban writer; all your novels have an urban setting; and yet you've got a hatred of big cities, it seems to me. Is this not right?

Baldwin: I've a distrust of big cities. I've a distrust of New York which is my big city. Why? . . . Well, because I was born there, grew up there. My experience of it, after all, it is pretty gloomy; and it is too big. It is one of the loneliest places in the world.

Mossman: Do you think there's any chance that Negroes with their psychology and emotional background would be able to resist this de-humanisation you've written about, this mechanised loss of freedom, more than white men in America?

Baldwin: The question hasn't really come up. Negroes are so effectively cut out of the mainstream of society, they're so effectively barred from most of the society's temptations.

Mossman: But looking ahead, how would you rate the emotional or psychological resources in the Negro character in America which might come in handy when this pressure gets too big?

Baldwin: Well, I would like to put it this way: I would like to believe that this is one of the things that will happen, that there is some kind of residue of emotional energy, of passion, of sensuality in the Negro people which will have the power to save an extremely sterile republic.But one can't be sure that the emotional qualities of the Negro people to-day will persist in the future.

Mossman Are you suggesting that they will—as they get more and more confidence and power in the accepted social sense—that they will take on the attributes of white people, their fears and their pressures?

Baldwin: It is, unlikely, one of the possibilities, that they will become as faceless as most of the other people in the country.

MacInnes: I don't believe this, you know.

Baldwin: I don't believe it, either, but it is one of the possibilities.

Mossman: Do you find that you who resist this very consciously are increasingly unpopular with your own people in America?

Baldwin: Well, let's try to get down to what you mean by one's own people.

Mossman: What do you regard yourself as, to start with?

Baldwin: Arbitrarily, you know, I'm an American Negro. The word "American" is kind of a conundrum, and the word "Negro" too. In any real sense one's got to assume that my people are the people on the American continent, because the American Negro problem is a kind of invention on the part of white people, which has no validity. One can say, and be perfectly truthful, that in fact there are no whites and no blacks in America, that all of us are mulattos or bastards. It is not a white country. And the only people, for example, who understand Americans at all, the only people in the world who have the least comprehension of what goes on in the American mind and heart are their black brothers and sisters. The great dilemma of being a white American precisely is that they deny their only kinship.

Mossman: But, therefore, I still ask: who are you? You're clearly not an American in the ordinary sense of a White American, are you? You're not an American Negro; that's not an identity, really.

Baldwin: Then I can't answer it. I'm part of a totally incoherent people at the moment, of African origin, with Indian, Spanish, and European blood in my veins. I'm part of a country which has yet to discover who and what it is.

MacInnes: Well, Jimmy, the last time I saw you (and I think this is relevant) I asked you a question to which you gave me a very sweet but, it seemed to me, slightly equivocal answer. You don't like White racialists and you loathe White Liberals. Where does that leave the rest of us, if there are any rest of us? Are there any rest of us?

Baldwin: I don't know in which camp you place yourself, Colin.

MacInnes: No camp, please, I'm camp enough as it is.

Baldwin: I can't stand White Liberals. Obviously I can't stand White Liberals. I don't intend to be converted again.

Mossman: Why? I don't understand that quite.

Baldwin: White Liberals, in my mind, begin to be frightened of you saying the words any more. I have one thing against White Liberals which is their assumption that their morality and what they take to be civilisation and their religion is something which I need. What I resent is the assumption I must be raised to their level. It seems to me that the only way we can deal with each other as human beings or as social units is to understand that we have to give to each other.

Mossman: If I may say so, in your work you seem to be preoccupied with the idea that the White and the Black in America and the world are locked together in an eternal sort of dance of hatred. Is this something you welcome almost as a way of identifying the relationships? It's completely pessimistic.

Baldwin: I don't think that. I don't think of Whites and Blacks as being locked together in a dance of eternal hatred. We are locked together in a kind of misunderstanding of each other. And I do think that in this kind of dance, as you put it, one is trying—both of us are trying to come closer to something human in each of us. We're afflicted by the terms we use. For example, if one would drop the phrase "Negro," one would understand one was dealing with just human beings, with people.

MacInnes: Well, Jimmy, look, let me take you up on this. Take Whites. A Norwegian can admire a Greek, can't he, and vice versa?

Baldwin: Yes.

MacInnes: So why shouldn't a white man admire a Negro

because he's a Negro? Am I not allowed to admire Negro qualities because Negroes are Negroes? And must I just think Jimmy Baldwin is just a man and not a Negro?

Baldwin: No, no, no. The only thing that operates between you as an Englishman and I as a black man which doesn't operate necessarily between a Norwegian and a Greek, is that once I worked for you. That when an Englishman or an American white man, in the main, looks at a black man, he is also looking at his own past, and a lot of what happens in the mind and heart of a white man looking at a black man is involved with his guilt, his guilt because I—after all— for nothing, went into the mines and I, for nothing, built the city.

MacInnes: Jimmy, are you sure of this? I'm not sure that it. . . .

Baldwin: Its a matter of historical record.

MacInnes: Yes, but listen. I don't feel guilty about slavery because three hundred years ago I would have been a slaver. I feel guilty about what my people and I do to-day, but not what happened three hundred years ago.

Baldwin: Yes, but, Colin, we're not talking necessarily just about you. We're talking about an historical fact—it is also a present fact— which controls the society in which we live. It is one of the reasons that my son, you know, my daughter, or my niece or nephew can't use a White waiting-room in the deep South.

Mossman: But when all that, assuming it's ever settled, is settled, what is the nature of the relationship between a black man and a white man that you consider right—if you despise the Liberal White and equally the racist White, and presumably the racist Black if violence is involved? What is the nature of the relationship you envisage or want?

Baldwin: I suppose I sound socially irresponsible. I depend very heavily on the mavericks, on the people who in one way or another have managed to liberate themselves from some of the terrors which bind us all. I don't depend, for example, on people in the Churches; I depend on people outside the Churches. The relationship one is trying to establish, hopefully, at least among a few people, as a model and a possibility and as an example for the rest, is simply a human one. Because colour really does not matter, and it doesn't have to be the affliction which it is in so many of our lives for all our lives. There are ways to break out of the nightmare if one is willing to deal with one's self and tell the truth to one's self.

MacInnes: Jimmy, in a certain sense colour does matter. Why is it that I'm attracted by Negroes and not by Indians, for example? Am I not allowed to be? That doesn't mean that I want to oppress people, that I want to be other than equal. I'm willing to work for them. Can I not like them because of colour?

Baldwin: Of course you can.

MacInnes: Provided it's a free liking?

Baldwin: Yes.

MacInnes: And not a condescending liking?

Baldwin: Well, God knows, I'm not trying to set up more barriers than there are already. I like people, you know, who like me. I like people because they're coloured too, and there's something very moving for me in some things I've seen on Lennox Avenue, or on the streets of Freetown—which is not to be found for me in the North of Europe. I think that one's instinct again, I think something in oneself recognises a kind of energy which is sensual, and of the earth, and something one cannot live without, which draws you. We romanticise it, and we lie about it. One has an instinct if one wants to live.

Mossman: Can I go back to the idea that you want to be an example of the way people should be towards each other? How far do you think that this mission, as it were, of being a living example is interfering with or obstructing your work as a creative writer, as a novelist?

Baldwin: That question keeps coming up and, of course, I may be deluding myself. For me it isn't the real question. It seems to me that life is much more important than art. By which I do not mean that art is not important, but it is only important because life is. And it seems to me that, anyway, given me, I can't hide in a room or a closet and cultivate my talents. I would assume that if my talent means anything it has to be tough enough to survive life.

MacInnes: You were very obsessed, I take it, with the case of Richard Wright, were you not? He was, in a sense, your precursor. And in two of your essays, I think you did, unless I misunderstood them, suggest that at a certain point he was an artist and at a certain point he became an emblematic figure. Right? Is there not a certain danger for you in the present context . . . ?

Baldwin: Oh, yes. . . .

MacInnes: . . . that something might happen? Could you speak

about it? There must be demands on you as a—to use a silly
phrase—"Negro leader"—that there weren't, say, ten years ago?

Baldwin: This is true.

MacInnes: Which must inhibit in a certain sense your freedom as
a creative artist, no?

Baldwin: It threatens to. It's a great menace, in many forms, but
part of it is the danger of beginning to take yourself seriously, and
beginning to quote yourself. And a graver danger when you're before
the typewriter, before that blank sheet of paper, to have a kind of
audience at your shoulders, invisible of course, saying to you—"What
will this do to the cause?" . . .

Mossman: But it's also a relief, perhaps, to leave the typewriter
and go to the balcony and make a speech. It's perhaps not, crea-
tively, so difficult?

Baldwin: I think at one time for me it was a kind of temptation, to
tell you the truth. But, in the first place, it's not so easy to go on to
the balcony unless of course that's what you want. As it turned out,
that isn't what I want. The great terror of public speaking is that you
begin to listen to yourself. By and by, since you are always telling
people what to think, you begin to forget what you do think. And the
moment that happens, of course, it's over. It's over. One's got to be
willing, one's got to be able to break it all up, crack it all up, throw it
all out, and start all over again as though you'd never learned how to
spell C-a-t.

MacInnes: Could we leave for a second the fascinating subjects of
religion, politics, and race, and come on to the even more fascinating
subject of sex? All writers have a certain sexual pattern, be it heterosexual, bisexual, or homosexual. To what extent do you think a writer
who may be bisexual or homosexual does identify himself with
minority movements in a way a writer who is heterosexual would
not? Do you think this plays an important part in the work of a writer
of that description?

Baldwin: Well, now we've really, you know, we've walked into
very marshy ground because those terms, homosexual, bisexual,
heterosexual are 20th-century terms which, for me, really have very
little meaning. I've never, myself, in watching myself and watching
other people, watching life, been able to discern exactly where the
barriers were. Life being what life is, passion being what passion is.

And learning being what that is. It would seem to me that in terms of the tremendous self-consciousness that all of us are afflicted by, this distrust we have of the affections and of the flesh, it's revealed most grotesquely in what we call the sexual deviates, the sexual minorities, who are really, simply the most vivid victims of our system of mortification of the flesh. And in such a desolate place, which is where we all are, it seems to me, the difference between a heterosexual who was miserable with his life and destroys his children and some poor lost creature, thrown out into the outer darkness of our society, it seems to me they are almost—they match each other.

Mossman: You raise two points there. One, I would have thought, that the heterosexual despite his sense of loneliness and misery, as you put it, if he has it, would draw some slight consolation from the fact that he wasn't involved in yet another pressure. And, the other, that the homosexual might draw some curious satisfaction and passion from this clear identity of what he would assume was wrong with him.

Baldwin: I don't. . . .

Mossman: I mean, in either case is either true?

MacInnes: No, I don't. . . .

Baldwin: I don't see it that way at all. It seems to me, in the first place, that if one's to live at all, one's certainly got to get rid of the labels. It seems to me an incredible way to live, to glory in the fact that one is heterosexual because it proves that you're not something else, or vice versa. It seems kind of suicidal. It seems to me that if one is going to deal with this, Colin, at all one's got to get to the root of all these assumptions. Of course, a writer who is bisexual or homosexual is probably but not surely going to identify himself with other minorities, but it's perfectly possible for him to become a fascist or a sadist, too.

MacInnes: Of which we've seen many examples. I'm not positive that the other minorities like particularly being identified with him very often.

Baldwin: That's true too. In the case of being a Negro or whatever penalty one is paying socially, the only way one can possibly make it less or even endure it at all is to examine the assumptions on which the penalities are based. No one, after all, has the right to judge anybody else's life. No one has the right to put himself outside the pale. And if one finds oneself outside the pale one has got to look very hard at the people who think they're safe. I think that your ostracisation makes them safe. That's their delusion.

Mossman: Can I switch to what sounds quite unconnected but isn't, talking of being put outside the pale—the whole matter of immigration into this country of people from the West Indies and other coloured former Colonies? From what you know of the subject, do you approve of controlling those immigrations?

Baldwin: As far as I know, the question of controlling immigration has never come up until now and applies, therefore, as far as I can tell, only to coloured people. If that's so, then obviously the question of controlled immigration is a question asked essentially in bad faith. The English people, after all, English history, has created these Black Englishmen, who have as much right to the capital as any White Englishman. They've paid quite as much for it as any White Englishman.

MacInnes: Yes. Could I stick up for our country a little bit over this? I mean, what other country has allowed, or encouraged, or admitted, a million coloured people in the last fifteen years and more or less not murdered them? I know landlords slam doors in their faces, I know they get the worse jobs, I know there have been riots (where, incidentally, nobody was killed). But what other country has done that? And behind the scenes there was a tremendous lot of work by rather stupid, well-meaning people trying to receive these people and make things. . . .

Baldwin: My dear Colin, I'm not trying to any way whatever to denigrate England. I don't know England well enough to be able to do that. In any case, I wouldn't. That's not the question. I understand what you're saying, and I do think as far as that goes, the English record certainly by comparison is honourable—and brave.

Mossman: But supposing the question is there: a principle as to whether people should be stopped coming in, basically on the ground of their colour, because this will create tensions and hatreds. Do you think that is a cowardly way out, or do you think it is acceptable and sensible?

Baldwin: I think it is not merely a cowardly way out, I think it is ultimately absolutely inefficient since they're going to come anyway. But the problem one is facing. . . .

MacInnes: They're going to come by birth, if nothing else, aren't they?

Baldwin: Yes, in any case here they are. There is no way effectively to keep them out. Here they are and that means that your societies, all of your societies will have to make room for these people because we have created them and they are here.

Mossman: You've said once, to my great surprise, that America was the most wonderful country in the world. Now that seemed to contradict almost everything else you've ever said or written. How do you account for that grand *cliché?*

Baldwin: When did I say that?

Mossman: You said it all right, in one of your essays which I was reading only the other day.

MacInnes: Well, whether you said it or not, you do think America's a wonderful country, don't you, Jimmy?

Baldwin: Yes, of course. It depends what you think I mean by "wonder."

Mossman: I'm asking you.

Baldwin: "America's the most wonderful country in the world." Well, I could have said it and I could have meant it. Then let me say it now. It is the most wonderful country in the world, it is the most extraordinary collection of ill-assessed motives and undigested history, the most peculiar system of moral evasions and tremendous innocence. There's something very winning and very moving and very beautiful about those people who don't yet know that the world is big and complex and dark and that you have to grow up and become yourself big and complex and dark in order to deal with it. Americans still believe they can somehow get through life without ever being corrupted. It is an insane endeavour and, of course, this is where the Negro comes in. The Negro, by his presence, being on the bottom, affords society almost the only coherence that it has. Since white people in the main cannot grow up our children must grow up by the time they're ten.

Mossman: Why does being at the bottom give coherence?

Baldwin: That means if I'm on the bottom and you can see me there, that means that you are not.

Mossman: If you've got something worse than you, you feel less "chaotic," is that it?

Baldwin: Yes. A poor white man in the deep South knows only one thing. This one thing that he knows has destroyed the labour movement in the deep South and almost in the country. The one thing that he knows is that he's White.

Mossman: Do you think you will be chaotic as well when you're not at the bottom?

Baldwin: Well, in my own case, you know, I. . . .

James Baldwin Breaks His Silence
Cep Dergisi/1967

From *Atlas,* 13 (March 1967), 47-49. Reprinted by permission of *World Press Review.* Translated from *Cep Dergisi* of Istanbul.

The U. S. civil rights front has had tortured and tu-multuous times, but for nearly three years now, novelist James Baldwin, one of the Negros' most biting spokes-man, has maintained a thundering silence. One reason is that Baldwin, a perennial expatriate, has spent most of that time in a villa outside Istanbul, where he granted this rare, if somewhat scattershot, interview for the third issue of *Cep Dergisi,* a new aggressive Turkish monthly covering the international scene.

Cep Dergisi: *Why have you chosen to live in Istanbul? Is there something about Turkey or Moslem countries in general you find congenial? Do you consider yourself an expatriate? If so, what are the advantages? Why have you been spending so much time out of the United States?*
    Baldwin: The principal reason that I now find myself in Istanbul is that I am a writer, and I find it easier to work here than I do else-where. I am left alone here. The people who recognize you on the street do not feel—presumably, as a reward for having recognized you—that they have the right to ask you if you write with a pen or pencil or whether you enjoyed your breakfast or if you can spare a month or two to read their latest, or their first, unpublished book. Walking around Istanbul is infinitely less hazardous than walking around New York; in fact, I do not walk in New York any more than is absolutely necessary, nor does anyone else who values his life and sanity. The Moslem question does not enter into my reasons for being here at all, except, perhaps, that it is a relief to deal with people who, whatever they are pretending, are not pretending to be Chris-tians. I am not now, and never will become—at least not by my own

desire—an expatriate. For better or for worse, my ties with my country are too deep, and my concern is too great. But I am an American artist, and I know exactly what Nathaniel Hawthorne meant when he wrote, from England, around 1861, that "the United States may be fit for many purposes, but they are not fit to live in." Nearly all American artists have felt this, and for very good reasons; but we have all—usually, anyway—gone home. The danger of being an expatriate is that you are very likely to find yourself living, in effect, nowhere. I am not, for example, responsible for Turkish society, and I can have no effect on it: it is not here that my social obligations can be discharged. This means that, as time goes on, the expatriate may find that he has no real or relevant concerns, and no grasp of reality. He is living, really, on the hazards and energies of other people; he has ceased to pay his way. In my case, I've got no choice but to shuttle back and forth between the New World and the Old. I gain something from both places, after all, and possibly I am simply far too proud consciously to side-step a danger. I have spent more time out of the U.S. than usual lately, principally because I have been concentrating on finishing a novel. I go home at the end of the year, to do a play. And then, sometime after that, I'll be back.

What do you think about Black Power and other recent developments in the civil rights movement in the U.S.? Who do you feel are the most effective people and organizations in the civil rights movement right now?

A great deal of hysterical and indefensible nonsense has been written about Black Power. It is a phrase which refers to an honored (!) canon of Western thought: The self-determination of peoples. It means nothing more than that. To limit ourselves only to the events of the last decade, the Negro in America has marched, protested, pleaded, sung, put his body before trucks and tractors, put his body before guns and hoses and dogs, put his body before billy clubs, put his body before chains, put his body in prisons where one would hesitate to house a pig, sent his children out to be beaten and spat upon and driven mad, has petitioned Washington, ceaselessly, ceaselessly, has seen his women humiliated, kicked, beaten (and sometimes they were pregnant women), his heroes, who were his hope, destroyed, and his children blown to bits before his eyes. And the result of all this, the response of the American people? The only response has been panic, rhetoric and lies. The ghetto is more heavily policed than it has ever been before, more brutally and more blatantly oppressed. As of this writing, and after all those prayers and petitions and bombings, neither the Negro child nor the Negro parent has anything resembling a future. The child has no school and the father has no job. And neither is likely to be supplied soon, no matter what the liberals say. The brutal fact is that the economy does not know how to make room for the Negro—it does not have room, after all, for many, many white people—and it would not know how, even if the bulk of the population were less brainwashed than it is. The American people are paying the price for the lie concerning Negro inferiority which they have told themselves so long, and which they have persuaded themselves is the truth. But the legend came about only to afford moral justification for slavery. If you buy and sell a man like an animal, then you must persuade yourself that he is an animal. The terrible thing about this dynamic is that the man who is being used like an animal exerts all his energy in not becoming one; while the man who is so using him fatally descends in the human scale and becomes something much worse than an animal. Black Power means the recognition that neither the American government nor the American people have any desire, or any ability, to liberate Negroes or—which comes to exactly the same thing—themselves. Well, the job must be attempted, we *must* save ourselves if we can; and if we can save ourselves, we can also save the country; it is now absolutely and literally true that the American Negro is America's only hope. As for organizations, I hope to continue working with SNCC.

What are your feelings about the Johnson trial arranged by Jean-Paul Sartre and Bertrand Russell in Paris?

I admire Bertrand Russell very much, and I certainly welcome any instrument which may help to arrest the American madness.

Elsewhere you have mentioned that you don't like the use of Negro soldiers in Vietnam. Am I correct in assuming that you don't share the views of some sociologists who say the U.S. armed services have provided opportunities for the poor and the underprivileged to rise in the social hierarchy?

I consider the American adventure in Vietnam a desperate and

despicable folly, for which future generations will pay very heavily. I
do not think that any American soldier should be fighting there. But
to send Negro soldiers there—to ask Negro soldiers to die there,
while one is busily destroying their kinsmen at home—is of an
impertinence so arrogant, an immorality so flagrant, as to take one's
breath away. As for the liberal sociologists to whom you refer, many
of whom, I imagine, consider themselves to be the Negro's "friends,"
they are, whether or not they know it, simply the hired mercenaries of
a chaotic and irresponsible economy, which, as it cannot employ
Negroes in any other way, prefers to send them out to die. See
Reagan's promise that the able-bodied will either accept state jobs or
be retrained. State jobs for the Negro or the Mexican, or the poor,
means whatever the state wishes it to mean. At the same time,
McNamara announces that those Americans classified illiterate or
poverty-stricken are to be retrained by the Army and used by the
Army. These clearly are not destined to be generals, or to die in bed.

*What are your present feelings about Robert Kennedy? Do you
think he has changed? What do you think of him as a presidential
candidate?*
    Robert Kennedy has made enormous progress along those lines he
deems most desirable, and will almost certainly—especially considering the enormous proportion of women in the United States who
have almost nothing to do *but* vote—be our President one day. I am
curious indeed to know if he will then find it expedient to visit any
American state and inform them that "apartheid is evil."

*Is there a relationship between developments in Black Africa and
the condition of the American Negro?*
    The relevance of Black Africa to the situation of the American
Negro is too complex to be dealt with briefly. We are slowly working
out—or so it seems to me—the precise terms of our relationship to
each other, for we know we need each other; but this endeavor is
complicated by geography and by history (or, in this case, really,
histories, many of them yet to be excavated) and by the fact that
White Power, when it seems to relax its grip in one area, tightens it in
another.

What do you think about demonstrations of violence against

Negroes organized by various minorities in Chicago, Brooklyn, Los Angeles and other parts of America?

The real attitudes of the American people must be brought to the surface before these attitudes can be changed. You refer to the anti-Negro demonstrators as a minority. Alas, they are not a minority.

Since the American Negro is in search of material equality in addition to social and legal equality, do you think he might be in danger of losing his rich spiritual heritage in his quest for material equality?

A man with no future is a man without a heritage. We will worry about preserving our heritage when we have set our children free.

What are your feelings about Christianity and the Negro? Communism and the Negro? Democracy and the Negro? Black Nationalism? Black Muslims?

Except insofar as the Negro transformed Christianity to meet the needs of his brutal situation, Christianity was a disaster. In no way whatever has it replaced, especially in Africa, what it destroyed. Since the word Communism can only here refer to the vicissitudes this concept has undergone in Europe, it has no present relevance to the Negro situation. What black men may or may not do with this concept is another matter. Democracy and the Negro have yet to meet. Black Nationalism ought, properly, to refer to nations, which makes it a rather muddy concept in the United States, and sometimes a dangerous one. One becomes a Black Muslim out of despair with the Christian world, and in order to create an identity which is not at the mercy of that world. In action, the concept has more to do with power than religion.

Are you planning to continue your fighting for civil rights? Do you believe you are in danger of being criticized for deserting the cause of civil rights?

I have never stopped fighting for civil rights, but I must do my work or I'll be of no use to anyone. I have been criticized for so many things, and for so long, that I am quite unable to look on the possibility of being criticized as a danger. The danger probably lies in the opposite direction.

Disturber of the Peace: James Baldwin— An Interview

Eve Auchincloss and Nancy Lynch/1969

From *The Black American Writer*, Vol. I, ed. C.W.E. Bigsby (Deland, FL: Everett—Edwards, 1969), pp. 199-216. Reprinted by permission.

It was reported somewhere recently that your friend Norman Mailer said to you, in anger: "You're little, you're ugly, and you're as black as the ace of spades." But your comeback was not recorded.

Oh, I just laughed. After all, it's true. But the point is, why, after all these years, did he have to say it? I mean, it's his problem, really, and I think it has to do with the fact that like most white liberals—though I'm not accusing him of being one exactly—he has always lied to himself about the way he really feels about Negroes.

Most people would say liberals have done more for the Negro than anybody else. Why are you so hard on them?

This has been on my mind for a long time, but it was triggered when I went on the Barry Gray show to protest the fact that the Anti-Defamation League had given a medal to Kennedy for his record on civil rights and to protest the fact that William Worthy was being indicted by the Justice Department for having re-entered his own country illegally, which as far as I know is an impossibility for an American citizen. And Barry Gray was very angry at me. What he finally said was that I should be picketing Governor Ross Barnett; I shouldn't be picketing my friends. And that made me mad, and I said that one of the hardest things anyone has to survive in this country is his friends. That made him madder. When it was over I began to feel there was involved in all this—in the case of a great many people who think they are on our side of the fence—a will to power that has nothing whatever to do with the principles they think they are upholding. They are operating in this part of the forest because this is where they find themselves, and it is easy for them—but it has nothing whatever to do with love or justice or any of the things they think it has to do with. And when the chips are down, it comes out. Their status in their own eyes is much more important than any real change. If there were no Negro problem, I don't know what in the world they would do. Their pronouncements have nothing to do with reality, that's what I object to. Reality is involved with their relationship to themselves, their wives, their children; but this they have abdicated entirely, and use, then, me, the Negro, as an opportunity to live safely.

Does this apply to people who work for CORE and such things?
Those people, in my book, are not exactly liberals. I'm not talking about them. You can't say they're accomplishing nothing, really, because they're indispensable on a certain level. But their work has no resonance. It's all sort of meaningless, you see, like that group of anarchists in *The Secret Agent.* They're in the back room and that's where they stay.

And when the revolution comes, it doesn't come from them?
It doesn't come from them. It comes from some place you never thought it was coming from. And this is what they don't seem to know. I don't know—between the kind of sad incompetence of most workers for the Lord and the rigid egotism of the self-styled leading liberals it's very difficult to choose. Some of these liberal columnists, the professional bleeding hearts, have the public ear, but what they do with it is simply to reassure it. They sound as though they're being daring, but they're not. If reality broke into one of those columns, God knows what would happen! And when it threatens to, they get up on their hind legs and say, "Don't attack your friends!" I watched one of them in Paris one night trying to pick up the toughest, most evil, black blues singer in the world. He was drunk and weeping and she was calming him as though he were five years old. A cat who doesn't know when he's facing one of the world's top bitches! He doesn't even know it? What else doesn't he know? If you don't know that, then what *do* you know? And what good can you possibly do me? They make no connection between what they do in nightclubs and what they say in print, no connection between the ruin of their children and their public pronouncements.

Well, what's this hypocrisy covering up? You've seen Norman

Podhoretz's article in Commentary, *telling how he grew up in a poor neighborhood alongside a large Negro population. And all through his childhood the Negro was someone who bullied you and beat you up on the one hand and on the other who enjoyed freedom of license no Jewish boy was allowed. And he says this animosity and envy is still buried in him.*

What Norman does in that piece is exactly what I'm asking all these high-minded white liberals to do: to tell the truth, what he really feels about Negroes—which is, as well, a confession about himself. But he is not lying about it. I'm sure that all the liberals I'm scoring off have stories very much like him, and they lie about it. But he says he hated and feared Negroes and that the little boy in him still does. The little boy in *them* still does, too, only they pretend he isn't there.

But what's the source of the bad feeling, basically?

It's very complicated, and a terrible, vicious circle, but there's no point lying about it. In any case, we all grew up with a great gulf fixed between whites and Negroes, and it makes Negroes per se exotic, strange, different, other. And whatever is "other" is frightening. The entire society reinforces this difference so that you have to be afraid of them; you aren't given much choice. And if you're afraid of them you've got to hate them. If it is so that no one really ever gets over his beginnings, then liberals are all liars, because this is true of them, too, and they pretend it isn't. And this is shown whenever you get to the personal level with them.

The sense of otherness is a fact we all recognize, anyway. But what can we do to overcome it?

In order for a person to cease to be other, you've got somehow to break through that thing which divides you and get into each other's lives. And this almost never happens. It doesn't never happen, but it almost never happens, and never at all within the liberal context, because the whole rhetoric is designed to prevent that from happening.

For instance?

Well, you certainly cannot talk to anybody in terms of great monolithic abstractions. You can't talk about The Negro Problem. What the hell are you talking about? Either we're talking about you and me, or we're not talking.

Do you ever worry that some of the things you say may only serve to reinforce feelings of guilt and fear in white people?

I think what I feel about guilt is that it is like a festering sore that must be worked upon until it's opened and the pus can run out.

But in criticizing Native Son, *you said you felt Richard Wright had made a mistake in presenting a character who would make people feel frightened and guilty. Yet you yourself have expressed a certain amount of pleasure in the way Black Muslims frighten white people.*

I know what you mean, but as a matter of fact the Muslims frighten me very much. I consider them really irresponsible in the most serious way—irresponsible in terms of what I consider to be their obligations to the Negro community, as all racists are irresponsible. They batten on the despair of black men.

You think they have nothing to offer, really?

No. If they were organizing rent strikes among the people who live in those ghettos in Harlem right now, organizing just one block not to pay the rent until the landlords did something about the rats and the houses; if they were spotlighting concrete things, proving to Negroes that there were certain things they could do for themselves . . .

But is there anything?

There is nothing they can do for themselves so long as they don't think there is. That's part of the price of being a Negro: you're de-moralized so soon. If the Muslims were operating on that level I would have no quarrel with them, perhaps, but they're doing something else. It's just another inflated store-front church. It has that emotional value and that practical uselessness, only it's more danger-ous. And another thing bothers me. I suppose it is the effect they can have on the country itself. Not so much the Muslim movement, but a whole area they represent—all the anguish that Negroes endure in this country, which no one wants to face. And the Muslims are the only people who articulate it for white people—and also for Negroes, I must say. And they frighten white people half to death. When you consider the ignorance that reigns in this country from top to bottom, it seems clear to me that the Muslim movement could act as a catalyst to turn the place into a concentration camp in no time at all.

How could that really happen?

If we'd been mad enough to go to war with Cuba, how many Negroes do you think you could mobilize out of Harlem? "Why should I go shoot Cubans? The government cannot protect me in Mississippi, but is willing to mount a whole invasion to bring freedom to the Cubans"—you really have to be an idiot not to ask that question. And God knows, if that does come about, the Muslims will not fail to ask it. You can put Elijah Muhammad and Malcolm X in jail, and maybe a couple of hundred thousand others. But if you've done *that,* then you might as well forget the war, because you've lost it.

Do you think the Negro can use the international situation as a power lever?
It depends on a great many other things, because you can use it as a power lever only to a very limited extent. The Negro situation here has not changed because of the cold war and the international situation, but the Government is aware of some things, and it is attempting to meet them by putting Negroes in the window, not to change things, but to create good propaganda. Of course, this doesn't help. What one needs is something that kids in the South are terribly aware of—some way of using such limited power as one has really to force the Government to investigate murders in Mississippi, and to bring pressure to bear on the cities to begin to deal with the Negro population.

How can it ever be done?
One's got to assume that it can be done, but how can it be done? Well, for example, in the South—which is clearer than the North—when a white man murders a black man, nothing can be done about it. But recently I went along with a field secretary of the N.A.A.C.P. in Mississippi to investigate a murder that had been hushed up. We rode around through those back roads for hours talking to people who had known the dead man, trying to find out what had happened. And the Negroes talked to us as the German Jews must have talked when Hitler came to power. It was a matter of turning the car around so that the license plate couldn't be seen from the road. And talking to people with their lights out. We had hoped to discover that the sheriff, who had forced the man to be buried without an inquest, had also murdered him. If he had, then *in principle* the Justice Department could have been forced to act. But it turned out it was not the

sheriff but simply the storekeeper, who was a friend of his. And there was almost no way for the Justice Department to act, because the law-enforcement interests in the South have very strong ties with Washington, and the whole political structure in Washington is partly designed to protect the Southern oligarchy. And Bobby Kennedy's much more interested in politics than he is in any of these things, and so, for that matter, is his brother. And furthermore, even if Bobby Kennedy were a different person, or his brother, they are also ignorant, as most white Americans are, of what the problem really is, of how Negroes really live. The speech Kennedy made to Mississippi the night Meredith was carried there was one of the most shameful performances in our history.

Why?

Because he talked to Mississippi as if there were no Negroes there. And this had a terrible, demoralizing, disaffecting effect on all Negroes everywhere. One is weary of being told that desegregation is legal. One would like to hear for a change that it is *right!* Now, how one begins to use this power we were talking about earlier is a very grave question, because first of all you have to get Eastland out of Congress and get rid of the power that he wields there. You've got to get rid of J. Edgar Hoover and the power that he wields. If one could get rid of just those two men, or modify their power, there would be a great deal more hope. How in the world are you going to get Mississippi Negroes to go to the polls if you remember that most of them are extremely poor, most of them almost illiterate, and that they live under the most intolerable conditions? They are used to it, which is worse, and they have no sense that they can do anything for themselves. If six Negroes go to the polls and get beaten half to death, and one or two die, and nothing happens from Washington, how are you going to manage even to get the ballot?

It seems very hopeless.

One cannot agree that it is hopeless. But that's the way it is. And the only hope we have is somehow to get in Washington, or *somewhere*, enough weight to begin to change the climate.

What happens to people like Meredith who put themselves in the front lines?

Aha. You can hold yourself together during all the action, but inevitably there's a great reaction somewhere. Some of them go to mental institutions. It's very hard to take. I got a taste of this only once. When I went to Tallahassee for you [MLLE, August, 1960] I was living in a motel on the highway and there were trees along the road, and my room was the very last one. I would come back around midnight. Since I was the only Northern Negro in town, I was terribly visible, and my light was the only light on late at night, because I was typing my notes. I couldn't avoid thinking about the highway and those trees. I couldn't get over it by saying "Don't be silly, Jimmy." And I was scared half to death. But I got through it and finally went to Paris. I was having lunch with a friend the day I arrived and suddenly I began to shake. And I stayed at his house for two days. I was afraid to be alone. And that taught me something about how much greater the pressure must be for those kids now. The reaction has to come, it has to come. Lately I talked to the only Negro boy in an integrated school in New Orleans. He stood and moved like a little soldier, and it was very impressive and very frightening. Because no boy his age can possibly be that controlled and not pay for it later on somehow.

Do you think school desegregation was a good place to begin? Putting all the onus of this on the children?

At this point there would be no good place to begin, really. But in another way those beautiful children are the only people who could have done it.

Movies and beaches, all that, seem like effort lost.

Well, it isn't entirely, though. What one's trying to do is simply make white people get used to seeing you around without a broom in your hand! I think it's just as important as the schools, because the wall has been built on every single level and has got to come down on every level. The Government, for reasons of its own, prefers that Negroes in the South work on voting registration rather than try to desegregate buses or bus stations or coffee counters or stores, and, God knows, not to have any boycotts. Well, of course, the Government's being very clever about that. It will take years to get the vote, in any case, and if you're doing that and nothing else, then the vote's safe another fifty years.

What do you think of the idea that Negroes can't get anywhere until they begin to mobilize as a real group?
I don't know on what principle it would mobilize itself, that's the trouble.

But whether you like it or not, you are thrust into a sort of role as spokesman for The Negro—a group that ought not to be a group. How do you feel about that role? Maybe you didn't elect it, and yet . . .
And yet it's true.

Can you speak for those millions?
I can't. I don't try to.

The neo-Africans don't seem to think you speak for them. What about them?
They are romantic American Negroes who think they can identify with the African struggle, without having the least idea what it's about. They want to see black men in power, simply, and it's more interesting to see a black statesman in his robes at the U.N. than to consider what kind of a statesman he is.

Do they actually want to live in Africa?
They think they do, but they don't stay. The Africans don't want them. They can't *use* them. You can't deal with anybody who pretends that he doesn't come from where he comes from; you can't respect him and you can't trust him. Maybe I can go to Africa and think that I'm an African looking for my tribe—and where is it? But they hear the way I talk and see the way I walk, and they don't like me any better for pretending I don't come from Harlem. And Africans remember, though neo-Africans do not, when American Negroes would not speak to Africans. But I do feel very involved with the students in the South. I don't consider myself a spokesman for them either, but I do think that they trust me and I can't afford to fail them. That controls me more than anything else in this context, because no one else seems to be doing it, really. And kids need somebody who will talk to them, listen to them. They want you to respect their questions.

What do they ask you?

Well, they ask real questions. "What would you do if your teacher
told you that instead of picketing and engaging in sit-ins, you should
get an education first?" one boy asked me. And I said, "I would tell
my teacher that it's impossible to get an education in this country
until you change the country." And the boy said, "Thank you." And
that does something for me.

*To go back to our fear of the Negro, haven't you also suggested
that sex is at the bottom of it?*
Yes, I think it has something to do with the whole Puritan ethic, the
whole idea that the flesh is something to be ashamed of. The burden
that is placed on you because you're a Negro male is terrifying, and it
says something about the poverty of the white cat's bed or the white
chick's bed, which today is very hard to believe.

But we love to talk about sex!
That's right, and that's where the Negro comes in. If a Negro is
present in a room, there's a great silence then. Sex is on everybody's
mind, but nobody's going to say anything. You can see people,
almost in the middle of sentences, shifting gears and making wild
right turns. They wanted to talk about sex, but now they're not going
to, because here sex *is*, right in the middle of the room drinking a dry
martini. And it all becomes extremely polite and antiseptic. But on
the other hand, at four o'clock in the morning, when everybody's
drunk enough, then extraordinary things can happen. It's very hard
to describe. It's something I want to do in a novel.

Why this poverty of the white cat's bed?
I have some hunches. It has something to do with Puritanism
again. It has something to do with the whole role of women in this
country since the country got here. Something to do with the scarcity
of women and the roughness of the country. I don't mean just
physical roughness, I mean the loneliness, the physical loneliness of
it. When you were crossing it, it must have been terrifying. And it has
something to do with the Indians. White men married Indians and
slept with them and killed them, too.

Do you think history operates this way in people's unconscious?
I think it operates this way *actually*. This has to be so. Because
when the chips are down in any crisis, what you have to draw on

finally is not what happened in the time that you yourself have been on earth, but what came before you. This is what gets you through your crisis finally. And somewhere in yourself you carry all of that. You have to be in great trouble to turn to it and use it, or to suspect that you have to; but when you are in trouble, that's what you turn to, which means it must be there.

In your writing you've always been hard on everyone, white and black, but lately you seem to be getting harder and harder on white people.
What I want to do in the play I'm working on now is somehow bring that whole thing together—what white people have done and also what black people are doing. And I don't know how to put that.

Well, everything you've said about white people has been negative; yet you say that blacks have something to give us without which we'll perish.
I think that's true. If the Negro doesn't save this country, then ,nobody else can. And if I can find another word than Negro it might be closer to what I mean. I don't mean the Negro as a person; I mean the Negro as an experience—a level of experience Americans always deny.

One of the most puzzling things you've said is that your darkness reminds white men of their death.
I meant what I said: if you are a Negro dealing with people all day long, all year long, all life long, who never look at you, then you have to figure out one day what they *are* looking at. Obviously it isn't you. When I was seventeen, working for the Army, I could not have been a threat to any white man alive. So it wasn't me, it was something he didn't want to see. And you know what that was? It was ultimately, yes, his own death. Or call it trouble. Trouble is an excellent metaphor for death. The white man knew he would not like to be me. People who certainly are not monsters on any other level will do monstrous things to you, semi-deliberately or deliberately, designed to protect their wives and children. This is what is meant by keeping you in your place. If you move out of your place everything is changed. If I'm not what that white man thinks I am, then he has to find out what *he* is.

Do we use status to make up for identity?

Exactly. And therefore I'm the only cat that has any identity, because it's in my skin. I've got a built-in identity for other people, which is more than they have for me, more than they have for themselves, too. And they fear and despise one for it.

How about when you look at us? Are we just blobs?

No. You never could be for me, because you all have too much power. I can be a blob for you, but you I have to study in order to survive. And this can kill you, but if it doesn't kill you it gives you a certain beat. It isn't a business of what people say. Listen to what they're not saying. A lot of Negro style—the style of a man like Miles Davis or Ray Charles or the style of a man like myself—is based on a knowledge of what people are really saying and on our refusal to hear it. You pick up on the beat, which is much more truthful than words.

They say that people deprived of the full use of their intellects make up for it with unusual powers of intuition. This would be true of the Negro, surely?

You live almost entirely by your intuition. It has to be highly developed. And the intellect, anyway, is one more way of avoiding yourself. One must find a way to get through to life or to experience, but that can't be done intellectually.

You must get a real sense of who you are, anyway. How would you define identity?

I don't know. It's some respect for the self, which has something to do—as my good friend Sidney Poitier says—with knowing whence you came. And really knowing that. And in some way, if you know that, you know something else, too. I can't tell precisely what it is you know then, but if you know where you were, you have some sense of where you are.

Evidently "whence you came" once stood between you and a sense of who you are.

It inevitably does, I think, for everybody. It has to. You have to accept it. You can't run. I know, because I've tried. And I think who you are has something to do with responsibility, too.

To whom and what?

The kind of responsibility that means you haven't got time to weep, because you have too much to do, the pressures are too great. It's learning very soon that there are no excuses, that if you fail, it's because *you* failed. And of course it doesn't mean you won't—one way or another everybody does. Everybody has to deal with this question of who and what he is. I have to deal with it because of the kids, the students, and I have to deal with it because I'm a writer. Writers have to make use of it all, every bit of it. That's all you've got. You take it or you die.

But in a way wasn't it easier for you to find out who you were because you were a Negro and had to face your suffering?

Yes. But there's something else, too. Hannah Arendt told me that the virtues I described in *The New Yorker* piece—the sensuality I was talking about, and the warmth, and the fish fries, and all that—are typical of all oppressed people. And they don't, unluckily, she said— and I think she's entirely right—survive even five minutes the end of their oppression.

And what we think of as the Negro's innate qualities are just desperate stratagems that people who have nothing else use to stay alive?

And you make do with nothing, and you get, if you survive, a kind of authority from that. You really have to know yourself to find resources to make do with the minimum. But you wouldn't do it if you weren't forced to do it. And the moment you're not forced to do it any more, you stop doing it.

And Negro millionaires are as far removed from reality as anybody else?

Insofar as they are pretending to be white.

You said you yourself once felt that you didn't know whether you were black or white. What did you mean?

Well, I meant I didn't know who I was at all. They used to say to me, "Don't act like a nigger." Acting like a nigger meant eating with your hands or scratching yourself or cursing or fighting or getting drunk or having nappy hair—all those things. And for a long time I spent a lot of effort trying not to act like a nigger. I slicked my hair down, never raised my voice, had perfect table manners, and of course it didn't help at all.

You were just being a cultured Negro!
I was being a cultured Negro. I was always wearing a sort of iron corset. And it didn't make me white. And it didn't make me a man either. And it means I couldn't talk to white people, because I was talking in a certain kind of way, and I couldn't talk to black people either, because I was too busy not being one of them. And I hated white people from the bottom of my heart. And I hated black people for being so common! I realized, too, that if a white man were doing any of those things I was not told not to do, no one would say he was acting like a nigger. It was only me who was acting like a nigger, because I *was* a nigger. No matter what I did, I was acting like a nigger. So I decided to act like a nigger, or at least act like *me*.

What did you mean when you said that a black person should cultivate the nigger within?
Well, I mean this. If I want to beat up a doorman, maybe I don't beat him up, but I have to know that that's what I really want to do. That I'm not being the poised, controlled, civilized cat that I dream of myself as being at all. That if a policeman hits me, I'm very probably going to try to kill him. And if I don't do it, it won't be because I don't want to. It will be because something else is operating and I know that I have to do something else. But I know it is *there*. That's my protection against it.

And it's not a matter of black or white at all?
It's a matter of not telling any more lies than you can help. And some black people know that and some white people know that; and for the rest . . . well, there are very, very few.

Is there any hope for the body politic?
No, not now. We'd be very lucky if we had a great man in the White House right now, *if* we had a great man. We do not, but *if* we did . . .

Have you ever known anyone who seemed to you great?
James Meredith. He's a very tough and loving little man.

Still loving? Has he repressed his hatred?

On certain questions I don't think that hatred any longer operates. I don't think I hate anybody any more. It's too expensive. I stopped trying to be white. It's a law that if I hate white people I have to hate black people.

Any other people you think great?
A man named Jerome Smith. He's one of the student leaders in New Orleans and one of the veterans of Jackson, Mississippi—beaten with brass knuckles until he was entirely numb; not simply out, but numb. He's still being treated for it. He's very young. He was a longshoreman. And he is a tremendous man.

Why is he tremendous? Because he survived?
No, he's tremendous because he knows what happened. If anyone has a right to hate white people, Jerome certainly does. But he doesn't hate. He does not.

You said you used to hate yourself. How did you get over it?
Well, I think it has everything to do with my brothers and sisters. You can't be involved with that many people so young without doing one of two things: either you reject it all, or sooner or later you begin to realize that it is part of you. And I loved them very much. I didn't always. At the very beginning I did. I did—and I do. In a way you take your worth from other people's eyes. And a friend in Switzerland did something, too. In a way he saved my life by refusing to allow me to be paranoid about my color. He did it by not being sorry for me. And my mother had something to do with it, too. I think she saved us all. She was the only person in the world we could turn to, yet she couldn't protect us.

She doesn't sound like that consoling black-mammy figure that we whites are so enamored of. The maids we know, for instance.
Yes, who's all wise, all patient, and all enduring. But it's emotionally too easy, because in fact those maids have sons who may by this time have turned into junkies because their mothers can get jobs and they can't. I'm sure all the people my mother worked for thought of her that way, but she wasn't like that at all. She was a very tough little woman, and she must have been scared to death all the years she was raising us.

Scared of what?
Of those streets! There it is at the door, *at the door!* Whores,
pimps, racketeers. It hasn't changed either, by the way. That's what it
means to be raised in a ghetto. I think of what a woman like my
mother knows, instinctively has to know, has had to know from the
very beginning: that there is no safety, that no one is safe, none of
her children would ever be safe. The nature of the ghetto is somehow
ultimately to make those skills which are immoral the only skills worth
having. You haven't got to be sweet to survive in a ghetto; you've got
to be cunning. You've got to make up the rules as you go along;
there aren't any others. You can't call the cops.

What about your father?
He was righteous in the pulpit and a monster in the house. Maybe
he saved all kinds of souls, but he lost all his children, *every* single
one of them. And it wasn't so much a matter of punishment with him:
he was trying to kill us. I've hated a few people, but actually I've
hated only one person, and that was my father.

Did he hate you?
In a way, yes. He didn't like me. But he'd had a terrible time, too.
And of coure, I was not his son. I was a bastard. What he wanted for
his children was what in fact I became. I was the brightest boy in the
house because I was the eldest, and because I loved my mother and I
really loved those kids. And I was necessary: I changed all the diapers
and I knew where the kids were, and I could take some of the pressures off my mother and in a way stand between him and her—
which is a strange role to play. I had to learn to stand up to my father,
and, in learning that, I became precisely what he wanted his other
children to become, and he couldn't take that, and I couldn't either
maybe.

Did he affect your ideas of what you could do in the world?
My father did one thing for me. He said, "You can't do it." And I
said, "Listen, m———— don't tell me what I can't do. I can't do it?
Don't tell me I can't do it. You'll see."

*Why couldn't you do it, according to him? Because you were
black?*
Because I was black, because I was little, because I was ugly. He

made me ugly. I used to put pennies on my eyes to make them go back.

But out of that an identity emerged.
Yes, all those strangers called Jimmy Baldwin.

Who are some of them?
There's the older brother with all the egotism and rigidity that implies. That tone will always be there, and there's nothing I can do about it except know it's there and laugh at it. I grew up telling people what to do and spanking them, so that in some ways I always will be doing that. Then there's the self-pitying little boy. You know: "I can't do it, because I'm so ugly." He's still there some place.

Who else?
Lots of people. Some of them are unmentionable. There's a man. There's a woman, too. There are lots of people here.

It's been said of you that you have two obsessions: color and homosexuality.
I'm not absolutely sure I have two obsessions. They're more than that.

Whatever they are, are they interrelated?
Let's go back to where we were talking about the Negro man and sex, and let's go back again to the American white man's lack of sexual security, and then let's try to imagine what it would be like to be a Negro adolescent dealing with those people to whom you are a phallic symbol. American males are the only people I've ever encountered in the world who are willing to go on the needle before they'll go to bed with each other. Because they're afraid of this, they don't know how to go to bed with women either. I've known people who literally died out of this panic. I don't know what homosexual means any more, and Americans don't either.

You don't think it's a disease?
This is one of the American myths. What always occurs to me is that people in other parts of the world have never had this peculiar kind of conflict. If you fall in love with a boy, you fall in love with a boy. The fact that Americans consider it a disease says more about them than it says about homosexuality.

What about societies where homosexuality becomes very open, as it has here or did in Germany during the Twenties?

When it becomes open as it has here, it becomes a disease. These people are not involved in anything resembling love-making: they're involved in some kind of exhibition of their disaster. It has nothing to do with contact or involvement between two people—which means that the person may change you. That's what people are afraid of. It's impossible to go through life assuming that you know who you're going to fall in love with. You don't. And everything depends on the fashion in which you live, on the things to which you will not say no, the risks you are prepared to take.

What's going to keep black people from becoming just like white people once they've broken down the barriers?

That's what frightens me when we talk about what we call The Negro Problem. I realize that most white people don't realize that the Negro is like anybody else, just like everybody else. And that when this situation ends, assuming we live to see that, something else will begin, which may be just as terrible as what we're going through now. And what some of the students in the South know is that it's not a matter of being accepted into this society at all. It is a matter of demolishing it in some way, which has nothing to do with the Kremlin. It's a matter of transforming it; it's a matter of not making your peace with it; it's a matter really of building Jerusalem again, no matter how corny that may sound.

Wouldn't most people rather escape it than transform it?

You can't escape. You have *not* walked out of the industrial society because you say you have or because you're wearing a beard. You're still right here where you were; you haven't moved an inch.

How about your years in Europe? Was that an escape?

I'll say this: I know very well I survived as a writer by living abroad so long, because if I had not been living abroad, I would have been compelled to make more money.

Are you ever tempted to go back?

All I can do is work out the terms on which I can work, and for me that means being a transatlantic commuter. What's most difficult is that you are penalized for trying to remain in touch with yourself. I have a public life—and I know that, O.K. I have a private life, some-thing which I know a good deal less. And the temptation is to avoid the private life because you can hide in the public one. And I've got excellent reasons for doing it, because what I'm doing is very admirable—you know, all this jazz. Except that that is not the most important thing! The most important thing is somewhere else. It always is—somewhere else. But it's not my life, and if I pretend it is, I'll die. I am *not* a public speaker. I *am* an artist.

You are stealing from the artist to pay for the Negro?
Yes. It's one of the prices of my success. And let's face it, I am a *Negro* writer. Sidney Poitier, you know, is not simply an actor; he's a *Negro* actor. He's not simply a movie star; he's the *only* Negro movie star. And because he is in the position that he is in, he has obligations that Tony Curtis will never have. And it has made Sidney a remark-able man.

Can a Negro ever talk about anything but being a Negro?
I get so tired of black and white, you know, so tired of talking about it, especially when you can't get anything across. What you have to do, I suppose, is invest the vocabulary with something it doesn't contain yet. Don't you see what I'm trying to do? I'm trying to find another word besides Negro to say what I mean, and I can't use tragedy.

Why not?
Because I haven't figured out the terms on which I can use it yet. All I know . . . I suddenly thought of all the Negroes who don't know anything either.

As we've talked now, you have translated Negro into terms which . . .
Which have nothing to do with *that*.

Which have nothing to do with that. And which is what we've really been talking about.
Which is the only thing *to* talk about. I don't know. Nothing will happen to change all that before we die—that vocabulary.

And we have to go on talking about black and white, and that's not it at all.

That is not enough, and it isn't interesting. I don't think much will happen, except disaster, to change things.

The fire next time?
Yes. People don't give things up; things are taken away from them. I'm not frightened of another war really. I'm just frightened of chaos, apathy, indifference—which is the road people took to Auschwitz.

Conversation: Ida Lewis and James Baldwin
Ida Lewis/1970

From *Essence*, 16 (October 1970), 23-27. Copyright 1970 by Essence Communications, Inc. Reprinted by permission.

James Baldwin is probably the most widely quoted black writer in the past decade. He is the author of numerous works, all of which have won critical acclaim. Among these are his novels: *Go Tell It on the Mountain,* his first work; *Giovanni's Room,* which was set in Paris, and *Another Country,* his first critical and commercial success. His latest: *Tell Me How Long the Train's Been Gone.* He also wrote a number of personal essays that were collected in book form; *Notes of a Native Son,* was his first collection, followed by *Nobody Knows My Name,* which brought him literary prominence. The third volume, *The Fire Next Time,* was regarded as one of the most brilliant essays written on black protest. Two plays, *Blues for Mister Charlie* and *The Amen Corner* were performed on the American stage.

From boy-preacher in Harlem store-front churches to famed essayist and novelist, Baldwin is now an expatriate in Paris. Why expatriate? What is he about now? While we were in Paris, *Essence* stopped to visit him and this is what he told us.

Ida: Jimmy, I'm here to probe, to find out what the new James Baldwin is all about?

Jimmy: Okay. I won't duck anything.

Ida: I am curious about why you are in Paris and not New York. Haven't you been this route before?

Jimmy: It's a difficult question to answer. But for exercise, let's begin back in 1948 when I first left America. Why in the world, I've been asked, did you go to a white country? When I first heard that question it threw me. But the answer is obvious; there were no black countries in 1948. Whether there are black countries today is another

83

question, which we won't go into now. But you know I didn't *come* to Paris in '48, I simply *left* America. I would have gone to Tokyo, I would have gone to Israel, I would have gone anywhere. I was getting out of America.

So I found myself in Paris. I arrived here with $40, scared to death, not knowing what I was going to do, but knowing that whatever was going to happen here would not be worse than what was certainly going to happen in America. Here I was in danger of death; but in America it was not a danger, it was a certainty. Not just physical death, I mean *real* death.

Ida: Would you explain this death you speak about?

Jimmy: The death of working in the post office for 37 years; of being a civil servant for a hostile government. The death of going under and watching your family go under.

Ida: These kinds of deaths were still part of black life when you returned to the States in '57. Why did you return?

Jimmy: I went back in '57 because I got terribly tired. It was during the Algerian war. My friends were Algerians and Africans. They are the people who befriended me when I arrived here broke. In a sense, we saved each other, we lived together. So when the war began, my friends began to disappear one by one. What was happening was obvious. When hotels were raided, I was let alone, but my friends were taken away. My green American passport saved me.

I got tired and I began to be ashamed, sitting in cafés in Paris and explaining Little Rock and Tennessee. I thought it was easier to go home. It was impossible to sit there and listen to Frenchmen talk about my Algerian friends in the terms that had always been used to describe us, you know, "You rape our women. You carry knives."

Ida: In a sense, all of us became Algerians.

Jimmy: Yes, in another language; but it was the same thing. So I went home. The rest, as we say, is history.

Ida: You became the famous James Baldwin, writer and black spokesman.

Jimmy: Yes, I played two roles. I never wanted to be a spokesman, but I suppose it's something that had to happen. But that is over now. And I discovered that the time I needed to stop and start again, the necessary kind of rest to get myself together, was not possible in America because the pressures were too great. So, I had to leave once more.

Ida: Could you be more specific?

Jimmy: Because of what I had become in the minds of the public, I ceased to belong to me. Once you are in the public limelight, you must somehow find a way to deal with that mystery. You have to realize you've been paid for, and you can't goof. I kept leaving for a short time—to do this, to do that—but to save myself I finally had to leave for good.

Ida: Can you recall that moment of decision?

Jimmy: One makes decisions in funny ways; you make a decision without knowing you've made it. I suppose my decision was made when Malcolm X was killed, when Martin Luther King was killed, when Medgar Evers and John and Bobby and Fred Hampton were killed. I loved Medgar. I loved Martin and Malcolm. We all worked together and kept the faith together. Now they are all dead. When you think about it, it is incredible. I'm the last witness—everybody else is dead. I couldn't stay in America, I had to leave.

Ida: What was buried in those graveyards?

Jimmy: That dialogue is gone. With those great men, the possibility of a certain kind of dialogue in America has ended. Maybe the possibility of it was never real, but the hope certainly was. Now, the Western world, which has always stood on very shaky foundations, is coalescing according to the principle under which it was organized, and that principle is white supremacy. From England to Sacramento, Ronald Reagan and Enoch Powell are the same person.

Ida: The other reasons?

Jimmy: I was invited to Israel and I'd planned to take my first trip to Africa after that. But when the time came, I had so many things on my mind I didn't dare go to Africa. After I visited Israel, I understood the theology of Judaism—and its mythology—better than I had before. I understood the great blackmail which has been imposed on the world not by the Jew but by the Christian. We fell for it, and the Jews fell for it. Let me put it this way. When I was in Israel I thought I liked Israel. I liked the people. But to me it was obvious why the Western world created the state of Israel, which is not really a Jewish state. The West needed a handle in the Middle East. And they created the state as a European pawn. It is tragic that the Jews should allow themselves to be used in this fashion, because no one cares what happens to the Jews. No one cares what is happening to the Arabs. But they do care about the oil. That part of the world is a crucial matter if you intend to rule the world.

I'm not anti-Semitic at all, but I am anti-Zionist. I don't believe they had the right, after 3,000 years, to reclaim the land with Western bombs and guns on biblical injunction. When I was in Israel it was as though I was in the middle of *The Fire Next Time.* I didn't dare go from Israel to Africa, so I went to Turkey, just across the road, and stayed there until I finished *Another Country.*

Ida: You sound as if you had been in spiritual trouble.

Jimmy: I was. It was very useful for me to go to a place like Istanbul at that point of my life, because it was so far out of the way from what I called home and the pressures. It's a funny thing, becoming famous. If you're an actor or dancer, it is what you expect. But if you're a writer, you don't expect what happened to me. You expect to be photographed all over the place but you don't expect the shit, the constant demands, the people's expectations. During my Istanbul stay I learned a lot about dealing with people who are neither Western nor Eastern. In a way, Turkey is a satellite on the Russian border. That's something to watch. You learn about the brutality and the power of the Western world. You're living with people whom nobody cares about, who are bounced like a tennis ball between the great powers. Not that I wasn't previously aware of the cynicism of power politics and foreign aid, but it was a revelation to see it functioning everyday in that sort of a theatre.

Ida: The Turks are poor people. It seems to me that they, too, are victims of many of the same prejudices that affect black men. Did you find any comparisons?

Jimmy: It's a very curious comparison. I would say, no, because of the fact that the American black man is now the strangest creature in history, due to his long apprenticeship in the West. For example, the people of Istanbul have never seen New York. *West Side Story* is an event for them. They know nothing about what the black man has gone through in America. They still think of America as a promised land.

The American black man knows something which nobody else in

the world knows. To have been where we were, to have paid the price we have paid, to have survived, and to have shaken up the world the way we have is a rare journey. No one else has made it but us. There is a reason that people are listening to James Brown, Nina Simone, and Aretha Franklin all over the world, and not to somebody from Moscow, Turkey, or England. And the reason is not in our crotch but in our heart, our soul. It's something the world denied and lied about, energy they labeled savage, inferior, and insignificant. But it has been proven that no matter what they labeled it, they cannot do without it.

The peoples of Turkey, Greece, even the peoples in Jamaica have not gone through the fire. They don't know that the dream which was America is over. I know that. What we have allowed to happen to our country is shameful. I'm ashamed of Nixon. I wouldn't hire him to become keeper of the gate in Central Park. There's no excuse for a man like Nixon to be put in charge of a country like the United States.

Ida: But don't we need all thinking and able-bodied Americans to change what has happened? We can't run away.

Jimmy: Okay, you're right. But it's like this: I believe that I've got a master stone in which I see something and I have to find a way of chiseling out what I see. I left America, finally, because I knew I could not do it there.

It doesn't matter where I do it as long as I do it. I don't believe in nations any more. Those passports, those borders are as outworn and useless as war. No one can afford them anymore. We're such a conglomorate of things. Look at the American black man, all the bloods in a single stream. Look at the history of anybody you might know. He may have been born in Yugoslovia, raised in Germany, exiled to Casablanca, killed in Spain. That's our century. It will take the human race a long time to get over this stuff.

Ida: That leaves blacks in a strange situation.

Jimmy: It certainly does. Because what has happened is that the party's over. All the pretenses of the Western world have been exposed. There is no way to convince me or any other black person in the world, to say nothing of people who are neither black nor white, that America is anything but an outlaw nation. It doesn't make any difference what one says about the Declaration of Independence, the Bill of Rights, the Magna Carta, when arms are being sold to South Africa, and the Vietnamese are being killed on their own soil by American bombs. The name of the game in America is banks and power. And one does not have to investigate too far to discover that the Western economy has been built on the backs of non-white peoples.

Ida: But to leave one's country, Jimmy, is traumatic.

Jimmy: I fought leaving for a long time. I didn't want to go. I had been based in New York for quite a while, my family and friends are there. It is my country and I'm not 24 years old any more. It was not so easy to pack up and leave. What probably convinced me that I had to leave was my encounter with Hollywood.

Ida: You went to Hollywood to write a screenplay on the life of Malcolm X?

Jimmy: Yes. I never wanted to go to Hollywood. And I would never have gone had it not been for Malcolm. When I was asked to write the screenplay on my friend's life, part of me knew that it really could not be done. But I didn't believe I had the right to turn down a possible opportunity to reveal Malcolm on-screen. I knew the odds were against me, but sometimes you take outside chances. It's better than thinking for the rest of your life that perhaps it could have been done.

Believe me, my Hollywood journey was a revelation. It was incredible to find yourself in a situation where the people who perpetrated his murder attempted to dictate his love, grief, and suffering to you. I believed Malcolm trusted me and that held me there. I tried to go down with the deal. I went the route. And when that battle was over, and I realized there was no hope—that they were speaking Hindustani and I was speaking Spanish—I was through. Day followed day and week followed week, and nothing, nothing, nothing, would penetrate. Not because they were wicked but because they couldn't hear. If they could hear, they wouldn't be white. Malcolm understood this. He said that white is a state of mind—a fatal state of mind. There I was in Hollywood. The things I was asked to write in the name of Malcolm, the advice I was given about the life and death of a friend of mine was not to be believed. So I left. I split to save my life. Ida, you once said that I was an actor. I'm an actor, but I'm also very determined.

Ida: Let's turn to another subject—your family.

Jimmy: I'd love to because my family saved me. If it hadn't been for my family, all those brothers and sisters, I'd be a very different person today. Let me explain. I was the older brother. And when I was growing up I didn't like all those brothers and sisters. No kid likes to be the oldest. You get spanked for what they do. But when they turn to you for help—what can you do? You can't drop the kid on his head down the steps. There he is, right?

So when I say that they saved me I mean that they kept me so busy caring for them, keeping them from the rats, roaches, falling plaster, and all the banality of poverty that I had no time to go jumping off the roof, or to become a junkie or an alcoholic. It's either/or in the ghetto. And I was one of the lucky ones. The welfare of my family has always driven me, always controlled me. I wanted to become rich and famous simply so no one could evict my family again.

Ida: So keeping your family from being thrown into the street was your inspiration.

Jimmy: That's really the key to my will to succeed. I was simply a frightened young man who had a family to save.

Ida: Have you remained close to your family?

Jimmy: The greatest things in my life are my brothers and sisters, and my nieces and nephews. We're all friends. They continue, in their own way, to save me. They are my life.

Ida: After you left America the last time you ended up in Istanbul. What could take a black American to Turkey?

Jimmy: There are several reasons why I went to Istanbul. One was that I had a friend there, a Turkish actor who worked with me at The Actors Studio in '58. He's memorable to me because at one point in the play version of *Giovanni*, someone had to spit on the cross, and no Christian actor was willing to do it. But my friend is a Moslem, so he loved it. Then he had to go away to Turkey to do his military service and I said, "Someday I'll visit you in Turkey." But I never really thought I would.

Ida: But wars will go on and on and on. . . .

Jimmy: Unhappily, we have yet to realize that nobody can go to war anymore and win. It's impossible. It's a dirty habit that mankind has got to give up.

But what is important to us as blacks is to realize that the kinds of

wars perpetrated today are quite different from those of the past.
Before Vietnam, the European wars were family affairs. Hitler's
Germany was no big deal until people feared that he might take over
all of Europe. He had murdered millions with the people's consent.
Nobody cared. Nobody. Only when Europe itself was endangered by
the madman it had created did it become moral. But right from the
start Vietnam has been a racist war in which all the West is impli-
cated. It was never a family affair. America's in the vanguard but the
war reveals where the West is really based. That's a crisis. I see it as
the beginning of the end.

Ida: Why have you chosen France as your refuge?

Jimmy: Laziness. Habit. I speak French; I became famous here.
The French are a very special sort. They will leave you alone, let you
do your thing. And all I want is to be left alone to do my gig. I
couldn't after all, pick Tokyo or Rome or Barcelona or London. They
don't know me as Paris does, or vice versa. Paris was actually the
only place for me to come.

Ida: Have you changed much over the last 10 years? What kind of
person are you now?

Jimmy: I could say that I'm sadder, but I'm not. I'm much more
myself than I've ever been. I'm freer. I've lost so much, but I've
gained a lot. I cannot claim that I'm a happy man. I'm terrified, but
I'm not unhappy. I've lived long enough to know what I have to do—
and what I will not do.

Ida: What won't you do, Jimmy?

Jimmy: I will never sell you . . . even when you want me to. You
follow me. You created me. You're stuck with me for life.

Ida: Let's talk about the meaning of being black today. What does
it mean to you?

Jimmy: I think that it is probably the luckiest thing that could have
happened to me or to anyone who's black. I was walking with my
brother David in London a couple weeks ago, and we were sort of
walking fast because there were a lot of people around us. We were
trying to get some place where we could sit down and have a quiet
drink and talk without having to go through all that. I said, "Davy, I
wouldn't dare look back. If I looked back, I'd shake." And then, we
both realized that if you are not afraid to look back, it means that
nothing you are facing can frighten you.

What it means to me? Nobody can do anything if you really know that you're black. And I know where I've been. I know what the world has tried to do to me as a black man. When I say me, that means millions of people. I know that it's not easy to live in a world that's determined to murder you. Because they're not trying to mistreat you, or despise you, or rebuke you or scorn you. They're trying to kill you. Not only to kill you, but kill your mother and your father, your brothers and your children. That's their intention. That's what it means to keep the Negro in his place. I have seen the game, and if you lose it, you're in trouble, not me. And the secret about the white world is out. Everybody knows it.

All that brotherly love was bullshit. All those missionaries were murderers. That old cross was bloodied with my blood. And all that money in all those banks was made by me for them. So, for me what it means to be black is what one has been forced to see through, all the pretentions and all the artifacts of the world that calls itself white. One sees a certain poverty, a poverty one would not have believed. And it doesn't make any difference what they do now.

The terrible thing about being white is that whatever you do is irrelevant. Play your games, dance your waltzes, shoot your guns, fly your helicopters, murder your natives. It's all been done. It may take another thousand years, another twenty years, another thirty years, but I've already worn you out. Whitey, you can't make it because I've got nothing to lose. What has happened is, I've stepped outside your terms. As long as it is important to be white or black in one's own head, then you had us. Nobody gives a damn any more. Western civilization's had to be defended by the people who are defending it. By the time you sank to the level of such mediocrities as presidents, whom I will not name, I'm sorry, you've had it. Civilization depends on Mr. Nixon and Mr. Agnew? We can forget about that civilization. There's not a living soul who wants to become Richard Nixon. There never will be in the entire history of the world.

Ida: What about the new black pride?

Jimmy: It's not new. Black pride, baby, is what got my father through. Drove him mad, too, and finally killed him. There's nothing new about it, and people who think it's new are making a mistake. Black pride is in all those cotton fields, all those spirituals, all those Uncle Tom bits, all that we had to go through to get through. There's something dangerous in the notion that it is new, because we can fall into the European trap, too. After all, I've been treated as badly by black people as I have by white people. And I'm not about to accept another kind of cultural dictatorship. I won't accept it from Governor Wallace, and I won't accept it from anybody else, either. I am an artist. No one will tell me what to do. You can shoot me and throw me off a tower, but you cannot tell me what to write or how to write it. Because I won't go. Most people talking about black pride and black power don't know what they're talking about. I've lived long enough to know people who were at one time so white they wouldn't talk to me. And now they're so black they won't talk to me. I kid you not.

Ida: What about all the new blacks?

Jimmy: Maybe they'll be white next week. They go with the winds, like a water wheel. I've lived nearly half a century. No dreary young S.O.B. is going to tell me what to do. Oh, nonononono. Of course, it is inevitable. On a certain level it's even healthy. But I'm somewhere else. Now, for the first time in my life, I suppose because I've paid for it, I really do know something else.

I trust myself more than ever before. And I suppose it's only because I had to accept something about the role I play, which I didn't want to accept. But now it's all right.

Ida: Well, how do you see yourself?

Jimmy: I'm a witness. That's my responsibility. I write it all down.

Ida: What's the difference between a witness and an observer?

Jimmy: An observer has no passion. It doesn't mean I saw it. It means that I was there. I don't have to observe the life and death of Martin Luther King. I am a witness to it. Follow me?

Are We on the Edge of Civil War?
David Frost/1970

From David Frost, *The Americans* (New York: Stein and Day, 1970), pp. 145-50. Reprinted by permission.

Frost: Where is home for you now? It's Paris more than here, isn't it?

Baldwin: Oh, no, I left Paris a long time ago. But to the artist, home is where he can work. And there are so many things happening in this curious country that it's hard to keep ahead of events, not to say assassinations. So, from time to time I have to leave to work, and at the moment I have a flat in Istanbul.

Frost: Is it a good place to work?

Baldwin: Yes, for me it's a great place to work. It is both in Europe and in Asia, which means it is neither Christian nor Muslim, neither white nor black.

Frost: Are you Christian or Muslim?

Baldwin: (*Laughing*) I was born a Baptist.

Frost: It's not *that* funny!

Baldwin: It is to me.

Frost: And what are you now?

Baldwin: I'm trying to become a human being.

Frost: And when does one know when one's reached that stage?

Baldwin: I don't think you ever do. You work at it, you know. You take it as it comes. You try not to tell too many lies. You try to love other people and hope that you'll be loved.

Frost: Do you feel as black now as when you were born? I mean, are you more conscious now of being black than when you were a child?

Baldwin: I think you should ask the question of our President.

Frost: Pardon?

Baldwin: You should ask the question of Richard Nixon, or the Attorney General.

I don't feel you're black or white, but I am a survivor in a way of—how shall I put it?—it doesn't matter how I feel, but I'm aware of

93

what's happening in the country, and if I say, "You should ask the President how black I feel," it's another way of saying, "Ask him to look at the record achieved in this country since 1956." I'm talking about the life and death of the civil rights movement.

I may feel in some ways blacker than I felt when I was younger, but that only means that I am on occasion determined not to allow black children to live the life I've lived. I assume the will of the majority is now represented in such places as Sacramento and Albany and Washington. I know the effect on the police in this country, the—how can I put it—the morale, the authority given them by the present administration, and that acts on black people and poor people and Mexicans and all of the dissidents and all of the pariahs of the society.

Frost: Presumably you feel there has been some progress since 1956, but you used the phrase, "the life and death of the civil rights movement." Do you think the civil rights movement is dead?

Baldwin: I feel the civil rights movement always contained within itself something self-defeating and Martin knew this finally, too. That's why he died in Memphis fighting for a raise for garbage men. In the beginning we thought that there was a way of reaching the conscience of the people of this country. We hoped there was, and I must say that we did reach several blacks and several whites.

We did everything in our power to make the American people realize that the myths they were living with were not so much destroying black people as whites. It's one of the things one lives with, to have one's head broken, but it is quite another thing to be a representative of the people in whose name it is done. It is one thing to be a victim, one thing to be one of our niggers, and another thing to be one of the people who are described when we talk about "our niggers." You see what I mean?

Frost: I think I see what you mean, but go on a stage further.

Baldwin: Well, after all, I am speaking as Jimmy Baldwin and, for this moment, as the representative of seven million [sic] black people in this country. I have not elected Nixon. I did not go to dinner with Agnew. I know a great deal about the Attorney General and yet more about the silent majority.

I am not a young man, but I'm a black American, and I know something about the crime of silence. I know what happens in San

Francisco and in Chicago and in New York when one of our representatives wants to protect the morale of the police.

I know what a no-knock, stop-and-frisk law means. It means
search and destroy. I know something about the history black people
have endured and are still enduring in this place.

It doesn't mean I hate white people, who are much more
victimized than I, but it is terrible to watch a nation lose itself.

(*Applause*)

Frost: You've got to add into that equation, haven't you, the white
people who've striven in the last ten or twenty years? They may have
been born with a feeling that people of another color are somehow
inferior, but they have progressed from that stand in the past years.

Baldwin: Look, I'm not talking about other blacks. That's the
great trick back into which America may tumble. We're not on the
edge of a racial war. We're on the edge of a civil war. Look, white
people may or may not accept it, but I am one of the descendants of
the slave-breeding farm. I know how I got my name. It's an old
English name, you know.

Frost: Very English, yes.

Baldwin: Well, then, I don't have anything to hide. Malcolm X said
that white is a state of mind, genealogically, historically. No one really
knows who's white or black, and when the chips are down, it doesn't
really matter. Who knows how many black people got pale enough to
pass across the color line? It's a buried part of American history. So, it
makes the American estimate of twenty-two million black people
extremely shaky. Nobody in this country really knows who his grand-
father is. No one can examine his history, which is the trouble.

Frost: What is the greatest problem we all face now?

Baldwin: Someone told me that in California in 1848 or '49,
there were something like a hundred and fifty thousand Indians, and
at the turn of that particular century, there were ten thousand, and I
was really astounded by this.

Martin Luther King was right when he said this nation was one of
the few nations, but not the only one, which had to destroy the
indigenous population in order to become a nation. But we're not a
nation yet. And if you're a black cat living in this place and in this
time, though you may spend your entire life knocking on the radi-

ators, knocking on the steam pipes to get heat, trying to get protection against the rats and the roaches and all of the horrible details one lives with in the ghetto and gets used to, you also know that if oil was discovered beneath the tenement in which you are living and dying, that wealth would not belong to you.

When the Indians were driven out of wherever they were into Oklahoma, and oil was found in Oklahoma, it did not belong to the Indians.

I'm saying that to be a black person in this century, and to be relatively conscious, is to recognize to what extent the wealth and the power of the western world depend on your condition, that your condition is in some sense indispensable to that wealth and power.

White people may not know, but I know, that the South African government, of which we disapprove, is based on slave labor and it would have a difficult time existing if we did not support it. I know what happened to Castro's Cuba. What white Americans think is happening in the world and what black people must deal with day by day are very different.

I don't like it, but I understand why a black cat refuses to talk plainly to white people. I understand that one is in a situation in which war has been declared on you, and it no longer matters about the life of someone my age.

Do you really think that I'm going forever to make pleas to the lesser of two evils? Do you really think that I expect anything from Richard Nixon?

And when a country gets to such a place, that country is in trouble.

Frost: That, alas, is all we've got time for, but you said, Jimmy—

Baldwin: I want to say one last thing. I would like to alert the American people to this fact, that they're not after me, but after you.

Frost: Well, I said you'd only have time for one sentence, but you've got to explain that a bit further.

Baldwin: Something very important is happening in this country now, and I think for the first time the people legally white and the people legally black are beginning to understand that if they do not come together they're going to end up in the same gas oven.

Frost: Gas oven?

Baldwin: Gas oven.

Frost: That's overstating the point, isn't it?

Baldwin: So were the Jews in Germany told that.

Frost: But there's no parallel, surely.

Baldwin: There is a parallel, if you were born in Harlem.

Frost: But you've never had a policy here like the one in Germany.

Baldwin: I will tell you this, my friend, for every Sammy Davis, for every Jimmy Baldwin, for every black cat you have heard of in the history of this country, there are a hundred of us dead.

I can carry you to some of the graveyards, where boys just like me. or brighter than me, more beautiful than me, perished because they were black.

Frost: But for every James Earl Ray in this country, there's ten or a hundred thousand other—

Baldwin: I don't think we want to discuss James Earl Ray, because I don't believe—speaking in my person as Sambo—that he could have swum across the Memphis River all the way to London by himself.

James Baldwin Interviewed
John Hall/1970

From *Transatlantic Review*, 37-38 (Autumn-Winter 1970-71), 5-14. Reprinted by permission.

Hall: In an interview with François Bondy in *Preuves* (October, 1963) you stated what would seem to be the novelist/political activist's dilemma, namely, the necessity for a spokesman to simplify the facts of his political case, in order to communicate directly, and broadly, as opposed to the novelist's need to remain faithful to the complexities of life in order to create a true image. Is this your dilemma, and if it is, how do you attempt to reconcile the conflicting roles?

Baldwin: It's true, I said that. And it is difficult, and would be more difficult if I thought the particular political issues with which I am concerned were capable of being simplified. Flags, and slogans and banners are always misleading, they have to be; and if one is forced, for whatever reason, to ally oneself with a public cause, it is still necessary to maintain a private point of view about it, you know, because in any case, you will be speaking out of that, no matter what you're saying. I always felt that when I was talking publicly, I was talking mainly to the children, to the young, which is to say to the future, and I was talking about people's souls; I was never really talking about simply political action, because I am not a political activist. I was talking about something else. So the dichotomy of my being a spokesman for civil rights and my being a novelist is not as great as it might appear. When you talk, you have to be much simpler than you can afford to be when you write, but your mind still works in a complex way, and the nature of the relationship of *rapport* with one's audience is still a very complex thing. Part of what one has to do is not to allow the audience to lead you, and tell you what to say. That's the strain. There's no essential conflict, except in terms of time, and the mechanics that surround speaking in public, and the results of it, which are misleading in another way, because they give you a kind of aura which is not exactly yours; but that doesn't make any difference, I think it probably applies to anybody who finds himself in that goldfish bowl which, in America, is called success.

Hall: I know you are working on a long essay about the civil rights movement in America. Your last essay, *The Fire Next Time* concluded that white liberals and relatively conscious blacks might work together to bring an end to the country's racial nightmare. Does that conclusion still hold good in the light of subsequent events?

Baldwin: I still hold that viewpoint; I still believe that. But the price will be high, higher than I might have thought when I wrote that. And high, I mean, in terms of human life. Nothing has altered in America, except that white people have simply raised the price, and raised it so high that fewer and fewer black people will be willing to pay it. That jeopardises everything we hope for, and everything the white man hopes for. It jeopardises the future of the civilisation. The presence of a man like Nixon in the White House is an unmitigated disaster, not only for black people in America, but for all the white hopes too, because it confirms, and makes official, and it seals an attitude that is essentially a racist attitude, but it is also, on a most sinister level, an attitude which is simply designed to turn the clock back; to hold back the sea. And you know, that can't be done. What people in power never understand is what people out of power are determined to do, and what people out of power are determined to do is, first of all, to survive you; to withstand you; and if they have to, kill you. And they have the advantage, because they have nothing to lose. The will of the American people, they believe, is like the voice of God. Well, the voice of God spoke out a couple of years ago, and put Nixon in the White House, and put Ronald Reagan in the governor's mansion, and it endures Spiro T. Agnew. And the effect on the American people of the presence of such men in high office is that they are justified in their bigotry, they are confirmed in their ignorance, they are all smaller or greater John Waynes.

Hall: That reminds me that you once remarked upon the difficulty of growing up in a world of John Waynes, once you discover that you're the Indian.

Baldwin: That's right, exactly. But it's not going to work the way it did before. They're not going to be able to kill off this particular

Indian. In fact they're not going to be able to kill off these particular
Indians.

Hall: What is the best thing for these particular Indians to do
about it? Oppose by force of arms, or perhaps establish a separate
nation within America?

Baldwin: Separatism is a dream. The transfer of power will begin
where it has to begin, on a local, community level. The school battle
of a couple of years ago was very significant in that respect. We want
schools, not necessarily equal but separate, just schools. Those
disaster factories in Harlem are not schools. I'm a survivor of one of
them, and they're worse now than when I was there. Of course that
transfer of power involved millions of dollars, and that's what the
battle was about. It means that instead of being administered to, I will
myself be responsible for the administration of a school. What black
people are plotting for is their autonomy, which they will have to get.
Now you talk about the separatist movement in America, and that's
like talking about the separation of a family, because the American
dilemma is not only that of the slave there. I'm related to the white
American by blood; I don't have an English name for nothing, and
the colour span of black Americans goes from you to people much
darker than me; every colour under heaven is represented by the so-
called American Negro. And we cannot separate. The tragedy of the
white people is that they always thought they could, and the result of
that thinking has been social chaos, which will get worse yet. You
can't deny your brothers without paying a terrible price for it. And
even then they are still your brothers. I do believe that what black
people have to do, and are doing, is what Malcolm X said we should
do. He said to some white liberal: "You educate your Community,
and I'll educate mine. By seeming to work separately, we'll really be
working together". And I think that's a very important concept,
because black people have been told nothing but lies in America—
lies about themselves, about their heritage, about each other, about
their mothers, about their fathers. And nobody can trust any longer
the really most well-meaning white person to teach his child, because
he brings his history with him. What he should do is teach his
children. I'll teach my children. Then his children and my children
can become friends. You see, the patterns of power are very hard to

lose, and it's a rare person who's able to liberate himself from something which is really in the gut; it's not in the head.

Hall: You're recommending a very moderate remedy. To what extent is moderation generally prescribed among black Americans, and what sort of support is there for a movement to achieve freedom by violent means?

Baldwin: Well, I'm going to ask you a question now: what happens in a society when those without privilege decide that they cannot endure their situation, and that their situation must be changed? What happens is that there has always been open conflict, because people in power just don't give up power. Now if I say anything abut a bloody conflict, everyone will accuse me of agitating, and stirring up hate, and advocating violence. But I'm not the man who has the gun; I'm not the man who has the helicopters; I'm not the man who has the mace, the tanks, the policemen; I might be a terribly violent person, but nothing could be more irrelevant, you know, because I've got nothing to be violent with. But I know that I'm facing a very violent people; the most violent people at this moment in the world. It isn't up to the black people whether it is violent or not, it's up to the white people.

Hall: And what do the white people have to do in order to avoid a violent confrontation?

Baldwin: Something people never do. They have to love my child as much as they love their child; they have to decide that human life is more important than their profits, more important than their safety, and they won't do that.

Hall: But failing to love another person's child has nothing to do with colour, surely? Isn't it just plain narrow stupidity? Just a human failing?

Baldwin: None of this has anything to do with colour, that's true. Colour is a great American myth. Babies and corpses have no colour. It's part of the great American masturbation. You see, it's easy to label a man this or that, maybe "nigger", and the label permits you to do all kinds of monstrous things to him because he's no longer a man; he's a label. But what the label says about the people's opinion of a man is what leads them to their doom. The old nigger is just something in people's minds.

Hall: You talk about a people being led to their doom by an attitude of mind, and much of what you say seems to repeat what you were saying seven years ago, in *The Fire Next Time,* when you said, in effect, OK, one more chance, but if it's not taken immediately, there'll be a holy conflagration. America seems to be fending off that doom pretty effectively, if at a high cost. What do you say now about the fire?

Baldwin: The fire is upon us. When construction workers in New York can walk, under the eyes of the police, and beat up kids and anti-war demonstrators, helped by the police really, and nobody cares, it's very sinister. Sinister as the Reichstag fire. When the police become lawless, and are allied with the visibly lawless, a society is in trouble. I'm chicken; I don't even want to say what I see.

Hall: Are there no grounds for optimism on any score?

Baldwin: I'm no optimist about the future of what we call this civilisation, because it seems to me that it has to go through so many transformations in order to survive. I think the transformations would be healthy, but I'm in the minority when I say that. And as it's not willing to undergo those transformations, you know, to make itself larger, then it will be destroyed. It's a process of evolution which nobody can stop. I'm optimistic about the future, but not about the future of this civilisation. I'm optimistic about the civilisation which will replace this one.

Hall: Well, having reached a Darwinian apocalypse, may we hark back a little to talk about Baldwin the novelist—a supreme artist of a defunct civilisation? Can you say what were your formative influences as a writer, what you have been doing lately, and why are you here in London now?

Baldwin: Formative influences: my father, the Church, and Charles Dickens. For the past year I've been in Istanbul, writing, as you know, a long essay on the life and death of what we call the civil rights movement.

Hall: It died?

Baldwin: It died with Martin.

Hall: But people are still going through the motions?

Baldwin: Well, we've marched and petitioned for a decade, and now it's clear that there's no point in marching or petitioning. And what happens I don't know, but when they killed Martin they killed that hope. They didn't kill that dream, but they did kill that hope. Now everybody knows one cannot reach the conscience of a nation that way. My book doesn't offer any answers about where we go from here.

Hall: And what are you doing now?

Baldwin: Well, I might make a movie, or I might do a play, I started another novel about which I know very little at the moment. I don't know what the movie would be about either, but it would probably be made with Joe Losey.

Hall: I believe you wrote a screenplay about the life of Malcolm X?

Baldwin: That's right. It's still in my trunk, and I will presently publish it. There were difficulties about making a film, which I would rather not go into.

Hall: Your fiction writing was generally acclaimed as great work until your last novel, *Tell Me How Long the Train's Been Gone,* appeared in 1968, when there was a feeling perhaps that you showed no obvious development, and that you tended to work away at the same propaganda. I think there was disappointment also that you were content to jog along in so-called traditional novel form. To quote a precis of many critics' notices, I recall that F.N. Furbank, in the *Times* Saturday Review, said that one couldn't help regretting that having spotted so acutely other deadnesses and self deceptions in American culture, you should not have spotted that this whole fictional genre was, in its own way, one of the worst. Don't you feel that this is the case?

Baldwin: Well, when a critic says that about you you're really quite helpless. People have been talking about the death of the novel, for example, since, well, as long as I've been around. This sort of thing involves the writer's sensibilities on a level at which he can't defend himself, because what the critic says might be quite true. I don't happen to think it's true, and I don't think *Trains* was such a conventional novel as people say, either.

Hall: Why not?

Baldwin: I don't think anyone knows enough about conventional novels first of all. My next book, and books to come, will certainly be different, I hope, and certainly the form will change. But it doesn't change from the top; it changes from the bottom. If it's not an organic change, it's simply a gimmick, and the only thing one can do is work within one's own limits, one's own sights, and do the work one can do. Maybe it will last for five minutes, maybe it will last for ever. Nobody knows. But if you begin to think about those things, like the form being conventional, you can't work at all. I disagree about the general assessment of *Trains*.

Hall: Then you don't find the so-called conventional form of the novel limiting?

Baldwin: Writers always have. I think real changes in form just occur, and I doubt if one's contemporaries are able to see a change when it does occur. The very people who clamour for new forms are also people who do not recognise them when they come. Since this is so, the only thing I can do is to work, and see where my experiments lead me.

Hall: At least you are experimenting then?

Baldwin: Any writer is. Writing is a polite term for it. Let me dare to say something else which I believe; to which in fact I am very soundly attached. Let's take *Another Country*: it's a safer subject as it's much older. A lot of people in that book had never appeared in fiction before. People overlook this fact. And there's an awful lot of my experience which has never been seen in the English language before. Rufus, for example. There are no antecedents for him. He was in the novel because I didn't think anyone had ever watched the disintegration of a black boy from that particular point of view. Rufus was partly responsible for his doom, and in presenting him as partly responsible, I was attempting to break out of the whole sentimental image of the afflicted nigger driven that way (to suicide) by white people.

Hall: You're suggesting he was the first fictional nigger in control of his destiny?

Baldwin: He was not in control of it; nobody is. It was simply too much for him, as it's too much for many people, as it may prove to be in the morning, too much for you, or too much for me.

Hall: The innovation then was to present the reality of an independent, talented, free Negro, partly responsible for his own disintegration?

Baldwin: Yes, as I say. It's a statement for which I can be roundly attacked, and of course it may not be true. But I think it's true.

Hall: Looking back on your own life, as a young, talented, independent Negro, you said in *Notes of a Native Son* that you always had in mind two apparently opposing ideas about life, and I quote you: "The first was acceptance, the acceptance, totally without rancour, of life as it is, and men as they are: in the light of this idea, it goes without saying that injustice is commonplace. But this did not mean that one could be complacent, for the second idea was of equal power: that one must never, in one's own life, accept these injustices as commonplace, but must fight them with all one's strength". You have clearly done your share of fighting injustice; do you still hold the same opinion about accepting life for what it is, and if so, how do you reconcile the opposing outlooks?

Baldwin: I don't think you do. I think it's a great mistake to be sentimental about human beings, and to be sentimental about one-self. One doesn't know what one can do until one does it. If you don't understand that about yourself and other people, then you can become a missionary, which is one step away from being a tyrant, and you can decide that because you cannot deal with your own life, then you can deal with other people's lives, and correct them according to some principle which you have yourself not quite understood. What I was talking about was human justice. It's not different from Dickens's indignation about children pulling carts through mines, and any society has its injustices, and there are always some people in it who are compelled, for reasons no one will ever understand, to point them out. I was talking about the way people treat each other, and especially about the way they treat their children. And, you know, there's no real conflict between knowing that I am able to do certain things, and everybody is able to do certain things, and fighting those things. You fight it for yourself first. You accept life as it is, you see it as it is before you can change it. In order to change myself, I have to admit that I am not six feet tall, I'm not blue-eyed. I've got to accept limitations before I can discover my possibilities.

Hall: And having discovered the possibilities, as a successful writer, the limitations are bearable?

Baldwin: Well, as a matter of fact, yes. It's not that one's talent is particularly important. I think passion is more important. The fact that I happen to be a writer doesn't mean as much as it's due to mean. I might be a bricklayer. I've known people in various stations of life who were extraordinary people; it was passion that made them that way.

Hall: But it must mean something to be the greatest Negro writer; you must at least feel a sense of responsibility.

Baldwin: I feel an enormous sense of responsibility, though I don't think I'm the greatest Negro writer alive today. I'm the most famous, which is not necessarily the same thing. What is important about my work, which I realised when I was a little boy, partly from the Church perhaps, and whatever happened to my mind all those years I was growing up in the shadow of the Holy Ghost, is that nothing belongs to you. My talent does not belong to me, you know; it belongs to you; it belongs to everybody. It's important only insofar as it can work toward the liberation of other people, because I didn't invent it. I didn't make myself, and I wouldn't have chosen to be born as I was, when I was, where I was. But I was, and you do what you can with the hand life dealt you.

Hall: Considering that you were raised in a particularly close, inward looking community, with which you obviously identify strongly in your fiction, it's interesting that you should have lived so many years in Europe. Or is it that you are able to see that community more clearly in exile, as Joyce was able to see Ireland?

Baldwin: Well, I'm just a displaced blackboy. I was driven to Europe, and my position is a misleading one. I'm not a European. I'm not French, though I lived in France a long time, and loved it. I learned things about France while I was there, but what I mainly learned was about my own country, my own past, and about my own language. Joyce accepted silence, exile, and cunning as a system which would sustain his life, and I've had to accept it too—incidentally, silence is the hardest part to understand. But I wrestle with it, as an exiled American, but I'm faced with a choice of exiles.

Hall: How so?

Baldwin: Well, if one is trying to become an individual in that most individual of countries, America, one's really up against something. To try to think for oneself, and act for oneself, and have as little regard as I was forced to have for the architecture of my prison . . . to go into battle with all that is to be very lonely. It's a sort of exile, and if you're lonely enough, you can perish from being lonely. The only places I'm really at home in the world are Harlem, where people know what I know, and we can talk and laugh, and it would never occur to anybody to say what we all know. Or in Europe, where I can talk with people I know, and we both know the same things. Laughing and talking, not about civil rights, anything in particular. Just enjoying each other, you know, meeting on a journey and wishing each other well.

It's Hard to be James Baldwin

Herbert R. Lottman/1972

From *Intellectual Digest*, 2 (July 1972), 67-68.

For over a year James Baldwin has been living in the south of France, in a large house among olive and orange trees, just outside the medieval hilltop town of St.-Paul-de-Vence. Once in a while Baldwin comes up to Paris on business, and on one of these recent trips we met for some talk in the dim, cloistered bar of the Pont Royal hotel.

Baldwin is small and wiry, with a dancer's build. You feel he can concentrate his forces that much more, being small. But if you watch him carefully, watch his facial expression, particularly his mouth, when he makes a joke or underlines the irony of a situation, you think you see something else, a vulnerability, a pain he works at concealing. The smile that follows is whistling a happy tune.

Q: Do you require the calm you seem to be getting in St. Paul?

Baldwin: I need a certain kind of privacy. It's very hard to describe or explain, but you know that it's also very hard to be James Baldwin.

Q: When did you last work in a city?

Baldwin: I suppose that would be Hollywood [in 1968]. What I'm trying to do has driven me farther and farther out of the cities. In America I've been considered not so much a writer as an angry young man. At 47 I'm still a dancing dog. You can't spend all your time on television and work too. By the way, I'm not complaining about that. But it's important for me to know what I am . . .

Q: Let's talk about your main project, *If Beale Street Could Talk*. Should I know what and where Beale Street is?

Baldwin: It's a street in Memphis that W.C. Handy wrote about in his "Beale Street Blues." You know,

If Beale Street could talk,

If Beale Street could talk,
Married men would have to take their
   beds and walk.

Q: Are you in this book more or less than usual?

Baldwin: A writer is always more or less in his book. You try to keep yourself out, or you try not to distort, not to let your prejudices distort. In *Beale Street,* for instance, the girl is telling the story. You can say I'm the girl, or the boy or their unborn child.

Q: Is she talking in your language or in her own?

Baldwin: She's a girl from the streets, as I'm a boy from the streets.

Q: What exactly is the story?

Baldwin: Her lover is in Attica, and a lot of her story is in her trips to the prison. Actually, I began writing before the Attica events. But I have a friend there. Part of the key to the book is the prison situation. She is wondering what is going to happen to the baby, and he is wondering too. He's in prison on charges of stealing a television set— he was sent up on a bullshit tip. He's still in jail when the book ends.

Q: Is he in prison for a limited term or is it one of those indefinite things?

Baldwin: Ask the American people that, don't ask me.

Q: Would you say that the book is giving you more problems than you usually have in your writing, or fewer, or what?

Baldwin: Luckily you don't remember the problems you had before, or you wouldn't continue. To try to tell a story from the point of view of a pregnant woman is something of a hazard. I tried to avoid it, but she's the only one who can tell the story. There are nine chapters, one for each month of her pregnancy. The book ends with the birth of the baby. *That's* what it's about, our responsibility to that baby.

Q: What other problems have you had with *Beale Street?*

Baldwin: You're always in difficulty with a book. There was the problem of interruptions, other projects, travel, illness. The trick is not to use these other things to get in the way of the book. You go through all kinds of shit before you actually sit down to write. And when you do sit down and these problems are all behind you, they were so painful that you cannot really discuss them.

As a matter of fact all writers have the same problems. The invention has to be organic, not a gimmick. It has to come out of your relationship to the subject. You work on it for years and one fine day, if you haven't lost your nerve, it works. It comes alive. And then it's over, and it doesn't belng to you anymore.

Q: Jimmy, would you say that new times require new media? Are you moving away from traditional literature?

Baldwin: Art isn't traditional. Mine isn't in any case. I'm not part of the television and tape age, but I can understand people 20 or 30 years younger than myself who grew up in it, whose minds have been formed by it. I'm not for or against it—I see these things as forms you have to learn how to use. I'm the kind of person who needs to *see* the page, but that's not a moral position or anything like that.

Q: Do you feel that you communicate better with readers as time goes on, or do you feel that words—or readers—are still difficult to attain?

Baldwin: I never thought of my reader in that way. He'd have to be a very particular reader in any case—even in the past that was so. Now all bets are off. What's happening in America was clear to me many years ago, and to many people. Now we can only wait until we see what happens on the other side of the holocaust. It's not American, by the way, it's global.

Q: But communication in itself. Does it come harder, or easier?

Baldwin: There's no sense saying communication is easy. What is communicated by television? It is always harder to communicate. If you see at all, I think as time goes on you see more, and it becomes more difficult to convey what you see because you yourself would rather not see it.

Q: Who is in your audience now?

Baldwin: I have no idea. I'd think it would be the young, white and black. I know that my books are read in the black communities, logically in paperback editions. I'm surely a problematical figure for many in the Afro-American world. On balance they trust me—I think. I know what my position is in any case. I know I love them. I don't know about them loving me.

A writer writes because he has to. It's not as calculated as it seems. A writer lives for years getting rejection slips, and if you're black . . . You don't think of your public. Something drives you. The turning point for me was when I left America. In two ways: something happened to me—I found out things I didn't know when I was home. And I was *here*, which made me a very odd object altogether. It was a turning point. I had been a published writer since 1946. Abroad I became freer. I trusted myself more and trusted my work. I ceased being corralled as a Negro writer.

Q: Have you found that your attitude has changed as the world changed?

Baldwin: I'm much sadder now, which doesn't mean that I'm discouraged. When you are 20 you see the world one way and when you're older you see it another way. You see yourself in another way as well.

Q: In what way?

Baldwin: I see myself as someone who is trying to become an artist.

Q: Do you feel that you are in opposition to those who think art should be secondary to protest? Are you still fighting that battle?

Baldwin: I'm not fighting with others at all. The only one I'm fighting is myself. I am my only problem. My integrity as a man is involved. If a man happens to be an artist, that's the terrain on which the battle is fought.

Q: Well, do you yourself sometimes feel that you should be a polemicist rather than a writer of finished works?

Baldwin: It's not one of my choices. I haven't done it, which means that I haven't wanted to.

Q: Among younger writers, whom do you admire?

Baldwin: There is Ernest Gaines, whose latest work is *The Autobiography of Miss Jane Pittman* and George Cain, author of *Blueschild Baby*. Nikki Giovanni has written four fine books of poetry. They are all black Americans, all very important. They're very important to me, and should be to everyone else.

Q: Do you have any followers?

Baldwin: I wouldn't be able to tell. I don't have a school in any case.

Q: May I ask what you think is going to happen back home?

Baldwin: I've already said that I see a holocause coming. That is the subject of my new book, *No Name in the Street*, which appeared in the United States this spring. It is the story of the civil rights movement up to the death of Martin Luther King, but it's not a documentary. It's a personal book—my own testimony.

Everyone overlooks the impact on the black population of our country of the present Administration, and that is very sinister. It's an insult to every black American that the President of the United States should be in competition with the governor of Alabama for votes. The civil rights laws? Bullshit.

Q: What do you mean by holocaust?

Baldwin: Americans who have managed to learn nothing are now about to learn a great deal.

A Television Conversation: James Baldwin, Peregrine Worsthorne, Bryan Magee
Encounter/1972

From *Encounter*, 39 (September 1972), 27-33. Reprinted by permission.

What does one actually hear when a discussion pro-gramme featuring reasonably intelligent conversationalists is televised? We asked Thames Television to give us a reasonably accurate transcript of the recent argumentative exchanges, broadcast in their *Something to Say* series (chaired by Bryan Magee), between James Baldwin and Peregrine Worsthorne, and the following are unedited excerpts, for what they are worth, from this text.

Bryan Magee: Well, before I ask our two guests this evening to discuss this question face to face let's go more deeply into the standpoint in which each one is going to argue. Peregrine Wors-thorne, why do you think that the black man is now as responsible for his plight, because plight is what it still is in most cases, as the whites?

Worsthorne: Well, first of all we actually talk about the ah plight of the black man in America.

Magee: Yes all right.

Worsthorne: Because of course there are different plights . . . .

Magee: Of course.

Worsthorne: And in Africa it isn't the same. But in America I would have thought that the situation had almost been reached when legislation has ah been passed and civil rights has been established and when opportunities exist which the Negro ah is in not very much a worse position than any other so-called immigrant group has been in the United States, in the last hundred years. I quite agree a bit worse but not all that worse. I think it would now be possible for the

American Negro to take advantage of the facilities. . . . In the middle
of the 19th century other groups with tremendous ah handicaps, the
Irish immigrants, the Jewish immigrants, the Italian immigrants, and
so on, who suffered ghastly ah discrimination and oppression and
economic exploitation, they made it—the Italian through a ah quite a
mastery if you like of crime, the Irish through Tammany Hall politics,
the Jews through great commercial skill—they all forced their way
into the mainstream of American social political economic life, and I
would have thought that the position had now reached ah where the
Negroes could do something comparable, if they're determined to
do so.

Magee: Well, thank you Peregrine Worsthorne. We must turn now
to James Baldwin. . . . What is your answer to his charge that the
Negroes have uniquely failed in the United States to work their way
up from poverty in the way that all other immigrant groups have?

Baldwin: Well the first thing I would say, we'll get to this later
though, is up to . . . (INAUDIBLE) . . . but we'll get to that as I say
later. . . .

All of the civil rights legislation is absolutely meaningless, and it was
meant to be meaningless, and furthermore, the situation of a black
man or woman, or boy, in any Northern ghetto is this: the school,
which is not responsible because it belongs to the city, to the board of
education, is a shambles, and in which no one is educated and in
which no one is meant to be educated—the house in which he lives
belongs to a landlord who is not responsible for anything but
whenever it's to collect his rent. Try to get through a one winter ah in
a Harlem ghetto. This is not either the black man's fault. Where do
you go to complain if you want to complain? And we might even
discuss the situation in the Labour Unions, which are geared to keep
black people in effect in their place. And if you were right if you were
right about the generosity of the American people then Governor
Wallace . . . (INAUDIBLE) . . . his conference in Florida the other day
and Nixon will not be President, I am talking about a system which is
not only historical but actual, I am saying in effect that the white
people without going into any further . . . (INAUDIBLE) . . . at the
moment have in their hands the means of production, and they have
the power, and they intend to keep it. And furthermore would you
not come to address yourself to at all, is what—this is a very serious

question—happens to a people whose history has been utterly
destroyed.

And furthermore the high income niggers such as you're really
talking about, are listen . . . I can name many high come . . . high
. . . income niggers whose name you would recognise, who can buy
a house anywhere . . . and do, and also . . . (INAUDIBLE) . . . of
them, by the population, by their neighbours, try to be Sammy Davis
and raise your children. What we are trying to get at, what I'm trying
to get at because I'm not talking about high incomes, I'm you see,
what I'm what I'm trying to suggest is I reject that particular standard.
I don't think a man's life is meant for that. I don't think. I'd rather die
than be Richard Nixon. I would rather die than make it in the American terms. . . .

Worsthorne: Another small point indicative really of the lack of
respect for words people use when they're debating these points. You
talk about black ghettos. It's a totally inappropriate word to use. A
ghetto which was the area imposed in central Europe on the Jews,
was where rich and poor Jews were forced to live by law. There is no
law in America or indeed no practice in America that makes rich
Negroes live in the New York as-you-call-it "ghetto." You are just
using the word in a propaganda sense as an equivalent to slum, and
of course we know that ah the emotive terms of ghetto means that
the whites are behaving abominably as the whites, as the Christians
behaved against the Jews. But there is nothing to stop you living
wherever you want in the United States, and indeed you do live
when you're there wherever you want as indeed does any other
black man who has got the money to live in other areas. It is these
kind of mis-use, this propaganda use of words that seems to me to be
part of the whole hysterical campaign in America of black power. . . .

Baldwin: Would you prefer it if I use the word Kasbah? I stick to
the word ghetto, and ghetto is the place you can't move out of. I'll go
further than that,
(INTERRUPTED) . . . .

Worsthorne: But how have you moved out of it? . . .

Baldwin: You talking about me, Jimmy Baldwin? . . .

Worsthorne: Well, haven't you moved out of it?

Baldwin: No I haven't. There is no way for any black man to
move out of it. Now wait a minute, I know my country a little bit. I

say ghetto, and I say ghetto because you can't move out, and I'll tell
you why you can't move out. The landlord knows whether you're
Harry Belafonte or Jimmy Baldwin or my young nephew. There are
many places you can move to, if I buy a house I pay 3000 more than
you will, and if . . . but my nephew tries at the rented apartment, he
has to put up with things that you would never put up with, because
it is a ghetto, he can't move out. . . . Let us say you're a school
teacher, let us say you are a grocer, let us say you have children.
Whatever it is, you're a menace, because the whole town knows that
you are going to vote, and if that when you do vote, that is to say,
when you get to the registrars office 'cos you don't manage to vote,
your houses are bombed, do you think all those housing of children
was some aberration, all this is a policy, designed to keep . . . (INAU-
DIBLE) . . . in America, a nigger in his place. As long as we pick the
cotton, and lie on the track, and build the cities, from nothing for
nothing, that was all right. But once you see a black human being, a
human being behind that mask, then you call that . . . (INAUDIBLE)
. . . ministry of yours which enslaved us in the first place, and which
intends to keep us slaves forever. And I tell you, I tell you frankly, I
speak with knowledge, Jimmy Baldwin, I reject your theology, your
history, your morality by which you don't live, your Gods and your
standards and in total all of it, lock stock and barrel, because you
don't live by them and I know that you don't live by them by the way
that you treat me.

Magee: Well, I suspect that this is really eloquent rhetoric,
meaning that you aren't genuinely trying to look at the truth. It is not
true that Negroes do not vote in the United States, the proof . . .
(INTERRUPTED) . . .

Baldwin: . . . story I told you . . .

Worsthorne: . . . ah . . . I'm perfectly prepared to agree that in
the South . . . (INTERRUPTED) . . .

Baldwin: And I ask you to . . . (INTERRUPTED) . . . .

Worsthorne: . . . In the South the situation is extremely difficult,
and indeed all over America it may be and it is extremely difficult, but
you can't simply pretend that Negroes who vote are shot down or
hosed down . . . (INTERRUPTED) . . . how . . . of course I have . . .
and I've read a lot of propaganda in them too . . . How many how
many black mayors are there in Northern cities? How many black
representatives are there in the legislative council! Well don't just sigh.

I mean are there any, or aren't there any? Are there any? Is it possible for any Negro to get elected to get successfully elected to high office in the United States. Is it or is it not? You answer me that question!

Baldwin: Oh I answer that question . . . .

Worsthorne: Or are they hosed out?

Baldwin: . . . depends which nigger it is.

Worsthorne: Well of course it depends on what niggers do, ah . . . which nigger it is. You can't elect a non-individual. Of course it depends on who it is.

Baldwin: It is very easy to put a nigger in the window, very easy indeed. Edward Brooke, for example, does not represent black people in America at all.

Worsthorne: Are you saying that anybody who gets elected who is black, isn't any longer black? . . . (INTERRUPTED) . . . .

Baldwin: . . . if he is black, if he is black, his career is in danger, and it will not last long or hasn't . . . (INTERRUPTED) . . .

Worsthorne: Every elected politician has an insecure life . . . (INTERRUPTED) . . . . Roy Jenkins would be the first to admit it. Not just a black man. This is democracy . . . (INTERRUPTED) . . . .

Baldwin: I refuse, I refuse, I refuse the proposition. I refuse the equation, 'cos what you are what you are avoiding is what I insist on. Colour is a fact.

Worsthorne: Certainly.

Baldwin: It is a fact of my life because I had to live a certain life because I am black. It is a fact that your life, because you see me in a certain way, because I am black, and it it amounts from the point of view of white people to a kind of absolute blindness. You would never treat a dog the way I watch you treat black people. You talk about democracy. How can you talk about democracy to me?

Worsthorne: But you can't talk to me about how I treat black people. You have absolutely no idea how I treat black people. You have no evidence. You're simply making a racist assumption . . . (INTERRUPTED). . . . Treat you like a dog? Well I don't usually spend an hour talking to my dog, or my cat.

Baldwin: . . . let us look . . . let us look at . . . .

Worsthorne: . . . It is purely a racist remark to say that I treat you like a dog . . . (INTERRUPTED) . . . . Have you any evidence that I treat you like a dog? . . .

Baldwin: Let us make it very clear.

Worsthorne: Why make these ludicrous remarks? . . .
Baldwin: Let us make it very clear that I have absolutely nothing personal against you.
Worsthorne: Well then why do you say I am . . . (INTER-RUPTED). . . .
Baldwin: . . . I am talking about your history . . . .
Worsthorne: Well, let us not talk about these generalisations. Let us talk about actuality. . . .
Baldwin: . . . A generalisation? . . .
Worsthorne: You know perfectly well that people don't treat you like a dog. Why do you go round shouting at people? . . .
Worsthorne: You mean me?
Worsthorne: Well, of course I mean you. I mean you. I'm talking about individuals, not talking about these abstractions.
Baldwin: I am not talking about . . . (INTERRUPTED). . . .
Worsthorne: I am sure that there are white people who treat black people like dogs. And judging by the propaganda which you lent your great authority to the Black Panther propaganda, you wish to treat my people like pigs. So far as an Englishman is concerned, it is worse to treat people like a pig than like a dog, so you don't get any benefit there. On the whole there are enormous numbers of white people who are leaning over backwards not to treat black people "like dogs". Why you have to go on shouting and saying white people treat black people like dogs. Some do, some don't. A lot of people don't, increasingly people don't. Why not recognise it? . . . (INTERRUPTED). . . .
Baldwin: . . . let us . . . clarify . . . let us clarify, let us clarify. . . .
Worsthorne: Let us talk of racist propaganda . . . .
Baldwin: Let us clarify my terms, let us clarify my terms. . . .
Worsthorne: I hope so.
Baldwin: You know very well I'm not talking about you.
Worsthorne: How do I know it? You said white people. I am a white person. How do I know?
Baldwin: Look, I only met you twice.
Worsthorne: Exactly, then why do you lead to . . . ?
Baldwin: I have absolutely no reason to attack you. We're not here to talk about each other. You know very well what I'm talking about.

Worsthorne: I certainly do not. . . .

Worsthorne: The American Press, if it can find an example of the police shooting a Negro, will not only shoot one Negro, it will say there would probably be 5 killed. The great American Press is exaggerating the iniquities of the whites to the blacks, even—I don't believe you can disagree—the *New York Times* or the *Washington Post*, the liberal papers, are wholly on the side of the American Negroes in this area, I mean, maybe not in other areas. But if they can find an atrocity by the white police against a black, they will certainly not fail to record it. And in fact, on the record, they will report it and duplicate it, in fact quadruplicate it, if that is the right word. So the idea that if they were being you talk about ah in America where American Negroes are being flung into prison and are being killed, if this was happening, do you not believe that it would be headline news all over the world, every day? Of course it isn't happening, and you know it's not happening.

Baldwin: Have you heard any news lately about . . . (NAME). . . . ? What news have you heard about American prisons lately. . . ?

Don't take my word for it, and I'm not making it into a racial thing. But in fact don't take my word, check out, check the record out, check out who was in prison in my country. I will tell you who. Take my word . . . the Mexicans, the Puerto Ricans and the Blacks, those are the people who are in prison. What do you think is happening in prisons all over America? Why do you think it's happening? I'm not being a racist, which is beneath me in any case. . . .

Worsthorne: Ah the proportion of Negroes in jail . . . (INAUDIBLE). . . . prison. . . .

Baldwin: Listen I don't want to hear that . . . don't want to hear it. . . .

Worsthorne: . . . is higher . . . American. . . .

Baldwin: I don't want to hear . . . .

Worsthorne: You may not want to hear it but the English viewers want to hear it. . . .

Baldwin: I don't want to . . . I don't want to hear that, I don't want to hear that. . . .

Worsthorne: Every law firm, white law firm in America, if they could find a Negro, they would be very glad to have him. . . .

Baldwin: I don't want to hear it. . . .

Magee: Now I'm going to intervene to put one final question ah to James Baldwin which, I think, we must say something about before we come to the end of the programme and that's this. Even if all that you say is true, what do you think should actually be done by the coloured people in the United States to alleviate this?

Baldwin: Now if I answer that question, first of let me answer the last thing. . . .

Magee: Well, I don't want you to go back, I want you to talk about what you've done . . . .

Baldwin: We we . . . Britons. . . . When I said I want to hear that . . . I know those . . . I know the price they paid. I know what happens to them because they are in neither community. They're neither white nor black. Now that that's all I want to say. . . .

(ALL SHOUTING AT ONCE . . . .)

Baldwin: I'm taken now as Jimmy. I, Jimmy, was assured that I was nothing until a white man found me, that I had no language nor use . . . no culture and no human value, and I was very lucky that the missionaries came and found me, and saved me from that terrible place called Africa, and civilised me and brought me over in this city so I could pick their cotton and line their tracks etcetera etcetera etcetera. I was very lucky now. When I try to protect my child, from this particular species of propaganda I am called by white people ah a dangerous fire-brand, an irresponsible Negro ah ah . . . .

Magee: Jimmy I hate to . . . Jimmy you're not answering my question . . . I I'm sorry, are you going to get there . . . ?

Baldwin: Yes, I'm trying to answer it. Now in order to do what you seem to be demanding of the black do, one has to attack the institutions, all of them which, in fact, are in your hands. You seem to assume that in some . . . (INAUDIBLE) . . . way which gives me no reason to believe in—not only your history—that you will give it to me. I don't believe you can give it to me. You can't give it even to your own. I know you can't give it to me. Therefore I've had to find a way of taking it. I don't know what way that will be. I'm not a Black Panther. I'm not a propagandist. I am not a violent man. But I do know that no matter what it may cost me and no matter what it may cost you I am not going to let you do to my children what you have done to me. Direct action is what is demanded. But when we try to do direct action you call this racist. If we were white and blowing up Detroit, you would understand it. When the Jews blew up, when they blow up to get Israel, you understood that. You understand everything when white people stand up. You understand your revolution, but you don't understand ours, and that's because history makes you feel in some occult way that we are not like you. There is a way in which we're not like you of course. The Irish don't like the Poles, the Russians don't like the Yugoslavs, but we are human beings and a child is a child. All this is really that children. . . .

Magee: Ah I'm only going to give you each another couple of minutes and then we must come to the end, so if you have . . . (INTERRUPTED) . . . a chance. . . .

Worsthorne: . . . talking like Jimmy, I can't understand how you should say that the whites don't give you, Jimmy, a chance. You've had a chance and you've made a splendid job. You're a great writer and you certainly demonstrated that ah as speaking as Jimmy that you've done very well. And although I don't think you've got any children but if you have any children I can only hope that they will do just as well. So I think it seems to me, illustrative of the whole theme of this discussion, that you make a point and you don't see how bizarre it must sound to many people that you, here you are, you've done very well and I'm . . . (INTERRUPTED). . . .

(SHOUTING OVER ONE ANOTHER . . . .)

. . . I'm congratulating you. I can't see how you can say that an American Negro, like yourself, has no chance. This is just denied by the very fact of your presence, by the very fact of you being a great man, and I would like to think that ah many more American Negroes would live by your example and by your words.

Baldwin: But you must understand that in the lexicon of the American Republic, a cat like me is a bad nigger, and a very bad example to someone you want to keep enslaved. And I will tell you something else that in my generation (and I'm not young) that there'll be one of me and thousands of us perished.

Worsthorne: But why don't you say: look at me, I've made it, and I'm . . . have escaped and I've . . . (INTERRUPTED). . . .

Baldwin: I've escaped. . . .

Worsthorne: . . . Dwell on this point rather than find some despair.

Baldwin: What I am saying . . . .

Worsthorne: There is such a source of hope in your own personal story. Why did it have to be, why did it have to be distorted, in this language of despair? Why?

Baldwin: Everything goes except, except the power, except the vital interests of the Western world. Now I've always been a slave in the Western world. Whether you think it's propaganda or not, I think that history will bear me out.

Worsthorne: How can you say you always . . . ? You've never been a slave in the Western world. It is just an inaccurate statement. You've never been a slave, have you?

Baldwin: Who?

Worsthorne: You.

Baldwin: You mean me, Jimmy?

Worsthorne: When you said, you . . . "I have always been a slave," why do you talk in this way?

Baldwin: Well let us say we then. To clarify the terms.

Worsthorne: So far as your own generation is concerned, none of you have been slaves. So why do you make a false statement which seems to me to be ah . . . I mean just . . . (INAUDIBLE) . . . false. But am I expected to say, yes of course you've always been a slave? Is that what you're accustomed to when you talk to all these white liberals? They say, oh Jimmy have you always been a slave, of course you've always been . . . You've never been a slave, and your father wasn't a slave. Why do we have to listen to this crap?

Baldwin: Because you don't know my father . . . (INTER-RUPTED). . . . Listen, listen, my father was. . . .

Worsthorne: . . . a free man . . . .

Baldwin: I beg your pardon, I beg your pardon. A man, who is strapped in, I repeat, a ghetto, who makes 27 dollars a week and can't make any more, not because he's stupid, who worked life away in a factory all of his life to support 9 children and cannot get out of the ghetto and cannot get out of the factory his only refuge is in Jesus Christ and this is not my father's fault, that man is a slave.

Worsthorne: A wage slave you mean?

Baldwin: No, I mean a slave.

Worsthorne: But in a sense that any very poor. . . .

Baldwin: No, I do not mean that. . . .

Worsthorne: But you . . . you have got out. . . .

Baldwin: Listen let us leave Jimmy Baldwin for the moment. . . .
(TALKING OVER ONE ANOTHER. . . .)

Worsthorne: Your father's generation people got out.

Baldwin: No, they did not get out. My father left South after a lynch mob wave. My father left the South to save his life. They were hanging niggers from trees in uniforms in 1919 and my father left the South therefore. Millions of us left the South therefore. And came to Chicago where we perish like rats, in New York where you perish like rats.

Worsthorne: So did the Irish.

Baldwin: No, the Irish, the Irish, the Irish. I'm so tired of hearing of the Irish. The Irish are white.

Worsthorne: Yes, I know, but they also perished "like rats" and they were also in miserable conditions.

Baldwin: Listen my friend, my friend, my friend. Angela Davis for example.

Worsthorne: Well let's not use Angela Davis. You'll call that propaganda too.

Baldwin: I'm a very famous man, and I can pay my rent. If my son or my nephew or my wife or my daughter walk into any room in the Western world, and nobody knows their name, she's just another nigger, just another nigger. Don't make no difference. If your son, your daughter, your wife walk . . . (INAUDIBLE) . . . they're white. You may have been starving you may, you . . . your . . . (INAUDIBLE) . . . you may have died in the potato famine. But that is not written on your brow. I wouldn't know you were Irish unless you say so. But to be black in a white man's world, it's quite a different thing. But that's what you were trying to avoid.

Worsthorne: No, I do accept that I think it is ah, it is a a great difference to to to other ah disadvantaged groups that the black skin is a disadvantage. Of course I recognise it. It would be ludicrous not to. But I really don't see that it's reasonable for you to argue that this is something which is . . . ah which can't be got over up to a certain point, I mean. . . .

Baldwin: Which point is that. . . ?

Worsthorne: You're perfectly right that there will always be a difficulty. Well, not always, there will be for quite a long time a

difficulty extra special difficulty for black people to make it in any
kind of white man's culture . . . (INTERRUPTED). . . .

Baldwin: Why's that?

Worsthorne: Why's what?

Baldwin: Mmm Mmm.

Worsthorne: I suppose it's because of the fact which I was ah, I
suppose, indiscreet enough to mention before, that white men don't
really respect black men in the same way as they respect other skins.
There is this prejudice. I would be perfectly prepared indeed . . .
(INAUDIBLE) . . . admit it is more difficult for blacks, much more
difficult. But this seems to me no reason to despair ah no reason to
reach the stage where you do, which is to say the only answer is to
kill white people.

Baldwin: And I said that?*

Worsthorne: No, but I think that you let yourself . . . .

Baldwin: . . . people who have said that. I beg your pardon.

Worsthorne: I think you have lent your support for the Black
Panther movement which does say that.

Baldwin: No, but have I ever said that?

Worsthorne: Well I'm . . . ah . . . .

Baldwin: Have they said that?

(TALKING OVER ONE ANOTHER. . . .)

Worsthorne: I read their publications, and they say that violence
and killing and bombing. . . .

Baldwin: Well, as a matter of fact what they've said . . . .

Worsthorne: They have said you said . . . .

Baldwin: The black man and the . . . (INAUDIBLE) . . . if we could
get on that for a moment . . . came into existence as a Black Panther
party for self-defence.

Worsthorne: . . . said they'd do it.

Baldwin: Will you let me finish? As a Black Panther party for self-
defence in West Oakland which is in the state of California . . . and I

---

*Ed. Note.—The disputed reference here is to a passage in James Baldwin's latest book, *No
Name in the Street* (1971), published by Michael Joseph, London, and Dial Press, New York).
On pp. 163-164 Baldwin wrote the following: "it is not necessary for a black man to hate a
white man, or to have any particular feelings about him at all, in order to realise that he must
kill him. Yes, we have come, or are coming to this, and there is no point in flinching before the
prospect of this exceedingly cool species of fratricide—which prospect white people, after all,
have brought on themselves."

know Oakland very much the same way I know Harlem. I know the cops in the ghetto and I know precisely what happens to the helpless. No cop will ever treat you as long as you live the way any cop will treat any black person, anywhere in the world really, but I'm talking about my country. And if you watch . . . (INAUDIBLE) . . . being beaten up, thrown into jail, ah dying day in and day out, which is a truth. Whether or not you want to call it propaganda that's up to you. I'm telling you what I have seen with these own, with my own, big eyes. Something has to happen. You've got to protect yourself and . . . (INTERRUPTED). . . .

Baldwin: The source of hope, my children, is a source of terror for you.

Worsthorne: Not at . . . you, you can't believe this. You can't believe, if you really think it, that the whites are terrified.

Baldwin: Prove me wrong.

Worsthorne: They're terrified of your weakness not of your strength.

Baldwin: Prove me wrong.

Worsthorne: I think that the tragedy of the white man in relation to the black is that it's the black weakness which is creating a sense of guilt amongst the whites. It's the black inability to take advantage of the possibilities, in that you're creating a despair and a frustration among the whites, though the opportunity is there. . . .

Baldwin: The opportunity to what?

Worsthorne: The opportunity to do what you have done, the opportunity to ah make a tolerable. . . .

Baldwin: Because you think I love . . .

Worsthorne: I think . . . God knows if . . . (INTERRUPTED) . . . that he would be for your children. . . Things are getting better and I think it's the most, I think it's the most bizarre and perverted role to counsel the young people that next generation after you in America. . . .

Baldwin: Do you . . . do you think. . . .

Worsthorne: . . . of your colour . . . . There is nothing for them to be but hosed down and shot down. This is not only untrue, it's a kind of corruption of the spirit . . . (INTERRUPTED). . . .

Magee: Peregrine, let James Baldwin have a last word in, and then we must finish.

Baldwin: Do you think, do you think that all those slaves, I repeat slaves, survived so long, because their eldest counselled them despair? Do you think that I would counsel my child despair? And let me tell you something. My kid knows what I'm talking about. You don't know what I'm talking about. I'm telling you that I'm going to raise my children to be men and women in spite of you, that's all I'm saying, and whatever it costs me or you. But I do know that the doctrine under which you really speak, which is called white supremacy, has come to an end. . . .

Worsthorne: Look, it is not a doctrine I would. . . .

Baldwin: Let me finish, let me finish, let me finish. . . .

Worsthorne: Not on a bad note, I hope. . . .

Baldwin: No.

Magee: Finish, then we all finish.

Baldwin: Yes. I'm only saying this the doctrine under which you speak, no matter what you want to call it, is betrayed by the way . . . the use of the word "give". You do not give anybody the opportunity really, you let him take it—you know. All one's asking—you know—is to be let alone. But in order to be let alone (INCOMP) . . . take over our schools and the ah labour unions and we have changed the shape of society, and in order to do that we are going to have a tremendous resistance even on the part of our friends. But that is what is happening. That is what my kid knows, and your kid and my kid may get to be friends.

Magee: Well thank you very much, James Baldwin. Thank you, Peregrine Worsthorne. Goodnight.

(MUSIC)

Exclusive Interview with James Baldwin
Joe Walker/1972

From *Muhammad Speaks*, 11-12 (September-October 1972). Reprinted by permission.

New York: The most famous contemporary Black American writer continues to be James Baldwin. During a recent visit here he granted this *Muhammad Speaks* correspondent an exclusive interview exploring his thoughts on Black literature and art today, events happening in the U.S. and the world, and his hopes and fears. The following four-part series is based on that conversation which took place on two occasions and lasted two and-a-half hours.

Part I 8 September 1972

Walker: How do you view what is going on in the United States today?

Baldwin: I have a feeling that the people in power are really figure-heads . . . I really do wonder in whose hands exactly the American people are. It is really striking in my experience that the government has been so blatantly contemptuous of the needs of the American people. Not only the Black people but the needs of the whole country.

Walker: Has the U.S. federal government *ever* represented the people? Doesn't it today represent the corporate elite as it did the big plantation owners in the South and the big manufacturers in the North in the beginning?

Baldwin: Until very lately I think it has made some attempt to seem to represent the people. And at certain moments, after all in our history, some pressures from below reflected themselves on high. It is not the case today. The government and the people have nothing to do with each other.

We hear about a silent majority and I am prepared to believe it exists but they aren't the only people in the country and besides I'm not sure Agnew speaks for them.

(Being in the United States) is a little like finding yourself in a backward nation and you read the company press and then you go out into the streets and they don't jive. What you're told is happening and what you see is happening are not the same thing. That can be a very eerie and frightening feeling.

Walker: Do you feel that what is reflected in the Gallop and Harris polls is the general mood of people in the U.S.?

Baldwin: What is reflected in those polls? I haven't read them.

Walker: They indicate that an overwhelming majority of people have lost trust and faith in the federal executive, Congress, the courts, governmental agencies and other institutions in this land.

Baldwin: I have a tendency to think that out of my own experience with the people.

Walker: As one of the Black literary giants of the day, do you see a renaissance in Black literature presently occuring?

Baldwin: All of those terms make me a little nervous. I have survived a couple of renaissances.

I would put it another way. I think there is a kind of ferment beginning in the whole society and I can't predict what will happen with it. It begins to show itself in the disaffection of youth.

I will get back to the question you asked me in a minute but one has to remember that part of the panic in America is the fact that these kids who are supposed to take over General Motors and Texaco seem to be copping out. The future of the corporate structure would seem to be in danger in a profound way because they are repudiating the moral and social standards of their parents. Out of that ferment I think something is beginning—perhaps the beginning of reconciliation between Blacks and whites, I don't know.

The renaissance we're speaking of certainly has something to do with the liberation in Black minds in the last 20-30 years and the freedom to become themselves. Some Blacks who are writing today would not have been thought of before World War II and they certainly wouldn't have been published.

It is only very lately that Black writers are being published in anything resembling numbers. It is far from a paradise but it is somewhat better than it was. Whether or not it is a renaissance is another question. Three or four swallows don't make the summer.

Walker: More than the printed word, motion pictures and television have captivated the masses. Of late there has been a boom in Black-oriented films. Have you seen any of these movies and what do you think of them?

Baldwin: I haven't seen any of them—my own reaction is one of uneasiness. I want and intend to see Van Peebles' and Ossie Davis' films. All I can say is that I hope for the best.

It all depends on finding out if a "Black" movie—in quotes "Blacks"—can liberate itself from the structure that produces movies. For example, a movie like "Uptight" with a Black cast and a white director was doomed from the get-go because we can't really tie the Black movement to the Irish rebellion. The given elements won't support the illusion. Blacks may act that way on the screen but we don't act that way in life. It is not the truth about us.

Hollywood has always, when they use Black actors at all, tried to painlessly incorporate them into the national fantasy. The question concerning the movies coming out now is to what extent they can escape from the psychological iron maiden (Black skins—white behavior.) As I said, I haven't seen any of the new "Black" films so I can't pass any judgement but I know that would be the problem or question.

Walker: What should be the role of the Black creative artist in the Black liberation fight?

Baldwin: First of all the hardest thing he has to do is to remain an artist. He shouldn't confuse himself with games he isn't equipped to play. I, for example, am not an organizer. I'm not a warrior. I'm not a banker; I can't count.

So I have to do what I can do and bear witness to something that has to be there when the battle is over.

Our battle has to be simple. You have to speak in slogans when you are in the middle of our situation. And yet you've got to be aware that a slogan is only a slogan. "Power to the people," for example, can be taken over by ConEdison.

Walker: And "We Shall Overcome" was taken over by Lyndon Johnson.

Baldwin: Precisely. So much for slogans!! What you have to do is to insist on complexity which people in the battle don't want to think about. You have to understand that they don't want to think about it (complexity) because in a certain sense they can't afford to—and yet they can't live without it.

Walker: When you say complexity, do you mean long-range goals?

Baldwin: Yes. A revolution can fail long before it gets off the ground if it isn't understood. After all, it does begin in the mind. There is no place else for it to begin.

It is the ferment occuring in hundreds of thousands of minds or hearts that begins to attack a society to change or overthrow it.

The people who are responsible for it, as distinguished from the people who are simply in the streets, have to be aware of what the revolution is supposed to accomplish. What values it is trying to destroy and what values it is trying to preserve.

Walker: In your opinion, what should the Black revolution in the United States be seeking? What values need to be destroyed? What values need to be preserved? What conditions must be changed? Should the whole system be scraped and reconstructed?

Baldwin: Well, that is a very large question. It is too complex to answer fully. Since I became a man I have felt that what Americans are most afflicted by is a kind of set of mercantile values. That sounds rather trivial until you really begin to examine the effect on a people living in what we call a consumer society.

One of the things it means at once is that you have no respect for labor. You can build a chair that will last a hundred years but don't because in a consumer society you have to buy another chair next year—that's how the society keeps going.

When a man has no respect for his labor, he has no respect for himself. When he has no respect for himself, he has no respect for others. This is what has happened in America because of something we call the profit system.

The way we have live now in this country is not only an affliction to Black people but to everybody in it. People weren't meant to live by the profit system. People weren't mean to drown in things.

These things don't have any value. So a whole collection of people are living in the United States with no values. They are only beginning now to discover what is happening to them and that there is a world—that other people don't want what they want.

Viet Nam is a very good case in point. As far as I know they don't have any vitamin pills, cod liver oil or steak but they survived for I don't know how many years with a bowl of rice. There is a great lesson in that.

Walker: Could not that lesson also have been learned by watching Black Americans?

Baldwin: True, if anyone here were awake. If we could have survived what we have survived at their hands and still do what we are doing, then they really should be able to suspect that we know something they don't know. . . . The values by which this country lives are invalid.

Part II 15 September 1972

Walker: Most newly independent countries in the world are moving in a socialist direction. Do you think that socialism will ever come to the U.S.A.?

Baldwin: I would think so. I don't see any other way for it to go. But then you have to be very careful what you mean by socialism. When I use the word I'm not thinking about Lenin for example. I don't have any European models in mind.

Bobby Seale talks of a Yankee Doodle-type socialism. I know what he means when he says that. It is a socialism created from the indigenous need of the people in the place.

So that a socialism achieved in America, if and when we do—I think you have to say when we do—will be a socialism very unlike the Chinese socialism or the Cuban socialism.

Walker: What unique form do you envision socialism in the U.S. A. taking?

Baldwin: I don't know, but the price of any real socialism here is the eradication of what we call the race problem. The usage of how that problem has been put has always had a terrible inhibiting effect on the development of this society.

Walker: You don't believe that racism in the U.S. was an accident, do you?

Baldwin: Racism is crucial to the system to keep Black and whites at a division so both were and are a source of cheap labor.

Walker: You have been living and working abroad for many, many years. You completed "Another Country" in Turkey and your next book in France. What other countries have you resided in, in recent years?

Baldwin: I lived in Istanbul for a while but in Paris most of the time. I have visited most of Europe and West Africa. In the last sev-

eral years I have been a Trans-Atlantic commuter (between Paris and
N.Y.C.).

Walker: Your writing has been done almost totally overseas. Is
there a reason for that?

Baldwin: In order to write you have to sit down and concentrate
on that. Which means you've got to turn your back on everything
else. It is impossible to do that in the situation in this country now.

For me it was also necessary to move out so that I could see it
because you don't see a situation very clearly when you're in it. You
can't. You spend all of your time reacting to it, resisting it or resenting
it, but you are not able to obtain any distance from it. Everything is
too urgent. It is a matter of life or death. You must react everyday to
what is happening. But that is no way to write a book or a sentence.

Walker: You have been called a Black expatriate. How do you
react to that label?

Baldwin: I don't feel like a Black expatriate at all. For me it is very
simple. I have a lot of work to do and I have to do it. If I could do it in
a shack in Vermont, I'd probably do it there. But I'm not the type to
go to a shack in Vermont. So I'm doing it where I can.

You can't be an expatriate anymore because America is all over the
world. I'm still an American citizen. And what happens here affects
people everywhere else and of course it affects me too, wherever I am.

It is really a matter of walking out of a situation and moving just far
enough back to be able to look at it in order to survive it and perhaps
help other people to survive it. It is not a question to be able to live in
France and leaving all the poor peasants here in their suffering. The
world isn't like that anymore.

Walker: When Angela Davis was imprisoned you penned a powerful and passionate open letter to her which was published in the
N.Y. Review of Books and widely-circulated by her defense commit-
tees. "For if they take you in the morning, they will be coming for us
that night," you wrote. That statement became a rallying cry in the
fight to free Angela and also served as a title for her recently-
published book.

I know that you also addressed large Free Angela rallies in France
and England. Now that Angela has been acquitted, what are your
feelings?

Baldwin: The government didn't have a case. I really don't think the government practically cares whether it is right or wrong or even if it can win the case. I think the whole attempt is to simply grind you down, a process of harassment and intimidation, a process of tying up peoples' energies and money so that nothing can be done.

Walker: To put you out of circulation.

Baldwin: Right. Like the case of Bobby Seale. His years in prison can't be returned. Still he is a man under a stigma. The whole adventure was so ambivalent so that there has to be a doubt left in the public mind—which is the point.

Walker: There are those who maintain that the jury system is working in America and point to the case of Bobby Seale and Erica Huggins who were released after a hung jury; the case of the Panthers in N.Y. who were acquitted on all charges; the case of David Poindexter who traveled with Angela and was found innocent of "harboring a fugitive;" and now the case of Angela herself. Do you share that evaluation of the U.S. jury system?

Baldwin: The American jury system has great limitations, especially as it concerns Black people. But I do think the government has discovered an unexpected resistance in the people. It reflects itself in those verdicts you mentioned in which the jury simply refuse to convict.

It is certainly a very healthy thing because if our situation were grimmer than it is, then the people would simply march along with what the government wished. For obviously, if the government brings forth a case it wants to win it, and it makes it almost a matter of patriotism to support the government. When the people refuse to do that, I am very happy about it.

Walker: Newspapers throughout the land have attacked these peoples' victories in court and critized the jurors' attention to public opinion. There are intensive efforts also underway in state legislatures to authorize convictions by less than unanimous verdicts, to deny defense lawyers the right to conduct their own examinations of jurors for prejudice and other legislation that strikes at the heart of the alleged constitutional guarantee of trial by an impartial jury of one's peers. What do you think about this backlash?

Baldwin: What they are seeking are ways to ensure convictions, in short. That's what it comes to, isn't it? Obviously they are totalitarian moves aren't they?

Such moves are aspects of the law and order cry.

Part III 29 September 1972

Walker: Since you wrote *The Fire Next Time* which was based on your reactions to an exclusive interview with the Honorable Elijah Muhammad, have you had any further reflections on the Nation of Islam?

Baldwin: The Nation of Islam is possibly the last remaining social force in America among Black people. I am looking at what has happened to the Black Panthers, the civil rights movement and a whole spectrum of movements which were operative until years ago and which in effect are not operative now.

I don't know to what extent Islam can work for most Black people. That is a question not a statement.

I have always been respectful towards the Messenger and his followers. What happens in the Nation of Islam and around it is very important. . . . The Nation of Islam has survived and that is a very significant development.

Walker: You have been an outspoken critic of U.S. involvement in Southeast Asia. President Nixon is withdrawing more and more U.S. forces, asserts that he is winding the war down and that in a matter of time the war will be ended and the U.S. will exit itself from Viet Nam. What is your reaction?

Baldwin: We have heard that song so long now. I am one who never believed a word Nixon has ever said—even before he was President. Leaving that aside, I don't see quite how we can hope to do that without confronting at one point the reasons we were there in the first place.

What Nixon is trying to avoid, I imagine, is an admission of defeat—that in fact we have been thrown out.

The reason we went in was to protect what we call our vital interests, didn't we? That is the only reason for that war—there isn't any other.

The problem of our vital interest, as conceived by Americans, still remains. The Vietnamization obviously isn't going to work. We are going to be forced to accept a coalition government and the fate of those people will finally be in their own hands.

So this costly adventure will have been not only a defeat but—what I always thought of it as being—a massacre for no reason.

Walker: Turning to the Middle-East, how would you describe the conflict and issues there—especially having been one who has spent some time in that area?

Baldwin: Israel, I have always felt, is a state created in the Middle East to protect Western interest. I never for a moment believed that it was created because England or America or Russia had a particular respect or affection for the Jews. But there they were and the conscience of the world was kind of bleeding because of the fate they had undergone, not only under the Third Reich, but in many other parts of the Western world. So that Jews were given Israel in order to help us control that part of the world. In fact, the Arabs are now paying for the world's bad conscience about the Jews.

Walker: Didn't you live in Israel for a time?

Baldwin: I didn't live there. I was there about nine years ago and stayed there maybe two months. Then I went there again when my play was on tour and stayed maybe a week.

Walker: Did you come into contact with any of the Black Jews there from Africa or Asia?

Baldwin: Yes, there was a sizeable number from Africa, Algeria, and Egypt. What is curious about it is that these people are all technically Jews, but a Jew from Russia, a Russian, a Frenchman and an Englishman at least as much as they are Jews. When they are confronted with a Jew from Egypt or Algeria, the fact that they are Jews doesn't in anyway soften the cultural collision or make it any easier for them to get along, as now is being proven in Israel. The darker Jews are protecting their situation there.

Walker: What about the freedom battles that are going on in Southern Africa—in Mozambique, Guinea Bissau, Namibia, Rhodesia and within South Africa? South Africa is the most heavily-armed and equipped country in that region and U.S. corporations have heavily invested there. Some people say that another Viet Nam will occur there because of its rich minerals and resources and the enormous Western capital investments. How do you see it?

Baldwin: It is hard to answer that because I haven't been there, for one thing. But I would think that it could very easily become another Viet Nam because of the reasons you stated and suggested and because the whites in Southern Africa are so completely marooned. They are surrounded by Black people after all and not all of them can be bought—in fact most of them can't be bought because there is nothing to buy them with. And because of the whole structure of white people's minds—they can't make any concessions to (Blacks)—they are afraid to.

So, of course, the freedom fighters are becoming more and more intranigent. Sooner or later there will be great trouble with American investment. It must be happening now. Then everything depends on what the U.S. decides to do about it. If we decide to go in and protect the investment or decide to make some kind of concessions. But I don't see what kind of concessions can be made for our investments. And I don't think American businessmen—unless we have learned something from Viet Nam—are gifted enough to understand the nature of the struggle which will inevitably overthrow them.

Walker: Will anything short of a bloodbath in South Africa itself change conditions there?

Baldwin: I wish I could say yes, but in fact I can't. Again though, if you have never been in a country you don't know what is really going on in it. What kind of forces are being created. But I do know the economy is lock, stock and barrel in the hands of the West. And you know what that means.

Walker: How would you assess the issues in the conflict in the Communist world between the Soviet Union and China?

Baldwin: It is a question I really don't know how to answer. I don't think of Russia as a Communist country when one speaks of a desirable form of socialism. I never had any respect for any of the Communist parties I've been in contact with.

If you strip the apparent ideology, it becomes just a very brutal question of conquest or control. In which case it would seem to be that Russia and America will have to go back to bed together, and I am sure this will happen. They will form a coalition to prevent the effect of China.

Walker: What is the effect of China?

Baldwin: The effect of China being at this moment anyway, the only faint hope that the Third World has. People in truncated revolts occurring all over the world can't look to Russia and America for aid.

Walker: But Russia reportedly gives substantial aid to Third World countries and freedom movements—so says the giver and the receivers.

Baldwin: Maybe be a given situation Rusia will give aid to shore us (U.S.) up but they aren't interested in those wars of liberation at all. Maybe China isn't either but at the moment it would appear that she is.

So the effect of China—much more than what is going on, on the Chinese mainland—in terms of freedom fighters all over the world is something I think both the U.S. and Russia would be determined to check and destroy if they can. Does that make sense to you?

Walker: It seems that what you are saying is that the three giant states in the world are maneuvering for spheres of influence or control over the developing and dependent nations. If so, that leads to the question—can any small country aspire to rule its own destiny unless it in some way links up or aligns with the Soviet Union, the United States or China?

Baldwin: It would seem to be something like that for the foreseeable future. I think the Cuban revolution would have developed differently if it hadn't had the most powerful country in the world on its doorstep and as its enemy.

Walker: But Cuba has survived attacks, boycotts and threats from the U.S. because of the will of its people and the military and other support—material, expertise and diplomatic—that it has received from the Soviet Union. Is this not true?

Baldwin: Those are interesting observations and no doubt with much truth but I haven't been there myself and I don't know what kind of options people have had or what the price has been for their proximity to the United States.

Walker: You have been to and lived in Turkey—one of the oldest inhabited regions on earth. What is life like today for the Turks? How does that country fit into the international picture?

Baldwin: Turkey is a U.S. satellite on a Russian border and facing Greece. It is trapped in its past and very poor and mainly illiterate.

If the populace becomes educated there is no telling what it will do. It would certainly break away from America and maybe not turn to Russia. But they can hardly hope to survive alone either.

Walker: Are you saying that underdeveloped and developing nations have to secure "Big Brother" assistance from large countries in order to make any go of it?

Baldwin: I suppose there has to be some grim coalitions between superstates and evolving entities.

Walker: Evolving entities?

Baldwin: I don't know what else to call them (the so-called emerging nations-J.W.). You can scarcely say evolving countries. When you break up the society you find you are dealing with tribes and languages, habits and histories, and so the nation becomes a very arbitrary concept, especially under pressures like that.

Walker: Do you think of Northern Ireland as a white colony of Great Britain?

Baldwin: They certainly think so.

Walker: How about you?

Baldwin: Again never having been there—let me put it this way, the Irish people I have met from Ireland certainly have a mentality which I recognize as being part of my own.

Walker: Would you describe that mentality?

Baldwin: The same kind of bitterness, the same kind of rage, the same kind of determination which finally has to become even extremely irrational, to be out from under the heel of an occupying power. . . . Yes, I think Northern Ireland would have to be classified as a colony.

Part IV 6 October 1972

Walker: Does the Black struggle in the United States need to be internationalized? Should Black North Americans struggling for bread and butter issues here be concerned with what is happening in Southeast Asia, in the middle East, in Southern Africa, in Latin America, and elsewhere?

Baldwin: What is happening there will determine a great deal about their bread and butter here. . . . If one doesn't understand the global trap, then you can easiy fall into such weird dreams as becoming a Black capitalist. That simply means that a certain number of Black people will be allowed to make a certain amount of money. But you can't be a Black capitalist unless you have a colony of your own. Unless you have people you are exploiting, you aren't really a capitalist. You are only a member of the club and they can always throw you out of the club.

Walker: Is it necessary for a Black involved in the Liberation struggle here to have a political ideology? Can revolutionary change be brought about without a political philosophy or outlook?

Baldwin: I don't have any coherent political ideology—nothing very doctrinaire. I know more clearly what I'm against than I can state what I'm for.

Walker: Does this result from what you earlier called "the colonial mind?"

Baldwin: I think it results from a certain kind of experience. What you have made of your experience. What your experience has made of you. So by and by without having thought it through, you have arrived at a political position, whether or not you have a political ideology. It is the way you have reacted to your life.

I don't think one can expect most people to have a political philosophy as such. There is something about me which mistrusts that level of political indoctrination.

People in some senses know better than their leaders what they need. The danger of trying to indoctrinate a population is that you then cease to listen to them. The lines have to be kept open so that you can be able to hear what the junkie has to say. He may not have a political philosophy but a great deal of political wisdom.

The whole point is to address yourself to the needs of the people. Any political philosophy should be open-ended—which is always evolving. The situation demands that.

I also think with attempts to indoctrinate populations, you alienate so much of the population that you destroy the purpose of the indoctrination.

Walker: How do you react to the projection of our literary figures and sports stars as Black leaders?

Baldwin: That is a part of America—I don't know what—I guess naivete.

Walker: You have been so projected even though you disclaim being a politician or organizer. How do you deal with being unwillingly thrust into a "Black leadership role?"

Baldwin: The only way to deal with it is to accept it.

Walker: To accept what?

Baldwin: You accept that what you do and say has an affect on other people, especially young people. It is not that you think of yourself as a leader, but that you have found that you are placed in a certain position where it would be criminal to not be responsible.

I'm a novelist, not a politician. People are not at all what politicians think they are, or what their leaders think they are. They are better and worse than that.

Walker: You consider yourself responsible in relationship to your work, don't you?

Baldwin: Well, yes. But there it is something I more or less chose. What came with it, I hadn't thought of. And I didn't in that sense choose it. I don't mean I'm complaining but it wasn't something I saw coming. You know, you write a book and you hope to get it published but you don't expect to become a leader because of that.

Walker: More than your Novels, your essays have had tremendous political impact.

Baldwin: I never used to think of them as political essays but now I see that they are. I was only trying to clarify a situation—first of all for myself and then for others. What happens once you've done that, the implications of where you are, forces you to move in a certain direction. That's politics. In that sense all action is politics.

Walker: Where do you see the world going from today onward?

Baldwin: I have too much faith in people to be hopeless but we are in for some very difficult times. The whole great power syndrome may be obsolete but nobody knows it yet. The world is heading for a certain kind of decentralization which I think is its only hope. But the powers that still rule the world don't see it that way or envision it that way. If I'm right, it will have to come about through one form or another of a holocaust. In a sense we wouldn't know where we are going until this present tension has been one way or another resolved.

Walker: Do you think the United States will go through a fascist stage before significant changes are realized here?

Baldwin: It could very well happen. It is such a strange and unwieldy country. Though it is a little difficult to imagine it, because partly one doesn't want to. A weird kind of decentralization could take place—concentration camps in California, concentration camps in New York, concentration camps in Philadelphia.

Walker: Many people say the U.S. is very close to it now.

Baldwin: True, but there is something else happening.

Walker: A counterforce?

Baldwin: Yes, which makes me doubt finally that America will really become the concentration camp which so many people would like it to become. I don't know but I think a lot of the white citizens of this country have undergone a kind of awakening—through the war more than anything else.

Walker: Do you consider yourself anti-capitalist?

Baldwin: I suppose, to put it briefly, I would have to say that. I think capitalism costs the world too much. I don't think that the economic arrangements of the world should be such that a Mexican peasant or a Turkish peasant should barely manage to live or nearly starve to death while so much of the world is eating far too much. It is not only a blatant injustice, but pure folly.

Walker: Do you consider yourself anti-Communist?

Baldwin: Yes. I was anti-Communist when America and Russia were Allies in fact. But again all the terms have to be revised. I'm anti-Stalinist, to be more accurate. I'm anti-Communist because the C.P. in the U.S., as I have witnessed it, is a party whose record, intellectually and internationally, is shameful.

Walker: Is there hope for meaningful Black advancement within the Democratic or Republican Parties?

Baldwin: Not as they are constituted.

Walker: If there was [SIC] a genuine Conservative and a genuine Labor Party, would that make a difference?

Baldwin: That might help to clarify things. At the moment we have something like four major parties—two Republican parties and two Democratic parties.

The Black Scholar Interviews James Baldwin
The Black Scholar/1973

From *The Black Scholar*, 5 (December 1973—January 1974), 33-42. Reprinted by permission.

James Baldwin was born on August 2, 1924, in New York City, the first of nine children, and grew up in Harlem where his father was a minister. He graduated from De Witt Clinton High School in 1942 and held a number of minor jobs—handyman, porter, elevator operator, office boy, factory worker, dishwasher, file clerk. At 24 years of age, he left the United States for Europe, returning here occasionally for business reasons. Staying mainly in Paris but traveling to many parts of Europe, he wrote and published his first three books. Baldwin has now written or co-authored more than a dozen novels, plays, essay collections and other works. His stories and essays have appeared in many magazines both in the U.S. and abroad, and four books—*Nobody Knows My Name, Another Country, The Fire Next Time,* and *Tell Me How Long The Train's Been Gone*—have been on national best-seller lists. Recognized as one of the country's finest writers, James Baldwin has also gained international prominence as a spokesman for the black freedom movement. This interview took place in October 1973 at his home in southern France.

Black Scholar: Brother Baldwin, you have been involved as an active observer in the movement of black people since 1955. What developments and differences do you see in today's movement?

Baldwin: Well, I really date my involvement from my birth, which was 1924, and there wasn't anything called a movement. But when I think about it again, I have to remember that I was born in New York because my father and my people had been driven out of the South. This was after the first World War when black people were undergoing a series of pogroms in the deep South and when black

142

soldiers were being lynched in their uniforms. It was a kind of convulsion all over the nation which drove my father, among many other people, North. That's why I was born in the North.

So I represent the first generation born in the North, of that massive migration. And you must remember that there was a tremendous dislocation. First, from the land to the city and, much more importantly, from the point of view of the question you are asking me, there was no articulation of what it meant to be black. It was an insult to be called black in those years when I was growing up, and part of my father's disaster and part of the danger which menaced the entire family was our relationship toward our own blackness, which was very painful. It was a matter of humiliation and self-humiliation which was not my father's fault and not our fault. It was the context in which we were born.

By 1955, when I was a grown man, something had begun to change. And what had changed was the relationship that black people had to each other. The fact that from that moment on, let us say, black people began to relate to each other more coherently than they related to white people. From that time on, what a white person's judgment of a black man was began to diminish in value. It did not end! And, it hasn't ended yet! But, it was a tremendous and perceptible shift. In a certain way around that time, which was 18 years ago, black people in America began to depend more on each other and began to create their own standards. It had become clear that one could no longer live by the so-called standards of white civilization.

By this time, in 1973, a whole new generation has grown up without these crippling handicaps of my generation; with certainly different illusions and certainly different dangers, but with a freedom which barely could have been imagined 49 years ago. And as time goes, that's a very short span of time.

Black Scholar: Why do you think these particular changes occurred?

Baldwin: I think for one thing, the breakup of the black family unit, which is tragic and one of the reasons that so many boys and girls are on the needle; why so many of us have been lost. But, perhaps like every convulsion, it had a positive side, too, in the sense that one is forced to deal with the city streets. The brutality of the

South is extreme, but the brutality of the North is extreme, too, and utterly impersonal. It's the same spirit but the technique is different and therefore you have to evolve different techniques to deal with those brutality problems as distinguished from the brutality of Georgia.

In this way another consciousness began to evolve. Something colder than it had been before. Something, in a word, more revolutionary, though that's a very hard word to use. If you had to come from Mississippi to Chicago or from Georgia to New York, you had to deal with questions you might not have in the South. The moment one begins to ask those questions, another sensibility begins to evolve; in the dark, as sensibilities always do, as many seeds of convulsions begin. But it began then, and by 1955 it had put down roots and was beginning, in a sense, to blossom. This may seem a misplaced word in such a grim context, but in short, black America had changed in those years and had changed forever. In some ways for the better and in some ways, perhaps, for the worse. But, then, that is something you can never really be definite about. In my point of view, it's for the better, on balance, because we know more about each other than we did before.

Black Scholar: Who do you see as being important leaders today? And why?

Baldwin: One of the things that has happened in the last five to ten years is that black people have begun to realize that a great many people who were called their leaders weren't, and we know that a great many of our real leaders were murdered. So, I think there's a general, though unspoken reluctance on the part of many black people, and certainly on the part of the young, to identify a leader, because identifying him is almost like putting the finger on him. In any case, I think the time for that kind of leader is probably past.

I think the leader now is to be found in all kinds of places. He might stand on the streets of Detroit, he might be an 18-year-old boy, it might be a 25-year-old woman, it might be a 75-year-old man. A leader is someone who is operative in changing things, and they are to be found in prisons; they are to be found in universities, for that matter, and on football teams. They work, and they must work (the situation being as grave as it is) in a kind of anonymity. Perhaps, if I go to Chicago next week, I might discover two or three leaders in various barbershops there. But, the nation won't know who they are, and the nation hasn't got to know. The nation has no way of reacting to them except with terror. And terror has brought death. The urgent need of the black community is to protect its leaders in order to protect its young.

Black Scholar: What is your evaluation of the civil rights movement between the years 1955 and 1964? What would you assess as its pluses and minuses?

Baldwin: To tell you the truth, the results of the civil rights movement to me has nothing to do with civil rights. (I'm talking with hindsight. I might not have said this two years ago.) The one thing it revealed to me was a profound nobility, a real nobility on the part of a whole lot of black people, old and young. There is no other word for it.

It was a passionate example. It was doomed to political failure, but that doesn't make any difference. The example will never, never die. And on another level, it exposed white people. Some of them understood it and some of them didn't. Some of them really understood what it meant to have all those kids cattleprodded and hosed and beaten and murdered and chained and castrated. The moral image of a cattleprod against a woman's breast or against a man's testicles.

It exposed some things for some people and on the other hand most of the people hid. They did not want to see it and don't see it until today. That's how we have Nixon in the White House and we see this hood Agnew on his way to jail. And then, once again, to keep the nigger in his place, they called it law and order. They brought into office law and order, but I call it the Fourth Reich.

I must say, I claim for the black people of America the example of nobility which I have never seen before and no one in this century has seen before. Malcolm was noble. Martin was noble. Medgar was noble and those kids were noble and it exposed an entire country, it exposed an entire civilization. Now we have to take it from there.

Black Scholar: With Stokely Carmichael's Black Power statement in 1966 various forms of militant black nationalism emerged. Do you see this as new development or basically a cyclical response?

Baldwin: It's such a very hard question to deal with, really, because Stokely at that moment was very, very young. I mean that only a young man would have been able to say it. And only someone who was forged in a crucible outside the United States. It is very important to remember that Stokely, like Marcus Garvey, is West Indian and therefore his relationship to the deep South and all those highways was a very different one, profoundly different one. I admire Stokely very much, but his frame of reference from his childhood was not Georgia or Harlem, it's someplace else. He had another sense of identity which allowed him to say, as Martin Luther King could not and as Malcolm had to say in another way, that if we don't have power, we can't change anything. That's a very good, logical statement coming from the West indies, and a very powerful statement coming from the deep South.

It is very important that Stokely said it but what was even more important was the convulsion in the white American breast because he really put his finger on the root of the problem. They ain't never gonna give us anything. Such people never do give. They have to be menaced into doing it. They won't set us free until we have the power to free ourselves. That was the importance of it. What one has made of it is something else, on both sides of what we call the racial fence. The dues that Stokely had to pay behind it were extraordinary because it really got to the heart of the American problem, which is, who owns the banks?

I'll put it another way. When the kids were marching down in the South, the North was vividly in sympathy with them. We knew that if it ever got to the North, the same Northern liberals, who praised all those kids on the highway and sent down all that money, would do the same thing in New York as was being done in Birmingham. And the same thing happened, except in New York, the enemy is in the bank. When the kids sat down in the bank, the very same policemen, for the very same reasons, did the very same things. That is when the movement changed. When Martin Luther King went to Chicago, they threw eggs at him and said we don't want dreams, we want jobs.

The importance of what Stokely said, and the importance of what's been happening in the last ten years is that people in the street from Birmingham to New York, especially their children, have learned to understand the nature of the American hoax.

Black Scholar: You are saying, then, that you don't think it was new?

Baldwin: No, it was old.

Black Scholar: What are the differences that you see in the kind of militant black nationalism that Stokely talked about in 1966 and the kind that Garvey talked of earlier?

Baldwin: Well, it is not so great a difference as it would seem. Garvey's era was the era in which I was born and grew up. Garvey was a West Indian adventurer; the boat sank, and we could pursue that but that's another question. The trouble has always been to arrive at some viable identity, some bearable identity, some identity which is not at the mercy of the people who despised you. Garvey was trying to do that. Whether it was wrong or right, and whether his tactics were wrong or right is another question because you cannot speak about tactics in such a tight situation, anyway. It is still a question of whether Booker T. Washington or W.E.B. DuBois was right. I wasn't there, but I know they were both produced by the same circumstances and reacted in different ways, or it seemed to be different ways, to the same trap. And they both bequeathed us something very important. The argument between them now is just as important as it was then.

All were dealing with America. It was a question then; it's a question now. One can't go back to Africa. You would never find your tribe; in any case your tribe would be different. Liberia proves this because American Negroes were used to go back to colonize Africa, and they all ended up working for the rubber plantation, which forbids you to be romantic about a return to any place. Monrovia is one of the most ghastly cities in the world, really, to tell the truth. And everyone in that country is owned by Firestone. Every acre, the rubber, is owned by Firestone.

The hard thing then is to recognize that if you can't go back, you must go forward, you know. And if you can go forward, you may be able to make a real alliance of your past and your present. You cannot possibly do it by going backwards. The past is irrecoverable. The American black man for the first time may be able to move forward into whatever his future is going to be, which means by changing his present. But he cannot do it by a romantic return to the past.

It's very difficult; all these questions have questions behind them. It's a series of parentheses and it cannot be answered, you know. It can only be faced. I don't have any answers. No matter how we play it, the question is who holds the power; and a deeper question than that is by what morality (and that's a very serious word) does whoever hold the power hold it. Which means, held to what purpose, to what end.

Black Scholar: What direction do you see the movement in the U.S. taking at this time?

Baldwin: I think it has become less domestic and more international. Marcus Garvey tried to articulate, after all, quite a long time ago, and even Frederick Douglass, that the situation of the black American slave was tied to the situation of the slaves all over the world. In a book called *Bury My Heart At Wounded Knee*, not too very many years ago, there was no connection between blacks and Indians. But when blacks started firing back at the Ku Klux Klan, so did the Indians. It was in the same month. That hit me in a very funny way because long, long before our day the Indians and the niggers (the Indians and the slaves) were friends and sometimes even married. I'm part Indian and probably so are you. But the Indians were almost destroyed and we were dispersed. So it is perfectly logical that a certain historical wheel should eventually come full circle; so that what began, arbitrarily speaking, with the black movement in the 1950s would spread first all over the country and then all over the world.

It is clear to anyone who thinks, and maybe even to the junkie who suffers, that the situation of black America is related to the situation of Mexicans, to all of Latin America. It's related to the military junta in Chile; with the misery of the people called the "have nots." It's not an act of God and it is not an accident. It is something which is deliberate. It is something which is necessary for the well being of the "master race" so that the poor of Latin America, or the poor of Vietnam, and me are in the same bag and are oppressed by the same people and for the same reason. And if they can be murdered in Latin America as we have been murdered for years and years in our own country, and murdered in Vietnam, then something begins to be very, very clear: that the salvation of the black American is also involved with the freedom of all the other slaves. And this, too, begins to evolve very slowly and in the dark, but I think it becomes clearer with every hour.

Black Scholar: What are your views on the sources of the oppression in Africa, Asia and Latin America?

Baldwin: My views? How can I put this? It is much more serious than my views. All of the oppressions that you speak of have the same root, have the same reason. Take the Israeli-Arab conflict or the so-called Israeli-Arab conflict because—it is very important, for me at least, to remember that they are of the same tribe, living in the same desert; they are both circumcised and have the same prophets, you know; and, when I was in Israel, fortunately I could not tell the difference between them. Now, all right, people will be what they are. They've been battling out there in that desert for a long time. But the situation became much more crucial at the point that their battle became useful to the Western powers which would use them against each other, which is exactly what has happened in the case of Palestine, now called Israel.

There is a level at which one can say that the guilty conscience of the Christian Western nations helped to create the state of Israel. A Jewish Zionist won't admit it but an anti-Zionist Jew will, that most Zionists who are not Jews are anti-Semitic, and in that sense the creation of the state of Israel was false. Many people knew it in France and America. It was a kind of final solution, and in any case was very useful for the Western powers. In a certain sense, the state of Israel was created to keep the Arab in his place. It's a very cruel way to put it but that is the truth. In any case, it is not acceptable to me that the people who have been in refugee camps for the last twenty-five or thirty years have no equal right to the land of Palestine where Jews and Arabs have been together for so long. I am not myself deluded that, *either*, in the case of Israel or in the case of Vietnam that the Western powers are fighting for anybody's freedom. They are fighting to protect their investments.

Black Scholar: Several people have seen the famine in the areas of Chad, Mali, Senegal, Niger, etc., as being a planned act of genocide. Do you believe such was the case?

Baldwin: It could be a planned act of genocide, but it is much more important to realize that it didn't have to be. The disasters of which you speak are built into the system of which we are speaking. A Western banker hasn't got to be wicked or even very clever, you know. Genocide is on one level, if you like, planned, but it is unplanned at the moment of real conflict. The rise of capitalism and the rise of Christianity created a dynamic which made genocide inevitable. The preacher and the missionary, individually, may be very honest and very sincere, but the dynamic they represent is what makes genocide inevitable. Whether or not they like it or whether or not they know it, that is what it was built to do.

Black Scholar: In your writings you have remarked that both black and white Americans are victims of an historical process which they do not understand. Further, you indicate that white America refuses to acknowledge the "horror," as well as the "beauty" of its history, especially in reference to race. Do you still hold this view?

Baldwin: Yes, I still hold that view except a little more emphatically. White America is unwilling to recognize its history. I don't think they can. I'm speaking about the generality, but the exceptions must be noted. You must consider that a lot of white people in America understand what's happening, especially young kids. But then to the extent that they understand it and to the extent that they act on what they understand, they become indistinguishable from the nigger. Indistinguishable, because, in a sense, they are worse than the nigger because they are traitors.

History is a very strange crucible and I don't pretend to understand it; but I do understand at least in my own mind that you are lucky if you are forced to understand your own history. A black American who has, in effect, or who is told he has no history has achieved some kind of identity in any case. And then you begin to recreate your history out of weapons you didn't know you had. This is what happened to black Americans, I think. I don't think that we were born with any particular sense of history. Yet when I realize that something had brought me from birth to maturity, someone had created me, and it wasn't anything I had been taught in school; it wasn't any history which was at anybody's fingertips. It was history which had been, in a sense, handed down to me, invested in me, and when I say me I mean all black kids.

History was someone you touched, you know, on Sunday mornings or in the barbershop. It's all around you. It's in the music, it's in the way you talk, it's in the way you cry, it's in the way you make love. Because you are denied your official history you are forced to excavate your real history even though you can never say that's what you are doing. That is what you are doing. That is one of the reasons for the life style of Black Americans, which is a real life style as distinguished from the total anonymity of white Americans who have so much history, all of which they believe. They are absolutely choked with it. They can't move because all the lies that they have told themselves, they actually think is their history.

We were able to raise our children because we had a real sense of the past. That is because we had to have a very real sense of the present and to have a hell of a lot of apprehension for the future so that the kid had to be prepared. All you have is your history, and you had to translate that through everything that you did, so the kid would live. That is called love, too. You try to become in a sense a model.

For example, I remember my grandmother because there was something she was trying to tell me and I knew she loved me. She scared me, you know. My father scared me, too. My mother some-times scared me, but I knew they were trying to tell me something, and I began to listen, which is the way a black kid grows up. You don't always know exactly what's happening or why it's happening but you do grow up respecting your father, whether or not you get along with him, and you do respect your mother and you begin to see when you get to be a man what they were trying to tell you, because now you've got to tell it. That's how history is handed down. You've got to be a model like they were a model. You've got to spank the baby; you've got to be responsible for him.

Someone told me once that there were no orphans in Africa and it was true. You can tell from the way the kids treat you. The kids treat you, in Africa, as though you automatically belong there because you are grown up. When I was growing up, the neighbors used to beat me and my brothers and my sisters when they thought we were doing wrong and would tell my mother or my daddy that "I just beat him." All of us brought up everybody else's children, you know, and none of us had any bastards.

Bastardy is a commercial concept which is among the most ob-scene in the world. It means that you can't inherit family property. Beyond that it goes a long way towards explaining the disaster of the South and the disaster of America, because it was white people who have had black children whom they have lynched, knowing them to be their children. If people can do that, they are doomed.

As Stevie Wonder says in his song (It will take a long time before white America can understand what his music is about at all; it's almost like a code. They don't really know what Stevie is singing about or what Stevie is saying. They can't afford to know.) Stevie says, "I ain't gotta do nothing to you; I ain't even gotta do nothing to you; you cause your own country to fall." And that's what's happening. Now, the rest is up to us because we are responsible *for* each other and *to* each other. We are responsible to the *future*, and not to Chase Manhattan Bank.

Black Scholar: How have you, a black man, found the experience of racism here in France as compared with the United States?

Baldwin: Well, it is very important to remember that *America* was *settled* by Europe. You know, it takes about five minutes for a European to become an American, and, as Malcolm said, the first word he learned was "Nigger." That puts it a little brutally, but it is very accurate. A black man from America in Europe is exotic. He doesn't pose any threat. In the first place, there aren't very many black Americans in Europe, when you take into consideration the population of Europe. Many of them are distinguished, one way or another, leaving aside of course the GI, but they don't depend on Europe. Therefore, they are no menace to Europe.

I was very poor when I got to Paris. I slept in the streets and under bridges and I slept with the Africans, the Algerians and the underside of Paris. It was very good for me. It was frightening, but it was very good for me. In France, the Algerian is the nigger. That's because of the relationship of France to Algeria for 130 years: A very complex relationship in which Algeria simply belonged to France and when an Algerian came to France, he was treated and is treated as a mule, especially now because he is doing all the dirty work that the Europeans no longer want to do. They need him for his labor, but they don't want him here as a man, they want him here as a mule. He didn't have his woman here, he didn't have his children. He had to work and send money back to Algeria. Of course, it is possible that something else begins to happen because the Algerians have been here long enough to have children and this begins to change the whole structure of France. France reacts the way England reacts, the way Americans have always reacted—with panic, and panic means cruelty, you know, death to the Arab. That overstates it a little, but not very much.

The French have (I can only speak of the French with some authority because I have lived here so long) one difference, which is not, when you examine it, a very great difference. They don't have the sexual hysteria of the English and Americans. They don't like Mohammed's presence, they don't want him to marry their daughters, but they don't have the American paranoia about your asking his daughter to marry you and her usually saying "yes," because she's just waiting to be asked. French men are too egotistical to imagine that anyone can take their women from them. But that doesn't make any difference in the day-to-day life of the garage worker, the factory worker, the mason. The difference is something which only I would observe, which makes no difference in their lives at all.

Black Scholar: What do you find is the level of political consciousness of Africans living here in France?

Baldwin: It depends on which African you are thinking of. The African laborer is articulate; I'm sure he's talking to his comrades. The African student or professional varies according to the extent to which he takes his standards from Europe. Many of them are still schizophrenic, which is perfectly understandable. The American black man has an advantage over him, having been born on the mainland, so that he does not discover when he is thirty that he is a nigger. He discovers it when he's five, or six, or seven. It's very different to be born in a colony and to be bright and to be sent to school in the mainland and then discover you are a nigger. It's much harder to get over. If you do get over it, you become a valuable weapon. Many people never get over it. One has to face that, too. I think that the generation you represent is freer from these hang-ups than my generation because it is much clearer for your generation how bankrupt the Western world is.

Black Scholar: Brother Baldwin, how do you see yourself as a black man here in the "sunny hills of southern France" and your relationship to black people who are struggling all over the world against racism and exploitation?

Baldwin: The south of France is not as sunny as people think it is. I know why I'm here but I could say, you know, that I have found a haven although I know very well that that's not true. You have to remember, first of all, that the world is very small, and it is no longer possible for an American, and certainly not an American black man, or an American black writer, and certainly not James Baldwin, to leave America. You have to remember that France and America are friendly nations and it may cost me more to live here than I am willing to tell. In any case, the most difficult thing for me to accept in my life was that I am a writer and that there are no excuses. I must get my work done. It is not up to the world to tell me how to do it, it is up to me. The important thing is the work. The world's judgment is something I have to live with. I learned how to do that a long time ago. In the meantime, I'm working. I can't do more than that and I am *not* in exile and I am *not* in paradise. It rains down here, too.

Black Scholar: Do you consider political themes or rather the influence of politics as playing an integral role in your writing process?

Baldwin: Politics was not very real to me when I was 19, 20, 22. It wasn't real to me because my situation was too tight and I was trying to survive in New York and I had my family to worry about and the rent to pay and I was dancing one step ahead of the devil. I still am but the difference is that when I moved out from America, I began to see it from a different perspective, which is very difficult to describe. I can see now what had happened to so many people who had perished around me and I could see that it was a political fact, a political disaster, and that I, myself, was in any case a political target; and menaced by forces which I had not seen as clearly when I was in America.

I also realized that to try to be a writer (which involves, after all, disturbing the peace) was political, whether one liked it or not; because if one is doing anything at all, one is trying to change the consciousness of other people. You're trying also to change your own consciousness. You have to use your consciousness, you have to trust it to the extent—enough to begin to *talk*; and you talk with the intention of beginning a ferment, beginning a disturbance in someone else's mind so that he sees the situation, which is what Malcolm was doing. Malcolm and I were very good friends, but we're not at all alike, and I am not comparing myself with him. What Malcolm was trying to do was make black people see their situation and then they could change it for themselves because Malcolm was only one man and I'm only one man.

A change, a real change is brought about when the people make a change. The poet or the revolutionary is there to articulate the necessity, but until the people themselves apprehend it, nothing can happen. When the people have taken the necessity, when the movement starts moving, then the world moves. Perhaps, it can't be done without the poet, but, it certainly can't be done without the people. The poet and the people get on generally very badly, and yet they need each other. The poet knows it sooner than the people do. The people usually know it after the poet is dead; but, that's all right. The point is to get your work done, and your work is to change the world.

Black Scholar: Is the poet necessarily one who is a literary figure, one who writes and composes poetry, or can a poet take other forms?

Baldwin: When I say poet, it's an arbitrary word. It's a word I use because I don't like the word artist. Nina Simone is a poet. Max Roach is a poet. There is a whole list of people. I'm not talking about literature at all. I'm talking about the recreation of experience, you know, the way that it comes back. Billie Holiday was a poet. She gave you back your experience. She refined it, and you recognized it for the first time because she was in and out of it and she made it possible for you to bear it. And if you could bear it, then you could begin to change it. That's what a poet does. I'm not talking about books. I'm talking about a certain kind of passion, a certain kind of energy which people produce and they secrete in certain people like Billie Holiday, Nina Simone, and Max Roach because they need it and these people give it back to you and they get you from one place to another.

Black Scholar: How do you see the role of the artist in general?

Baldwin: The role of the artist is exactly the same role, I think, as the role of the lover. If you love somebody, you honor at least two necessities at once. One of them is to recognize something very dangerous, or very difficult. Many people cannot recognize it at all, that you may also be loved; love is like a mirror. In any case, if you do love somebody, you honor the necessity endlessly, and being at the mercy of that love, you try to correct the person whom you love.

Now, that's a two way street. You've also got to be corrected. As I said, the people produce the artist, and it's true. The artist also produces the people. And that's a very violent and terrifying act of love. The role of the artist and the role of the lover. If I love you, I have to make you conscious of the things you don't see. Insofar as that is true, in that effort, I become conscious of the things that I don't see. And I will not see without you, and vice versa, you will not see without me. No one wants to see more than he sees. You have to be driven to see what you see. The only way you can get through it is to accept that two-way street which I call love. You can call it a poem, you can call it whatever you like. That's how people grow up. An artist is here not to give you answers but to ask you questions.

Black Scholar: Speaking of black artists and writers, you were very close to Lorraine Hansberry. Is there anything you would say about her life and work?

Baldwin: It is hard for me to talk about Lorraine in a way because I loved her. She was like my baby sister, in a way. I can't think of her without a certain amount of pain.

Every artist, every writer goes under the hammer. But under ordinary circumstances, since a writer's real ambition is to be anonymous and since his work is done in private, one arrives at some way of living with the hammer. But the black writer is by definition public, and he lives under something much worse. The pressure of being a writer is one thing, but the pressure of being a public figure is another—and they are antithetical, too. The strain can kill you. It is certainly one of the things that killed Lorraine, who was very vivid, very young, very curious, very courageous, very honest. But she died, as you know, subsequent to the eruption in Birmingham, as the country, in fact, began to go over the cliff. Many of us began to realize then that there was no way of redeeming the American Republic. It was bent on destruction.

This was one of the things that killed her. It was the incomprehension of her country and the disaster overtaking the nation, which, after all, she, like I, had many reasons to love. We were born there, and our ancestors paid a great deal for it.

Black Scholar: What closing words would you like to leave with *The Black Scholar* readers in several countries round the world, and particularly brothers and sisters engaged in active struggle wherever they might be?

Baldwin: This may not answer your question exactly but it's the only way I can get into it. I have an actor friend, a black actor friend who lives in California with two or three kids who are my godchildren, and a beautiful wife. The faces of his children, his three boys, when they look at their father, are very proud faces. They are very proud of him, in a way that was very rare, very rare to see when I was growing up. And they don't care if he's poor. They are not upset by that. They know who he is and what he's trying to do and he's their daddy. That all gives me a certain resurgence of consciousness that I was trying to talk about before; and also the necessity that we have to take care of each other because no one else is going to do it.

The importance of the black family at this hour in the world's history is to be an example to all those other dispersed all over the world because in a sense, the American Negro has become a model. In a very funny way the vanguard of a revolution which is now global, and it does begin with what you call the black family. My brother in jail, my sister on the street and my uncle the junkie, but it's my brother and my sister and my uncle. So it's not a question of denying them, it's a question of saving them.

I think the revolution begins first of all in the most private chamber of somebody's heart, in your consciousness. I think that what is happening now is that a new vision of the world which has always been there, but a new vision of the world, is beginning to be born. And if that is so, then the little boys that I am talking about will be the architects of that world.

There have been civilizations which have lasted for thousands of years without policemen, without torture, without rape, where gold was an ornament, not the summit of human desire. It has happened before and it can happen again. I really begin to look on the 2,000 year reign of the theology of this system, which is coming to its end, as a long aberration in the history of mankind, which will leave very little behind it except those people who have created an opposition to it, if that makes sense. What it can give it has given. In America, what it gave was us and the music which comes to the same thing. Now, it's not even worth translating. It has translated itself. It was doomed.

But those three little boys who are living in California, my godchildren, will not be doomed. We must take our children out of that civilization's hands. That will be easier than we think it is because this civilization is on its death bed.

There are new metaphors, there are new sounds, there are new relations. Men and women will be different. Children will be different. They will have to make money obsolete; make a man's life worth more than that. Restore the idea of work, which is joy and not drudgery. People don't work for money, you know. You can't work for money. When you work for money, something awful happens to you. But we can work, and understand. The world begins here, entrusted in your head and in your heart, your belly and your balls. If you can trust that, you can change the world, and we have to.

James Baldwin Comes Home
Jewell Handy Gresham/1976

From *Essence*, 7 (June 1976), 54-55, 80, 82, 85. Reprinted by permission of the interviewer.

Long ago James Baldwin ran away from this land. It was not, however, a permanent leave-taking. For although he makes his home in the South of France, he regularly comes home to feed on what France cannot give him—the warmth and love of his own homefolk, including that large clan of mother, sisters, brothers, nieces, nephews and friends who live for the most part in the Harlem community in which he was born. This is the account of one such trip home.

On his last return Baldwin visited Riker's Island. On this stretch of land in Manhattan's East River roughly 5,000 men and 400 women, the overwhelming majority Black, are imprisoned. Baldwin had accepted an invitation to speak with members of the Women's Development Unit, a smaller group within the prison.

The Riker's Island women's facilities may be unique in this country. The chief officer, Superintendent Essie Murph, and the majority of the correctional staff are Black. Their drive and initiative are responsible for programs meant to introduce constructive change in the lives of prisoners.

The average female inmate's age is 25 although one quarter is adolescent, ranging in age from 16 to 21. Most have made it no further than the tenth grade before becoming drop-outs or shut-outs. Blacks constitute 81 percent of the prison population, 13 percent are Spanish speaking and six percent are white. Mothers who, in most cases, represent the sole support of their children represent another alarming (67 percent) figure; ten percent are pregnant when they enter. Most have a history of having sustained early sexual violations.

In this predominantly youthful audience gathered to hear Baldwin, one face stood out, an older woman, exceptional because usually no one at Riker's is over 50. The lines were gentle in her face; her expression was quiet, reserved and sad. She might have stepped out of a Charles White drawing. She had been jailed for participating in a fight while intoxicated. She was unfortunate; alcoholic, suburban matrons do not usually go to jail for unruly behavior during drunkenness.

Some of the women were very vocal. From a corner now and then, however, would come other, somewhat shyer voices.

Baldwin: Thank you, I'm very glad to be here. I'm not very good at making speeches, so I just thought we'd sit and rap awhile. I don't quite know what's on your minds and I'd like to. We all have to find out how to deal with and change the positions we're in. The most important thing for me is how to save our children. They only have us to do that. We all got here through many dangerous toils and snags. Our fathers had to go through death, slaughter and murder—things we still see around us. But there is more than that behind us. If not, we wouldn't be able to walk a single day or draw a breath. I'm only trying to say that one can change any situation, even though it may seem impossible. But it must happen inside you first. Only you know what you want. The first step is very, very lonely. But later you will find the people you need, who need you, who will be supportive. I don't want to talk anymore, really. I'd like you to just throw questions at me, and we'll see what we can see. OK?

Question: James, what was your main goal? What did you want to be?

Baldwin: I wanted to be a writer. But I didn't even know what that meant when I was a little boy. I used to write Christmas shows for the church and school. I wrote the school song, and my brother David, sitting over there, had to sing it for years and years. He never forgave me. I wasn't a dancer, I wasn't a boxer, I can't sing. And as it turned out I wasn't very good at carrying a mop. So I wrote.

Question: Was it hard for you?

Baldwin: It's still hard.

Question: Did people accept you on your qualifications or was it a matter of who you knew?

Baldwin: In the first place I didn't know anybody. And the people I got to know later I didn't like. When I was young, the idea of being a Black writer was a strange one for Blacks to accept. My father was very opposed to it. Not because he was opposed to writing but because he thought I'd get my heart and my head broken. It took me a long time to understand where he was coming from. But you have to do what you have to do. I had to start writing.

In a sense I wrote to redeem my father. When I was a kid I didn't understand his rigidity and I *had* to understand that. I mean, I had to understand the forces, the experience, the life that shaped him, before I could grow up myself, before I could become a writer. I began my first book when I was 17, and it took me ten years to write it. But I became a writer by tearing that book up for ten years.

Question: Could you share with us what you received from your father as well as your mother to sustain you?

Baldwin: Well, my father was a very strong-willed Black man from New Orleans who moved North after the first World War. He never reconciled himself to New York and to Harlem. And he was perhaps too old to have as many children in a strange land as he had. The world was changing so fast, and he was in such trouble that he could not change with it. He was sometimes a very difficult man. As children we didn't realize what his working day was like. He would get dressed in the morning as a preacher, which is what he was on Sunday, with a well-brushed black hat and polished shoes. And with black lunchbox in hand he would go to the factory where he worked all day as a laborer. He had nine children he could hardly feed. His pain was so great that he translated himself into silence, rigidity . . . sometimes into beating us and finally into madness. He died in the madhouse. I didn't understand all that when I was growing up. But he taught me something. Without him I might be dead because knowing his life and his pain taught me how to fight. My father used to say, "You didn't call me to preach; God called me to preach." Many years later I was battling with an editor and I said "You didn't call me to preach, God called me to preach."

My mother was very different. She's still alive, thank God. She was very gentle. We all thought she was a little too gentle and forgiving, but actually she was very, very strong. To raise nine children under those circumstances she had to be. And she knew that James and

George and Gloria and Wilma were very different people. And that's not easy. She taught us what we needed, which is a simple thing, but not so simple when you get older. "You have lots of brothers and sisters," she used to say. "You don't know what's going to happen to them. So you're to treat *everybody* like your brothers and sisters. Love them.

Question: Do you feel, as you look back, that you deserve your success?

Baldwin: There is something very dangerous about the world's acclaim. If you believe everything that people say about you, you can be carried on a trip—out—and you can stay out to lunch for days. I think I'm learning how to write. We're always learning. I think I know from whence I came, what I don't want . . . what I won't do. I think, though it sounds very pretentious, the only reason to try to become a writer is not to tell the world how *I've* suffered, because who cares, but it's an act of "I love you." That's what it's about to me.

Question: What about the process of writing?

Baldwin: Sometimes it comes very quickly. Seems almost to come from the top of my head. But in fact, it's been gestating for a long, long time. Most of the time it's not like that. Usually it's a matter of writing, recognizing it ain't right or it won't move. You tear it up and do it again and again. And then one day something happens—it works.

Question: Did you have very many friends when you were growing up?

Baldwin: No. I didn't have many friends but I had my family.

Question: What was your greatest difficulty in writing your first book?

Baldwin: The difficulty was a kind of language barrier. I come from a certain street in Harlem, a certain place and time. And the people I grew up with, my mother and father, my aunts and uncles, all those people in the streets, the people in the church, had a certain life. The English language as such was not designed to carry those spirits and patterns. I had to find a way to bend it the way a blues singer bends a note.

Question: Yet many of your readers and critics feel that you are a particular master of English prose. How do you explain the inconsistency?

Baldwin: When I wrote my first novel, I was living in Switzerland, in the mountains, in the snow. I had Bessie Smith and Fats Waller records, which I played all the time. I had come out of the church and the blues. Black people speak in a certain cadence, and you can't get it on the page by dropping *s*'s and *h*'s and *t*'s and so forth. You have to listen to it very, very carefully to get the essence and flow.

When I realized that music rather than American literature was really my language, I was no longer afraid. And then I could write.

Question: Do you speak any other language besides English?

Baldwin: I learned French in self-defense.

Question: In one of your plays you talk about a young boy in church having flashbacks. Did you write that out of personal experience?

Baldwin: That's a very good question. You're talking about *Go Tell It on the Mountain*, my first novel, which concerns itself with John, his father and mother and the church people. The point of the book, in a way, is what experiences shaped his aunt, his father, his mother. All of these lives were shaping John's life. *His* choices are defined by things that have happened to other people, not him. Not yet. In short he's walking into his ancestors' lives and experiences. Obviously at some point in my life that was my situation. And in order for me to assess and surmount it I had to face it. That's why you write any book, in a sense, to clarify something. Not merely for yourself. What I have to assume is that if it happened to me it happened to someone else. You have to trust your own experience, which is all that connects you to anyone else.

Question: How did you become a writer, and were you discovered by any particular person?

Baldwin: I can't really say I've been discovered as much as I've been washed up. Actually the most important person in my life in that sense was and is a very great but not very well-known Black painter named Botha Delaney. He was much older than I and a real artist. I was about 16 and he believed in me. Following him around, watching him work taught me something. Without him an already rocky road would have been much rockier.

Question: Does a Black writer, painter, artist stand a better chance in Europe?

Baldwin: Not really. It can be a terrible trap. There are certain

American impressions and legends of France, of de Gaulle, French girls, elegance—a pattern of myths. You have to be there to realize that Paris is a part of Europe. All of Europe was involved in the slave trade. Now it is perfectly true that in Paris I, as a Black American, was not treated the way a man from Senegal or Algeria, former French colonies, was treated.

I was an exotic. I was from somewhere else. They don't know, in fact, that I come out of the slave trade, which comes out of Europe. So for a while, in Paris, you can slide because nobody is bothering *you*. On the other hand, if you have the sense to look around, you see that what's happening to the Algerians, the Senegalese and to any nonwhite person in Europe is the same thing that's happening to you here. So you have not really escaped anything at all. The battle I had with Richard Wright was probably about that. He was much older, and he'd gone to France before I did. We were both living in Paris before the Algerian war. And if you just opened your eyes, you could see what was happening. You could see the way the police treated the Algerians. You could see why they were being thrown in jail and dropped in the rivers like flies. Now what the French did to Algeria is no different from what whites do to Blacks here or what the British do to a Jamaican in London. That's part of the cement as well as the crisis of the Western world. All those Black Englishmen who were created by England when she was an empire are now trying to go to London, which is where they're supposed to "belong." But there is no longer an empire to support them. England is nothing now but a damp little island and they can't support their ex-slaves. What is happening there is happening all over the Western world.

Question: Do you like Paris?

Baldwin: Well, I don't really live in Paris anymore. I live in the country, near a town called St. Paul about a half hour outside of Nice. I don't like cities anymore. That's probably because I'm getting older, and it's harder for me to write than it was before. I love and hate New York. I was born in New York. A lot of me is in New York although I'm not sure I'd ever live in the city again. If I were living in the United States, I'd be living in the hills. I can do without the cities. I can live without going into another bar.

Question: What made you go on to playwriting?

Baldwin: To see if I could—although I had to do *Blues for Mr.*

Charlie. It's based roughly on Emmett Till. It's based on much more than that but that was the catalyst. I knew it couldn't be a novel or a short story or an essay. It had to be a play because I wanted people to see it, react to it. I wanted Black and white people to look at it together. I wanted to try to get inside the mind of the murderer. No man is a villain in his own eyes. He thinks what he's doing is right even when he knows it's wrong. That was one of the things I tried to do with it.

Question: How do you feel about some political prisoners like Eldridge Cleaver and Angela Davis?

Baldwin: Well, Eldridge Cleaver and Angela Davis are very different people. Angela obviously was a political prisoner. Many others don't have the title but are, in a real sense, political prisoners. Sometimes, however, the term "political prisoner" is used as a propaganda label, a way of intimidating or guilt provoking other people.

Question: What advice would you give young people like us who want to be writers?

Baldwin: I might buy you some paper and a pen and say "sit down." But there's really no advice to be given. When I'm writing, I usually show my work to my brother. I know he'll tell me the truth. He can't really give me any advice. All he can say is this does or doesn't work. It's true or it's not true. Or why'd you do this—what did you mean here? It's that kind of tug-of-war. At that point nobody can really help you except by being there and helping you go through it. Nobody can do it for you. There aren't many helpful hints. You learn by doing and then you gotta unlearn all the tricks in order not to rely on them.

Question: Someone said it's better to write about personal experiences than to fantasize.

Baldwin: That's probably true, but even that depends on what kind of writer you are. You know, some people were meant to write fantasy. In any case fantasy is also truth. All of us are much more devious and mysterious than we think we are.

Question: Do you ever feel strange reading some critic's opinion of the way you write and what you say?

Baldwin: What other people write about me may be correct, I don't know. In any case it's irrelevant to me. If you think I'm a good

writer, so much good for me; if you think I'm a bad writer, so much
the worse. It can't make any difference to me because I have to write
anyway. I would think that for a writer it's better to read his own
books than read what others write about him. I've read very little
about myself.

Question: You prophesied in the *Fire Next Time* that this country
was headed for an apocalyptic end if it did not realize how brutally it
treated Black citizens and therefore how horribly it corrupted the
national soul. Do you feel there is any possibility that the American
people possess the potential to change course?

Baldwin: Every American city is in trouble mainly because whites
are fleeing from Blacks. That's how we got the inner city, which is
bankrupt. White America brought that on herself.

Any fool could have told her she could never win in Viet Nam. She
should have figured that out since she'd never been able to conquer
us. But just as America didn't know about us, she didn't know about
Papa Nam, Mama Nam and Baby Nam. America's trouble is that she
created a myth, locked herself inside it, and now she doesn't know
how to get out. The world is not the world Americans think it is. For
example, the world is not white. Colonialism may not be dead but it
is certainly dying. The structure that held the Western world together
is crumbling. All that's left now is naked power. That's the beginning
of the end. No kingdom can endure that way. No kingdom or country
can endure against the will of life, against the will of the people who
are trying to subvert, to change it. It needs those people. It needed
them as slaves. It needs them as a free people. In any case we'll
never be slaves again, although it'll be a long time before we're free.
But that's something else. The basis—moral or spiritual—on which
the Western world was built is gone.

There was a day, for example, when a Black believed he was a
nigger, when he was really trapped in the fantasy in the white man's
mind. But that day is gone. Nothing will ever make him a nigger
again. Nobody's ever been able to turn back time. What is going to
happen to England now that she has no colonies, only the good Lord
knows. The fall of Portugal, the disasters in Italy and Spain, the
tension in France and all that these imply involve the end of the Western world as we now know it.

Question: Mr. Baldwin can you tell us what the title of your next novel is?

Baldwin: Oh, the one that's coming out is a long essay entitled "The Devil Finds Work." It's about the role played by Black people in American films beginning with *Birth of a Nation* and ending with *Lady Sings the Blues*. It discusses *The Exorcist* too.

Question: Will you be writing another autobiography?

Baldwin: I don't intend to. I'm not that fascinated with myself. I have a lot of work I want to do, and I haven't got 2,000 years.

Question: What happened to your play on Malcolm X?

Baldwin: I wrote it. I went to Hollywood to do it for Columbia Pictures and they and I did not agree. To make a long story short, I walked out with my script. To put it brutally, if I had agreed with Hollywood, I would have been allowing myself to create an image of Malcolm that would have satisfied them and infuriated you, broken your hearts. At one point I saw a memo that said, among other things, that the author had to avoid giving any political implications to Malcolm's trip to Mecca. Now, how can you write about Malcolm X without writing about his trip to Mecca and its political implications? It was not surprising. They were doing the Che Guevara movie while I was out there. It had nothing to do with Latin America, the United Fruit Company, Che Guevara, Cuba . . . nothing to do with anything. It was hopeless crap. Hollywood's fantasy is designed to prove to you that this poor, doomed nitwit deserves his fate.

From the Audience: Say something in French.

Baldwin: Bonne nuit, mesdemoiselles, à bientôt. Vous avez été très gentilles.

Question: What does that mean?

Baldwin: Good night, ladies. I'll see you soon. You've been very, very nice.

The Artist Has Always Been a Disturber of the Peace

Yvonne Neverson/1978

From *Africa: International Business, Economic and Political Magazine* 80 (April 1978), 109-10.

James Baldwin is one of the most famous black writers of our time. Born in Harlem, New York, his particular experience as a Black person who has the abilty to create images with words encouraged him to draw from his own personal experience and to reflect more profoundly on the wider issues of the Black experience.

The role of the Black writer is a constant subject of Baldwin's thinking . . . and he (has) explored with honesty and precision the curious situation in which an artist of the Black Diaspora finds himself.

Since Baldwin's earlier writings in the 1960's he has been primarily an observer and sometimes committed participant to the tremendous sociopolitical change that Africa and the Diaspora have experienced.

Africa magazine recently went to meet James Baldwin. Yvonne Neverson initiated the dialogue. Some excerpts:

Q: Africa is keenly interested in observing the process of cross-fertilisation of ideas among artists in Africa and the Diaspora. Do you think that this is an on-going process which originated in the Civil Rights struggles of the 1960s and if so how do you feel this can best be fostered?

A: I would set up exchange student programmes through institutions if they are willing to do it, but if not then we need to set up our own institutions, to do it ourselves. I have a nephew born in New York who recently went to Africa. It had a tremendously liberating effect on him, and although that is an individual example, that kind of experience ought to be more actively fomented. I see this as something which the African media could promote in a positive way. What I am talking about is cultural interdependence. If one were to really examine it, it is conceivably much deeper than the common experience of colonialism or neo-colonialism. The colonial experience certainly in America, Europe and in Africa created another identity and maybe, perhaps, it forces us to recognise how much we need each other in order to examine the foundations of a new world. The first step is knowing that it's there. I would think, that this kind of cultural interplay and cross-pollination is much more vivid for this generation.

Q: In those areas where a common language is utilised, say in music and literature, there is a growing body of artists whose works are widely known in the Black world and are shared by most Black people. This, however, does not seem to be so apparent in the area of the visual arts where the language of symbolism does not seem to be as universal. What is your view?

A: I do not claim to know a great deal about this, but there is little doubt that this sense of common identity is one of the principal impulses. Of course America is vast by itself, and yet the sense is that one no longer wishes to be isolated on the American continent for there is another nation or another world which is much larger than the one into which we are born, and literally all need each other. We have to know what is going on in the Caribbean, we have to know what is going on in Africa and Africa has to know what is going on in Black America.

Q: This sense of common identity between contemporary artists of Africa, the Caribbean and the Americas is perhaps manifested visually by their returning to African traditional themes as a source of inspiration. Do you see this as an important element in their artistic development.?

A: That is what excites me. There are no rules about it. That is what is happening. In my own work; in any creative work you are driven to the first principles. You are driven to where you should really come from, what you really feel apart from all the things which you think you have learnt and forgotten. But when the chips are down and you are really trying to work out of the soil that you've been given, there is no place else to go. Whatever you have learnt to gain it is irrelevant at that pressure. The passion that creates a work of art is really not cerebral.

Q: How do you see it manifesting itself more concretely?

A: That I cannot answer really. I would like to see a change in the educational system in America which allowed, or at least did not penalise, the energy we are talking about. In fact I think what I am talking about is occurring in various southern states of America but it is also happening, oddly enough, in places like Detroit, Chicago, Philadelphia and New York where there are abandoned waste grounds and the kids have taken the remaining wall standing. Some of the kids in the various cities painted what they call a wall of respect. It was absolutely spontaneous. The kids themselves decided to do this. This graffiti which is both political and satirical, is a very important creative endeavour which is another aspect of this communal spirit which I mentioned earlier.

Q: In Africa this is very similar to the popular art which is to be found in sign writings and some of the decorative works in public buildings. Would you say that this mode of artistic self-expression using new symbolism is similar to the observable popularisation in literature such as the rejection of standard English?

A: It depends on the level of rejection. I am not so sure that it is important to reject like that. I think it is important to reject it as a standard but whether to reject it in toto is another question. It is a standard that obviously does not work, for it is not big enough to carry your experience and in that sense one is forced to snatch the language and do things with it that cannot be done within the confines of the Queen's English. There is a reality of a painting. There is a reality of a Black life that is not that of Rembrandt. Everything must be learned but to be put to your own purposes.

Q: This popularisation is in some cases influenced by the belief that Blacks should communicate with Blacks only. Do you agree?

A: That is too crippling and I deem it unnecessary. I think you communicate, you do your work. There it is and it is for everybody because, you know, in all this talk about Blackness one tends to forget or let me say it this way; the terms you have lived with so long is the same point of view from which one can suggest, to overstate it. But I mean it when I say there are no White people and that it is a myth.

The sense of history, the sense of reality even the sense of religion under the umbrella heading 'White' has is really a metaphor for safety and for power and that is why people are White. The idea of speaking only to Black people seems unnecessary. No one in love or trouble or at the point of death is only a recognisable colour. What he is at that moment is his experience. It is himself.

Q: Often the artist is in an ambiguous position for his self-expression can be constrained by other factors. Have you experienced this with regard to your own work?

A: I have some feeling that there is on some level a greater respect for artists. A greater understanding of them than there was twenty years ago. Although I do not want to minimise the conflict with the artist's own struggle for existence, there is a danger of conflict between the private vision and the public role. But I think that conflict is irreducible and I don't think it has been crippling. It can become that given social and political vigours, given time and places and it is part of the secret behind the jailing of the playwright, Ngugi, in Kenya who has offended the State. The artist has always been a disturber of the peace in some way, but that seems less important at this moment than the beginning of the flowering which is something unprecedented.

James Baldwin: No Gain for Race Relations
Hollie I. West/1979

From *The Miami Herald*, 16 April 1979, pp. D1,3. Reprinted by permission of *The Washington Post*.

"If we do not now dare everything, the fulfillment of that prophecy, recreated from the Bible in song by a slave, is upon us: God gave Noah the rainbow sign, No more water, the fire next time!"
—The Fire Next Time, 1963

NEW YORK—James Baldwin, the avenging prophet of American letters, the novelist-essayist who warned of a racial Armageddon in the 1960's, is still foretelling famine and gloom in race relations.

Though civil rights laws are on the books and the black middle class continues to grow, Baldwin says really not all that much has changed.

"To be very honest about my experience in the last decade," he says, "a great deal has changed on the surface. But nothing has changed in the depths. A great deal has changed on the surface in Atlanta, but nothing has changed in Georgia. Maybe we're in worse trouble than before."

The trouble signs he sees:
• the middle-class tax revolt and what he sees as racial implications;
• the Bakke decision;
• campaigns against anti-discrimination measures in general.

He is sitting in the New York offices of his publisher, Dial Press, near the United Nations complex. He shifts his 5 foot 6, 135-pound frame within the narrow confines of a Danish-modern chair. His eyes, always big, look as if they're about to explode.

Baldwin is nearly as articulate in his speech as in his celebrated writing. And on this day his words have painted a paradox. All during the interview he has said he's an optimist. So why is he voicing such pessimism? "It's a contradiction," he concedes.

"When I say I'm not a pessimist, I mean that I don't consider that everything is lost even though I don't see how we're going to have a

172

future, or even a present. Except that in some ways so much of it is up to black people now. And we're in a terrible position. I know that. "The responsibility can't be placed anywhere else. We have to save our children by whatever means come to hand, or they will attempt to save us, and those results will be cataclysmic.

"No one's going to clarify the situation for black people. They know that very well—the situation of the kids in the street who have no jobs and no future. We have to articulate that necessity because Mr. Carter can't do it. He never sees those people. Those people are numbers in the bulk of the American population. I suppose that what I'm suggesting is that we're going to have to create the help."

In the political history of this country, groups have created help for themselves by forming coalitions, it is suggested.

"Yes," he nods, "but you can't form a coalition in Boston now between poor whites and blacks. And I doubt very much you can form a coalition between poor whites and blacks in this country, as of today.

"A coalition of rich whites and blacks is even more dubious. That leaves the great unwashed. That leaves us, the Puerto Ricans, the Mexicans, the handful of Africans that are here."

Baldwin has always seen his mission as that of spokesman for black Americans. Ever the moralist, he skillfully translates his personal experiences into group significance.

The Christian Sciene Monitor once said, "Perhaps no other Negro writer is as successful as Mr. Baldwin in telling society just what it feels like to be a Negro in the United States."

Baldwin burst upon the American literary scene in 1952 with *Go Tell It on the Mountain*, a partly autobiographical novel about his days as a boy preacher in Harlem.

It was followed in 1955 by *Notes of a Native Son*, a collection of graceful and biting personal essays.

And thereafter followed the novels, *Giovanni's Room*, a study of homosexuality, and *Another Country*, a nightmarish account of race and sex in Harlem and Greenwich Village and more essays, *Nobody Knows My Name* and *The Fire Next Time*.

By 1963, when the civil rights movement was in high gear and people were marching and demonstrating against racial discrimination, Baldwin had become a literary force. His fiction and essays stamped him as the chief black literary spokesman of his generation.

Robert Kennedy conferred with him on race relations, and Baldwin spoke to audiences of thousands, passionately arguing for black-white understanding to head off a race war.

"Few Americans have been called on as has James Baldwin in the last decade to function as the public voice of rage or frustration or denunciation of grief," said the Saturday Review. "The writer means to create an image of his people that will not only recover their dignity, that will not only spell out what they have to teach, but that will sting all sane folk to jealousy."

Today, at age 54, Baldwin is no longer the lionized literary figure. The lines in his face are heavier now and his hair is filled with patches of gray.

The civil rights movement, for which he polemicized and marched, has taken a turn from street confrontations to boardroom negotiations. Now there is talk—much of it controversial—of the idea that race has been superseded by class as an important factor in determining life chances among blacks.

Nevertheless, Baldwin still speaks with the old fire. His message, delivered in taut apocalyptic tones, is the same: that whites had better recognize the "full weight and complexity" of black humanity before the world explodes over the issue of race, for the momentum of the civil rights movement has ground to a halt.

"Once Martin (Luther King) was dead, the situation had been irrevocably altered," he continues.

"A great many friends of mine got completely wasted. . . . Some of the leaders I've worked with in the Deep South and the North. There've been nervous breakdowns, ulcers, divorces—madness. Some are literally starving. Their whole frame of reference and reason for being was shattered that day in Memphis when Martin was murdered.

"It was being confronted with the brutality of the American decision," he says quietly, almost in a whisper. "So they simply had had it. . . . And when you see that, you see how little, after all, has changed.

"You see what they want to tell. The history of school desegregation. You're confronted with an overwhelming record of bad faith. And there is no other word for it. Look at the situation in the cities, and you're confronted with American panic vis-a-vis blacks. . . ."

His home recently has been in the south of France, but he hasn't lived in this country since 1969. That's when he left, aggrieved over King's death and disappointed over Hollywood's rejection of his screenplay on the life of Malcolm X.

"I didn't know for a long time whether I wanted to keep on writing or not."

"What I said to myself was that Martin never stopped. So I can't either. It was as painful as that."

So Baldwin resumed writing. He has just completed a novel, *Just Above My Head*, the story of a gospel singer, that's scheduled to be published this fall.

Dial Press has inaugurated a fiction prize in his name, and Raymond Andrews was recently named the first recipient for his novel, *Appalachee Red* (Dial Press, $8.95).

But though the prizes and association with America continue, and though he insists it's hard not to stay in touch with America ("More and more of Europe is becoming more American") Baldwin has been trying to leave America since he was a young man. He first left for Paris in 1948 when he was 24.

"I left America because I doubted my ability to survive the fury of the color problem here. (Sometimes I still do.)," he has written. "I wanted to prevent myself from becoming merely a Negro; or, even, merely a Negro writer . . . In my necessity to find the terms on which my experience could be related to that of others, Negroes and whites, writers and nonwriters, I proved, to my astonishment, to be as American as any Texas G.I. . . ."

His first stay in Europe was critical. He lived in one of the poorest sections of Paris, one inhabited by transient workers from Algeria. For the first time he was brought face to face with who he was. In Harlem he had had the comforting surroundings of family, friends and his people.

"I know," he wrote in *Notes of a Native Son*, "in any case, that the most crucial time in my own development came when I was forced to recognize that I was a kind of bastard of the West; when I followed

the line of my past I did not find myself in Europe but in Africa. And
this meant that in some subtle way, in a really profound way, I
brought to Shakespeare, Bach, Rembrandt, to the stones of Paris, to
the cathedral at Chartres, and to the Empire State Building, a special
attitude. . . ."

James Baldwin: Looking Towards the Eighties
Kalamu ya Salaam/1979

From *The Black Collegian*, 10 (1979), 105-6, 108, 110. Reprinted by permission.

James Baldwin, like an old testament prophet whose insistent voice refuses to fall silent, has been one of this country's most persistent witnesses. He is a witness in that he testifies to everything he thinks and feels as we move through the minefields of love/hate, Black/white, rich/poor relationships in twentieth century America.

His complex prose style has often been favorably compared to the King James version of the Bible (primarily the fire and brimstone Old Testament). Although books such as *The Fire Next Time* have earned Baldwin a reputation for being a harsh critic, James Baldwin is actually most concerned with the problems and possibilities of finding and holding love.

While he has not found it easy to live and work in this country, Baldwin continues to prolifically produce novels and essays. Most often he writes from a small town in France, but on occasions he has sent work to us from Turkey. The important thing is that he is not running away but rather searching out a rock, a desk, a stone table from which he can find the needed moments of silence and rest out of which will come rushing full force another letter, or a new nerve-jangling essay, or perhaps a huge and rich novel (such as his latest *Just Above My Head* which some critics think is his best since his first novel *Go Tell It On The Mountain*).

Having crossed the half-century mark, he is no longer an angry young man; he is an elder. He is a seer who has seen much. There is much we can learn from the visions he has, visions which have been tempered by a long time coming.

James Baldwin, a witness, a writer, a Black survivor: listen, he speaks and it is life-song he is singing.

Q: Now that you are back in this country, do you plan to stay?

177

Baldwin: I'll be here for a while. I'm sort of a commuter.

Q: Why do you choose to commute?

Baldwin: I'm not sure I chose it. I went to Paris a long time ago, didn't stay away as long as people thought I had. I came back home in 1967 and was based here until 1969. Since then I have been more or less commuting because it's very hard for me to write here.

Q: What makes it difficult to write?

Baldwin: Well, there are so many other demands which have to be met. There is no way to sit in an ivory tower.

Q: During the sixties there were a number of people who attempted to say what the role of the writer was. I remember a quote of yours which said that the "role of the writer is to write." Do you still think that quote encapsules what should be the role of the writer?

Baldwin: The role of the writer *is* to write, but this is a cryptic statement. What I meant is that a writer doesn't dance. His function is very particular and so is his responsibility. After all, to write, if taken seriously, is to be subversive. To disturb the peace.

Q: Why do you say that?

Baldwin: "What it is" must be examined. Reality is very strange. It's not as simple as people think it is. People are not as simple as they would like to think they are. Societies are exceedingly complex and are changing all of the time, and so are we changing all of the time. Since to write implies an investigation of all these things, the only way that I can sum it up is to say that the role of the writer is to write.

Q: In essence then, the role of the writer is to point out how things got the way they are and how. . . .

Baldwin: . . . how they can continue and change.

Q: You're teaching at Bowling Green College now. Have you taught school before?

Baldwin: No. I'm doing a writer's seminar which is a catch-all term that means whatever you make of it.

For a very long time until Martin died, I was operating as a public speaker in the context of the civil rights movement. And when Martin died, something happened to me and something happened to many people. It took a while for me and for many people to pull ourselves back together. Then I had to find another way to discharge what I considered to be my responsibility. I've been working on college campuses and in prisons; which is why I don't bring my typewriter across the ocean.

Q: The responsibility on the other side of the ocean is to be a writer in the sense of a craftsperson who puts words on the page. The responsibility on this side is what?

Baldwin: On this side my responsibility is, well, it's very difficult to answer that because it involves being available, it involves being visible, it involves being vulnerable, it involves my concept of my responsibility to people coming after me and to people who came before me. . . .

Q: To, in a sense, tell their story, so that others can understand from whence they came.

Baldwin: Yes. I consider myself to be a witness.

Q: On one side of the ocean you can write about what you have witnessed, and on this side of the ocean you bear witness to that which you would write about.

Baldwin: That puts it about as well as it can be put.

Q: Looking at our current situation, in your opinion, what are some of the key themes that need to be expressed?

Baldwin: That is so vast.

Q: I understand that it is vast, but, for example, after fifty-four and going into the sixties, it was critical that people understand the necessity of the civil rights struggle. Do you think there is anything that has a similar cutting edge for us today?

Baldwin: I think that what you've called the civil rights movement, although it is an acceptable term, well, it might clarify matters if one thought of it as, in fact, a slave insurrection. When one thinks of it in that way, in the first place, one is prevented from descending into despair. On one level the civil rights movement was betrayed, but on a much more important level, we all learned something tremendous out of that effort and out of the betrayal something important about ourselves.

Q: What are some of the things we learned about ourselves?

Baldwin: That the people who call themselves "white," I must put it that way, well, as Malcolm X said, "white is a state of mind." The implications of that statement are enormous because it finally means that the people who call themselves white have really invented something which is not true. The key to this is European power which is a very complex thing and which involves the history of the church. White people invented Black people to protect themselves against something which frightened them.

Q: Which was?

Baldwin: I don't know. Life, I guess. All the legends about Black people are very revealing. They are all created by white people: "Aunt Jemima," "Uncle Tom," "Topsy," the Black stud, the nigger whore. Those descriptions, which are labeled legends, do not describe Black people at all.

Q: They describe the creator.

Baldwin: That's right. Whatever you describe to another person is also a revelation of who you are and who you think you are. You can not describe anything without betraying your point of view, your aspirations, your fears, your hopes. Everything.

Q: As you pointed out earlier, if white is a state of mind, then there are many of us who have a Black legacy but who also can be very much white.

Baldwin: Yes, you can not tell a Black man by the color of his skin.

Q: Let's talk about that betrayal of civil rights. In your opinion, who did the betraying and how was it done?

Baldwin: It was inevitable from the moment it started. From the moment it started, we came up against a tremendous political and economic machinery which was not going to dismantle itself. The attempt was made by some very well meaning people. I'm not putting down or condemning Black people, but finally, these estates could find no way to accommodate this discontent and no way to respond to it. All of the civil rights acts passed during that time, including the supreme court decision outlawing segregation in school, were all gestures attempting to ameliorate something which could not be ameliorated without a profound change in the state and that profound change in the state involves an absolutely unthinkable revision of the American identity.

Q: Drawing that out then, there are some of us who believe that the present state of the entertainment arts is in fact a true reflection of what those who think they are white would like to believe about those whose faces are Black?

Baldwin: Precisely. That is why there are only minstrel shows on Broadway now. And white people flock to them in droves to be reassured of their legends, to be reassured of their state, their identities. That's the brutal truth and the bottom line.

Q: So, how do you assess the seventies? The civil rights period and the sixties brought our struggle to a point of sharpness, so much so, that it was unthinkable to believe that we didn't have to struggle.

Baldwin: But of course. Out of that something was clarified for us and even more importantly, for our children.

Q: Which was what?

Baldwin: That one was no longer at the mercy of white imagination. I was born fifty-five years ago. In a sense I was born in the nightmare of the white man's mind. All of my growing up and all my early youth was first that discovery and then the bloody struggle to get out of that mind, to destroy that frame of reference for myself and for those coming after me. I'm the oldest of nine children; this is very important. I know that my great-nieces and great-nephews are living in a different world than the world in which I was born. They can not imagine the world which produced me, but I've seen the world for which they are going to be responsible.

Q: So although they can't imagine the world that produced you, you understand the world which produced them and understand still the state which remains to be dealt with?

Baldwin: Precisely. And I trust them to do it. We have so far. There's no reason to despair now.

Q: When you say we have so far, how does that correlate with your assessment that the civil rights struggle was betrayed?

Baldwin: The civil rights struggle was betrayed and the people who betrayed it were responsible for that betrayal. We are not.

Q: If I understand you correctly, you are suggesting that although there was a betrayal of the civil rights struggle, there was also a profound impact whose shock waves are still being felt. In fact, although the state may have not toppled at the first blow, it is still tottering and the winds are still blowing.

Baldwin: Oh yes. In fact, the winds are getting stronger because it is not only this particular state, it is the whole western world.

Q: You are obviously very hopeful about the eighties.

Baldwin: Yes, but that doesn't mean it's going to be easy. But I'm far from being in despair. We cannot afford despair. We have too many children. Despair is a luxury only white men can afford.

Q: You mentioned the church. In your new novel you suggest that the church has proven not to have been the redemptive force. . . .

Baldwin: This is something very complex. It depends. When I said the church, I was thinking about the overall, two thousand year history of the Christian church, one of the results of which was the enslavement of Black people. On the other hand, what happened here in America to Black people who were given the church and nothing else, who were given the bible and the cross under the shadow of the loaded gun, and who did something with it absolutely unprecedented which astounds Black people to this day. Finally, everything in Black history comes out of the church.

Q: Given that the church, in the classical sense of church, was both an offer we could not refuse and also has not fulfilled its role as a redemptive force for our people, but at the same time, at the juncture where our people took the church, it did serve as a bridge cross troubled water. . . .

Baldwin: Yes it did. The essential religion of Black people comes out of something which is not Europe. When Black people talk about true religion, they're "speaking in tongues" practically. It would not be understood in Rome.

Q: If you believe that the church is the foundation for our people. . . .

Baldwin: It was how we forged our identity.

Q: What do you see for the generations who are here and who are to come, who have no sense of church?

Baldwin: This is an enormous question. In the first place, I'm not absolutely certain that they have no sense of church, although I hear you very well. I know what you mean when you say that. I don't know if one can divest one's self of one's inheritance so easily. I would go so far as to say it's not possible. Things are changing all of the time. The form changes but the substance remains.

Q: What do you think about the current group of students?

Baldwin: People are very critical and very despairing of the young. But I can only say that in my own experience, and admittedly it's limited, and even admitting I'm in somewhat of a special situation. I must say that my experience in all these years on campus has given me a great deal of hope. Kids ask real questions. I begin to suspect that, in fact, the elders who are so despairing of the young are actually despairing of themselves. Kids ask real questions, very hard questions. Those questions imply a judgement of the man of whom you're asking the question. All you can do is be as open as possible and as truthful as possible and don't ever try to lie to the kids.

Q: You know in the early sixties, if someone had come along and judged the then current crop of students in the Black colleges, they might have felt the same way some people feel about students today.

Baldwin: Of course, and I must repeat myself, that's a luxury one can't afford. I've dealt with junkies, lost girls, exprisoners, people ruined by bitterness before they were eighteen years old, ok. But that's not all there is to that.

Q: What would you note about the prison experiences?

Baldwin: The candor of the prisoners, their knowledge, and I'm not being romantic about prisoners. People get lost. But, I've encountered very few prisoners, and of course this is not a Gallup poll, but I've encountered very few people who did not really understand their situation.

Q: The college situation sets up the type of environment that leads to questioning and the prison situation sets up the type of environment that leads automatically to reflection, whether or not you want that.

Baldwin: Yeah, you could put it that way. The college situation is exceedingly difficult. The Black kid in college, no matter how we cut it, risks paranoia, risks schizophrenia because there is no way for this society to prepare them for the same future that the white boy is prepared for.

The real meaning of the word progress in the American vocabulary, for the most, and there are exceptions to this rule, but for the most part when they say progress they're talking about how quickly a Black kid can become white. That's what they mean by progress. Well I don't want my nephew to grow up to be like Ronald Reagan, or Richard Nixon, or Jimmy Carter.

Q: Let's discuss the relationship, the understanding, the reality of sex and sexual relations in our people's lives. On one level our relationships have been vulgarized. . . .

Baldwin: In the lives of Black people—everyone overlooks this and it's a very simple fact—love has been so terribly menaced. It's dangerous to be in love. I suppose, anytime, anywhere. But it's absolutely dangerous to be in love if you're a slave because nothing belongs to you, not your woman, not your child, not your man. The fact that we have held on to each other in the teeth of such a monstrous obscenity, if we could do that, well I'm not worried about the future.

Q: So you would think that the so-called sexual revolution that's going on. . . .

Baldwin: What do you mean "sexual revolution"?

Q: What I'm basically asking is for a commentary on the current situation.

Baldwin: All I can tell you is that, as regards for example gay liberation, I'm very glad that it seems to be easier for a boy to admit that he's in love with a boy, or for a girl to admit that she's in love with a girl, instead of, as happened in my generation, you had kids going on the needle because they were afraid that they might want to go to bed with someone of the same sex. That's part of the sexual paranoia of the United States and really of the western world.

Q: Homophobia.

Baldwin: A kind of homophobia, but it's . . .

Q: Actually it's life-phobia.

Baldwin: Yeah, that's what it is.

Q: Afraid of someone who is living.

Baldwin: Everybody's journey is individual. You don't know with whom you're going to fall in love. No one has a right to make your choice for you, or to penalize you for being in love. In a sense, I think they've put themselves in prison.

Q: That's what you meant in your story about the sheriff who could not love his wife ("Going To Meet The Man")?

Baldwin: That's right. He was going to meet the man!

Q: Yeah, he was going to meet the man, and everytime they meet men or women they try to kill them.

Baldwin: Exactly.

Q: There is a technological revolution happening. Do you think there is a future for writing within this revolution?

Baldwin: The technological revolution, or rather the technological situation, I am not as worried about it as some other people are. First of all, it depends entirely on the continued validity and power of the western world. I don't think it is in our power to eliminate human beings. And although it may seem at this moment that the television has rendered everyone illiterate and blind, the world can not afford it. When you talk about writing today, you're talking about the European concept of writing, you're talking about the European concept of art. That concept, I assure you, has had its day. There will be different things written in the future, coming out of a different past, and creating another reality. We are the future.

Q: Thank you very much James Baldwin the witness and James Baldwin the writer. We encourage both of you to continue.

Baldwin: Thank you very much and keep the faith.

James Baldwin Finds New South Is a Myth

Leonard Ray Teel/1980

From *The Atlanta Journal*, 22 April 1980, pp. B1-2. Reprinted by permission.

Now, when James Baldwin has just declared that, no, there is no New South, a young pro-Atlanta dashiki-clad brother can't persuade the author to change his mind.

The gentlemen's dispute Monday night at Emory University ended calmly when two women, Atlanta friends of the author, each grabbed an arm and escorted him away from a reception and toward a much-delayed late-night dinner.

Baldwin, one of America's foremost writers, is defiantly ready for a verbal fight. In the course of a long day in Atlanta he not only refused to accept the existence of a New South, but declared that "Gone With the Wind" was obscene.

Earlier Monday, across town, he declared to a packed auditorium of mostly black faces in Clark College's Davage Auditorium: "We are inhabitants, if not citizens, of a most illiterate country—a country which in my lifetime does not read . . . and has no respect for literature and not very much respect for life."

And to the same audience: "I don't want to mount an attack on Western literature—at least not this morning, in your presence."

He smiled his huge smile, and the people laughed.

After all, the purpose of Baldwin's visit was to help kick off the 11th annual writers workshop, which continues Tuesday (with a second talk by Baldwin) and Wednesday with an address from poet-playwright Imamu Amiri Baraka (Leroi Jones).

Baldwin, who since fleeing Harlem in 1948, has published 14 novels and non-fiction books, explained his philosophy of writing:

• "The only reason art is important is because life is more important. And what the artist is trying to do is bear witness to the endless possibilities of the human spirit, and therefore is always working in an utterly hostile climate.

• "I am saying that literature comes out of life. And the nature of (the writer's) value is how close he responds to life. Responds—his *core* response.

• "The poet is created by the people. He is created by the people because the people need him. And the people may often dislike him, the poet they have created. They may even put him in jail. They may even stone him to death. But they created him because they needed him.

• "There is a division of labor in the world. Some people drive trucks or run banks or run cities or read contracts. I can't do any of those things. But I can try to give back to you what you give to me. It is an act of love. It's an act of faith.

• "Someone told me once, 'If you can describe it, whatever it is, describe it. If you can describe it, you can get past it. You are not at the mercy of something you don't understand; if you can describe it, you can outlive it.' And that is what life is all about. That's *all* life's about—really—to understand where you are and how to get from where you are to somewhere else."

At both campuses, Baldwin wanted to be questioned "so I can find out what's on your mind."

At Clark College, a young woman rose to ask him why he left his family in Harlem and moved to Paris. Was it because "society prevented you from flourishing?"

"The only honest answer," Baldwin told her, "is, first of all, I was 24. That's very young. And I knew—I'd been in enough fights, enough precinct basements, to have known at that time that on one particular Tuesday, or one black Monday, some cop or somebody would call me 'nigger' once too often and one of us would die.

"Becoming a black writer was a very long shot, but it was the only shot I had. So I went to Paris to get myself together and to take a deep breath, to finish the book, so my sister would know at least that I was serious. And I was lucky. Again, I had some sense of myself."

At Emory University, after an open-air jazz concert in his honor, Baldwin's audience in White Hall was predominantly white, together with black faculty members and students of the Black Student Alliance, co-sponsors of his visit.

He said he tried to keep an open mind about Atlanta and the New South before returning. He said he told himself, "Maybe it is true that there is the New South. I profoundly doubted it, but in order to be fair I suspended judgment. I'd already been to cities with black mayors. I know how the process works. The mayor has very little power over the state."

"Mr. Baldwin. *Is* there a New South?" one woman asked.

"No!" he boomed.

Baldwin also underscored racism to the black students at Clark College.

"The Western morality, the Western power, is in terrible trouble," he declared.

"That's right, we're in trouble," echoed a young man in the front row.

"And they're in trouble because," Baldwin continued, "nothing worse happens to a man or a woman, a person or a people, than to deny, to lie about, to make a fantasy out of, one of the central facts of their lives. That man, that woman, that person, that people atrophies.

"The romance they have made of our struggle with the Indians . . . called genocide—the romance they have made until today on television in endless movies—that romance is one of the greatest obscenities of our age. And the romance made in such films as 'Gone With the Wind'—and until today—of our slavery is obscene."

There were laughs and some applause when Baldwin said:

"And we are the only people in the world—the only people—who know anything about the white American, and the only people in the world who care about him. What white Americans, therefore, do not know about the world is the price they are paying for lying about us.

"I don't know—I have not been to Atlanta for an extended period. When I was here before, when I was working down, down in the civil rights movement, it was physically speaking—or cosmetically speaking—a very different scene.

"It *now* would appear to, let's say, a foreign observer or a casual observer from the North, to be a vastly more liberated city. But since this is not true in Detroit or in Boston or New York where I come from, or anywhere else in the nation, I think it's something else.

"You have to have an awful lot of money to be on Peachtree Street at all. In any case, the bulk of Atlanta is not to be found in Peachtree Plaza. And the state of Georgia is still the same Georgia."

"That's right. Racist," said the same man in the front row.
"I don't know. I'm no prophet. I don't know what the future holds.
I am no politician either, but I know that politics is a give-or-take
thing. But I know this—the world's not white. It never has been."

James Baldwin, an Interview
Wolfgang Binder/1980

From *Revista/Review Interamericana*, 10 (Fall 1980), 326-41. Reprinted with permission of the author and Inter American University of Puerto Rico.

The sometimes unorthodox punctuation, particularly comma usage, reflects Mr. Baldwin's speech rhythm and deliberate pauses. The interview as held at Cannes, October 23, 1980.

Wolfgang Binder: Your last novel *Just Above My Head* is being published in Europe. When did you start writing it, and how long did it take you to write it?

James Baldwin: It is very hard to answer a question about a novel which is over. I guess I started it somewhere around 1974, and it took between four and five years to write.

Binder: Why did you write it? What were you trying to say?

Baldwin: I grew up with music, you know, much more than with any other language. In a way the music I grew up with saved my life. Later in my life I met musicians, and it was a milieu I moved in much more than the literary milieu, because when I was young there wasn't any. So that I watched and learned from various musicians in the streets.

When I was under age I was listening to the very beginning of what was not yet known as bebop. And I was involved in the church, because I was a preacher and the son of a preacher. And all of that has something to do with *Just Above My Head*, with an affirmation which is in that life and is expressed by that music, which I have not found in that intensity anywhere else. The book has something to do with the journey of a people from one place to another, a kind of diaspora which was unrecognized as yet, and in that journey what has happened to them and what has happened to the world as a

190

result of their journey and is still happening to the world. They brought themselves a long way out of bondage by means of the music which *Just Above My Head* is at bottom about. So in a sense the novel is a kind of return to my own beginnings, which are not only mine, and a way of using that beginning to start again. In my own mind I come full circle from *Go Tell It On the Mountain* to *Just Above My Head*, which is a question of a quarter of a century, really. And something else now begins. I don't know where I go from here yet.

Binder: How do you see the whites in *Just Above My Head*?

Baldwin: There are virtually no whites in this novel.

Binder: What about their effect on black people?

Baldwin: It all takes place within the relationships of the brothers, the two families. And the rest is really a kind of cloud of witnesses to a particular assessment of possibilities, perhaps. And implicit in the story is the fact that they all love in one way or another to depend on each other as the gospel quartet does as it goes south. And then you have the meaning of the loss of Red who becomes a junkie, and the meaning of the loss of Peanut who is murdered. And white people are outside this world, they are never visible except in the vast terms of the sheriff and his men, the people on their motorcycles, the people who are absolutely inescapable, but in a sense faceless. The only white person in the American part of the book is a boy named Faulkner, who is one of Hall's not co-workers but afflictions in the advertisement agency. And there is Arthur's affair with Guy in France. Guy is French, and in the context that Arthur is operating, he is not yet white. He has not yet become an American, though there is implicit in the whole Algerian-French thing, in the whole scene of the nightclub, a kind of incipient culmination of all these concerns which are not conscious yet in Arthur's head, or Guy's head, or are in some other way beginning to become vivid in Julia's journey to Abidjan, which is not quite Africa, she says. Finally, Arthur dies, in the middle of his journey, and all the rest are left with his legacy, which is still an enormous question. The question is: What is history, what has it made of us, and where is a witness to this journey?

Binder: In *A Rap on Race*, your dialogue with Margaret Mead, you state that no people nor individual can really escape, if that person is honest, history and the effects of history.

Baldwin: Well, it is impossible.

Binder: In which sense does this apply to whites and blacks in America?

Baldwin: I have been living with those questions for a long time. You see, the trouble I am having right now is with the word itself. History means one thing in a European head. It actually means something else in an American head, and yet again something else in a black man's head. To leave it at that is enough for openness. I am not sure any longer what the word means. Especially as the white world now is calling on what it calls history to justify its dilemma without having the remotest sense of how they got to where they are. In spite of their adulation of history. So history in the context in which the French, or the English, or the Germans are operating is an enormous dead letter. Because if history means something, it means that you have learned something from it. If you haven't then the word has got to be changed. History in England, or France, or Germany, or indeed in Europe is now meant as an enormous cloak to cover past crimes and errors and present danger and despair. In short, it has become a useless concept. Except that it can be used as a stick to beat the people without history, like myself, over the head. That worked as long as I believed that you had history and I did not. And now that it is clear that that is not so, another kind of dilemma, another kind of confrontation, begins. Perhaps history has got to be born for the first time. It is certainly true that all the identities coming out of history with a capital H are proven to be false, to be bankrupt. We cannot live with them for another five minutes, they are going to carry us from here to the corner. And no one knows how we got here, from Maggie Thatcher in London to Ronald Reagan in America. If that is not the bottom of the barrel! And in terms of America, the Americans are even more abject than the Europeans who are stifling among their artefacts, their icons, which they call history. The Americans have never even heard of history, they still believe that legend created about the Far West, and cowboys and Indians, and cops and robbers, and black and white, and good and evil. There is a reason that the most simple-minded men, Mr. Carter and Mr. Reagan, who might be considered to run a post-office, are the only candidates America can find to run the world. If the Europeans are afflicted by history, Americans are afflicted by innocence.

Binder: Are they innocent?

Baldwin: The Americans would like to be. Go back to the beginning of the country, go back to the last of the Mohicans. It was poisoned from the beginning, and no one has been able to admit it.

Binder: Could you comment on how blacks interpret, see, feel their history? Do you feel that blacks as a group are becoming more and more aware of their history?

Baldwin: It is very important to recognize that whatever is happening among black Americans at the moment is not occurring within the western frame of reference. I could say, which is true, yes, black Americans are assessing their history, but then you have to consider that they are assessing something which does not exist officially in what is called history. Our presence is a proof of the failure of history with a capital H. We have never been recognized by history, and the present is doing its best to pretend we do not exist.

Binder: Even though you have a vast body of literature in print?

Baldwin: Oh, yes. Indeed, there would be no American speech if it had not been for black people. But the Americans pretend that none of this is so and imagine they can steal an inheritance, a word I prefer to use. That's the word I have been looking for. They prefer to steal an inheritance and not pay for it. But Aretha Franklin is Aretha Franklin. Barbra Streisand is not Aretha Franklin and nothing can make her Aretha Franklin. In order to become Aretha Franklin you really have to be able to assess an inheritance and find yourself able to use it. The proof that you are able to use it is, when you use it, to move it along, to hand it down the line. And there is nothing in the western world that can be handed down the line to its children, except perhaps IBM machines or the atomic bomb. But there is nothing to assess an inheritance, unless one wants to liberate oneself from the western language, from the western frame of reference. There is something much more various, much older and much more tenacious than that. And much more human. The pragmatism that rules America, that rules the western world, is an entirely false god. The rest of the world is going to smash the western world on the rock of its pragmatism. I was never what you said I was, I the black. Which means that you were never what you thought you were. And I can prove it, because I watched you when you did not see me.

Binder: Were or are you in favor of what has been called black cultural separatism?

Baldwin: It is not possible in any case, whether I am for it or against it. Black culture is an amalgam of many things. The truth about history—here is a way the word can be used—is that history is common, belonging to all of us. We are talking here about history, they are talking about power, which is not the same thing. And this power is all held together from the Vatican to the chain gang by the same principle.

Binder: You were very active in the Civil Rights Movement. How do you see that period now?

Baldwin: Malcolm X asked a very important question years ago, which I did not quite hear at that moment. We were doing a radio program with young students in 1961 when there were the two poles in America, Black Muslims on one hand, and the very beginning of the student sit-ins on the other. And I was there as moderator, because it was Malcolm and the students who were talking. And Malcolm was very good with a kid when he said: "If you are a citizen, why do you fight for your civil rights? If you are a citizen, you have civil rights. If you don't have them, you are not a citizen." Very harshly put, but absolutely correct. Therefore, the Civil Rights Movement is a misnomer in a sense. It clarifies matters at least for me to think of it as the last slave rebellion, for that is what it was. The last slave uprising, and the very last time that the American black people, who are no longer alone as they were even twenty years ago, will petition the American government.

Binder: Are you optimistic about the black situation in America?

Baldwin: The black situation in America has escaped the American context. Washington cannot operate as it did when I was born without any reference to the rest of the black people in America, because there are black people all over the world whom they have in one way or another made an attempt to see. They certainly cannot ignore Ethiopia as they did when I was twelve. And as Malcolm X once put it: "The chicken has come home to roost." The energy crisis is a matter of bankruptcy of the western world. The bankruptcy of the western world is simply the end of the possibilities of plunder. So great corporations are leaving what we now call "off-shore operations" to build cheaper cars in other parts of the world, because labor is cheaper there, will be cheaper there for the next ten minutes. But that's now the bottom of the barrel, too. There is nothing which will prop up this system, nothing, nothing. It depended on slave labor and it lost its slaves. And by the year 2000, which is only twenty years from now, the power of the western world will be over. It will be chaos, and what we will have to go through will not be pleasant, but it is the price we are going to pay to get something else. And for people who have been through what some of the people I know have been through, nothing in the future will terrify. The future will be strain, death, terror. In any case, this system is doomed. The human race cannot afford it.

Binder: How do you see the state of the black ghetto in the inner cities in America?

Baldwin: It is a ghetto and white people turn them into ghettos to get away from the niggers. It's a vicious circle: they move out, the entire economic basis of the city crumbles, because nothing is taken care of in Harlem. The City has no responsibility for the ghetto, the cops don't live in the ghetto, tax-payers don't live in the ghetto, so nothing comes in. What little was coming in is lost. Nothing is owned by black people in Harlem, or a fraction of what is owned in Harlem is owned by black people. It is owned by banks, by real estate, by vast organizations including the Catholic Church, including universities. So houses are boarded up, and presently what will happen, what is happening in other cities is that bulldozers move in, move the niggers out, somewhere else, and the land is claimed by white people. Atlanta is a special case. What they have there is simply a tremendous kind of showpiece within Atlanta, but the street half a mile away is exactly what it was before, if not worse.

Binder: Do you think, like some of my friends in New York, that hard drugs are channeled into the ghettos by the FBI and other agencies?

Baldwin: I would tend to agree with that, but of course I can't prove it. For me there is no question about it. I can't prove it, so time will prove it. It is between the Mafia and the government. It is an open secret; anything will do to keep the niggers asleep.

Binder: Do you feel that there are poor whites who are just as oppressed as poor blacks?

Baldwin: I would love that! I wish *they* did! Yes, on the day they will realize this, things will begin to change.

Binder: What are your feelings on the role of the black woman in the black family? Do you share the opinion that the black woman is overly strong?

Baldwin: That's all very curious. Women have a certain type of strength, men have another. As Otis Reading once said: "Try a little tenderness." He understands much better than most sociologists do. The whole myth, the whole confusion is, I think, mainly on the part of white people. There is a certain kind of vehemence between black women and black men; I would not want to go so far as to say distrust, that is not true. You see, a black man is both a man and a black man in a white society, and his options for a time—for I think really something else is happening now—seemed to drive him away from the black woman into the arms of white women. I think that may have run its course, that particular snare. But I think it is a mistake to put it quite in these terms. The black woman has been accused of something I don't think she is guilty of, a certain kind of domination, a certain kind of dominance. She did have to hold the family together, she had to deal with her father, her mother, her husband, her son, somehow. And as Richard Wright worked out in "A Man of All Works", she could be hired when a man could not. Her terrible dilemma was to treat a man as a man and protect him from being lynched, which is quite an assignment. And I resent in a way the whole myth against black women, the myth being made about them. They are much more various than that.

As for the black cat, in the twenty or thirty years that interracial sex is being practised, we are talking mainly about the north, obviously, and only about a certain milieu. We are talking really about two milieus. I could be talking about the pimp and his whore and I could be talking about the academy, about those two levels, and very rarely about the middle. And on both levels, on the bottom and the top, so to speak, people are terribly compromised by a whole series, a whole system of assumptions, a whole system of other utilities they treat each other with, and a certain kind of vengeance, a certain kind of paranoia even. But the root of my argument is that the black man and the black woman have somehow managed until today not to lose each other in spite of all the things which might have destroyed both in many ways. And as against that, the black cat could never become white. Sooner or later he had to deal with that or be destroyed. The black woman admittedly suffered enormously in all this, and her bitterness is understandable. But at bottom I don't think that black women finally blame black men as much as it is alleged that they do. If they did, they would have to commit suicide. I don't think that I

would be here or that any black man would be here if the women
had not understood something about the men. That is finally what
you go back to.

Then it gets to be tricky, because that seems to be putting down
white women. They are very complex, too. The Women's Liberation,
let us put it on that lebel, does not include many black women,
because black women's problems are much more complex and much
more down to earth. The Women's Liberation Movement is a little
like the Gay Movement in that it is essentially a white middle-class
phenomenon, which doesn't have any real organic connection with
the black situation on any level whatever. I have nothing against
Women's Liberation or Gay Liberation at all, but they are essentially
à côté, they are not really one of my prime concerns. I have not really
got to join a club in order to go to bed with a man or fall in love. My
life is my life, and I have only one of them. It is hard enough just to
deal with this. The dangers my sisters face, my mother faced, have
nothing to do with what Women's Liberation think it is about, nothing
at all. And those white women are not to embrace my mother and
my sister, unless my mother and my sister happen to work in the
same office and are as bored as most white middle-class women are.
So it is not one of my concerns. I wish them luck. Then they should
do something about Ronald Reagan if they want to be liberated. He
is their creation, not mine, and their problem, not mine.

Binder: Would you agree to the idea that the black woman writer
has more difficulties in expressing herself and in getting published?

Baldwin: Yes, first of all to express herself, and then being published. I think that would have to be so. It is less true for white
women.

Binder: They, too, say it.

Baldwin: Yes, I am willing to accept that. A black woman would
have tremendous difficulties, like a black man, to go to the nitty gritty,
to express what is really going on inside. Because what happens is
that you are being treacherous. By telling the truth about myself I am
telling the truth about my father, my mother and a whole lot of other
people, too. You can get crucified for that.

Binder: Which is in more than one way sick.

Baldwin: Well, it's one of the things that happen when you live in
a sick society. And some black women like Gwendolyn Brooks, Toni

Morrison and Paule Marshall have gotten beyond that at whatever price, but they got beyond it. Their testimony is there, and part of the importance of a testimony is that it is for others. That carries a testimony further. So the whole black macho thing is essentially a false argument. I think that if you leave black men and women alone, they can manage very well. They have so far, and under awful circumstances. I think it's a red herring. Society's problems, black problems, white problems, are much, much deeper than that.

Binder: When you grew up in Harlem, what were some of the forces, some decisive moments that shaped you, that are still very much with you?

Baldwin: The music and the church, my family, certainly. My family was crucial, because it was a matter of being forced to make what I would call now moral choices, but I wouldn't call them that then.

By the time you are seven, you know why you are in the ghetto. You can't explain it, but you know what it means to be a nigger. What ever it means, that is what you are. That is it! And this is very bewildering and very painful, something I can't quite explain. It makes you look at everybody in a way you would not have before. And the first reaction is not hatred, it is wonder, pain. But I suppose, instinctively you begin to figure out how you are going to handle what everybody is. And you begin to look at people, you know. You study them, because they are mysteries for you now. Every white person is a mystery.

Binder: That is what Maya Angelou wrote about in *I Know Why the Caged Bird Sings*. Whites were strange, unreal things to her.

Baldwin: Strange beings, and you watch them, too, because you have to watch them. As a result of this you are beginning to understand them. By the time you are fourteen, if you get to be fourteen, for better and for worse they can't surprise you. They can't surprise you except by not doing what you would expect them to do. And that can be devastating. That's another part that you have to learn.

Binder: Can you give a concrete example when the pattern of expectations was broken?

Baldwin: Well, what comes to my mind seems a rather awful story. My brother and I used to sell shopping bags down on Fourteenth Street. I guess I was about thirteen. Anyway, it was against the law. We bought them for a cent and sold them for two or three. We were the only black kids on the block, and the trick was to get the door. There was a tremendous battle between all the kids on the block. A cop would come around and chase us off. He was a big cop, a big, beefy man. And I noticed that he never chased the white kids, he always chased me and my brother. At one point I turned round and said: "Why you never chase the white kids, why do you chase us?" And he said: "You stand out better against the daylight." He said that! I started to laugh, and he laughed. And I can't explain it, it was a curious moment. He was about eighteen feet tall, and I was smaller than I am now. And I couldn't stop laughing, and he couldn't stop laughing, and that was the last time he chased us. I'll never forget that. Take that for whatever it means, it was my first memory of bewilderment. But that is a very strenuous way to live. Nevertheless, something very healthy happened that moment: he moved himself out of that monolith of white people. The proof being his conduct subsequently, because he did not have to go that far.

   The other example is that of a teacher of mine, a white school-teacher. But she was in the context of school and not in the context of the streets. I write about her in *The Devil Finds Work*. She was something else altogether. My life was really in the streets. We had to sell shopping bags, because we had to bring home money. George and I knew we had to sell our shopping bags.

   Binder: Was your mother the saint in the house?

   Baldwin: I would not describe my mother as a saint. That is a terrible thing to do. I think she is a beautiful woman. You have to be my age, I guess, to know your mother really well. When I think about her I wonder how in the world she did it, how she managed that block, those streets, that subway, nine children. No saint would have gotten through it! But she is a beautiful, a fantastic woman. She saved all our lives. She is somebody.

   Binder: Do you consider yourself a political writer? And do you feel that a certain amount of combativeness can conflict with writing literature? Is there a tension between message and literary expression?

   Baldwin: Yes, there is a tremendous tension between two aspects of reality, really. It has nothing to do with whether I think of myself as a political writer or not. The state thinks of me as a political writer, if only because it is in itself a political act to write, and a black writer is always a political target. So it takes that as given. The real problem is finding a way to combativeness, which comes very early, even before you are a writer. It is a matter of learning every day, a terrible kind of discipline. So that you don't let your rage or your anguish tear you, tear your sentences to pieces. There are days you would rather blow up a police station than sit at a typewriter. And then you have to do something difficult, you have to accept that for you to blow up the police station, which you are not going to do at any rate, would not be the real application of your responsibility. So that you have to think yourself beyond the details of the day of disaster, which exists daily, then react again to your own reaction and try to find a way to engrave it in stone, to make certain that it will not be forgotten.

The other day the police shot a Moroccan kid in Marseilles, a seventeen year old kid. The cop doesn't know why, he hasn't done anything. It is happening in France, it is happening in America, it is exactly what is happening in London, what is happening in Germany. The doctrine of white supremacy comes from Europe, now it is coming back. And so one would like to go that day to Marseilles, for example. My plane was just leaving Miami, Florida, when the court acquitted the murderers of the black cat Macduffy, and Miami blew up. You see, every day it's like that, and you have to do your work somehow, as long as you can do it. So at the bottom it's a question of clarity and discipline, and it is very important to realize that whatever is happening to you, the effect of this danger, terror, anguish, it is very important to recognize it, connect it to the human condition of the people and not divorce it from it. It is very important to recognize that your anguish is not spectacular, not unprecedented, by no means new. And everyone has in one way or another to deal with it.

Binder: Would you agree to the fact that this transcends race?

Baldwin: Race has absolutely nothing to do with it. Race is a concept, which has no validity whatever. It is cowardly—all racists are cowards. It is a word which arose with the rise of the western nations, with the justification of slaughter. "Manifest Destiny" in the United States is simply a way of saying, we have the right to slaughter everything in our path, because it is obvious that we will control this part of the world, so that I became a thing, my father became a thing, and the Indian became a corpse.

Binder: Would you go crazy if you could not write?

Baldwin: Yes, certainly. That has always been true. My mother realized that long before.

Binder: And she supported you in that as a youngster?

Baldwin: Yes, with fear and trembling. She never opposed it. My father did.

Binder: Why?

Baldwin: He thought quite rightly that this would get me into terrible trouble. It's true. The only fight which my father and I really ever had and which I inaugurated was about my writing.

Binder: Did he feel that this was unworldly?

Baldwin: I learned a lot from him during that particular passage. That was a pretext, that it was worldly. What he really meant, or what the word worldly really meant, was that it was dangerous, and that I would get myself killed.

Binder: Why would he say that?

Baldwin: Well, because that's what he would have seen. My father was the son of a slave, and I am the grandson of a slave. In the northern ghetto he never reconciled himself to it. It was impossible for him to do this. There wasn't even the question if he should have, he could not. He was much too old for it. We as children had never been to the South, and children are children. Seeing me move in the direction I was moving, was moving into the shadow of death. He was a very difficult man, but I can understand him now better than I did when we were not getting along. But that was what he felt. It scared me, because I had absolutely nothing to contest it, except again my schoolteacher, who was only one frail white woman. But in any case, I knew by the time he died that that was what I would have to do, there was nothing else I would do.

Binder: When did you leave America, and could you give some of the reasons why you did?

Baldwin: Nothing very spectacular. I simply came to the end of a certain rope. I realized that I could not work as a waiter any more, all my nerves came out of the edge of my skin. I could not be called a nigger. Since I was small and all that shit, it was fun to beat me up— well, they couldn't always beat me up either. I'm not a small boy in the street, as a street boy will tell you. Since he knows that he is going to be killed, he is going to try to kill you. So my life turned out to be a nightmare by the time I left the country. And I left the country because I knew two things. I knew that if I went on like that I would go under, if I stayed I would certainly kill somebody. And that would have been the end of me and the end of my family, my five sisters, my three brothers, my mother. I was twenty-four when I left, and they were all kids.

Binder: What were your impressions of Paris?

Baldwin: I came to Paris in 1948, and it came right out of World War II. Paris was on bicycle, it was a very poor city, a frightening city, very cold.

Binder: Were you much alone?

Baldwin: I was entirely alone. All I had was forty dollars. Well, it is not true that I didn't know anybody, I knew Richard Wright. But I did not know anyone very well. Richard was much older in any case. It turned out that everybody had in one way or another problems of identity. I didn't have any money, so I went my way; I didn't want to be pitied. I don't know how in the world I survived that first year.

Binder: Did you get America out of your system?

Baldwin: Oh, I never will. I don't even know if I wanted to get America out of my system. I finished my first novel, *Go Tell It On the Mountain*, there and it was a turning point in my life, because it proved to me, not so much to the world but to me and my baby sister that at least I was serious. A black writer in the world that I had grown up in was not so much wicked, he was insane. So when *Mountain* finally came out in 1953, at least I had proved something to people. And then the real battle began. But nothing that happened to me afterwards was quite as terrifying as the very beginning. I knew that if I could not finish *Mountain* I would never be able to finish anything after that. But that was my ticket to something else. I finally had gotten it. At least I was a writer.

Binder: A great amount of commentary has been written on your relationship with Richard Wright. How do you see him today?

Baldwin: I don't know if my opinion has changed an awful lot, really. As concerns Richard himself, I met Richard in 1944 in Brooklyn. I met him, because I wanted to meet him. I was working on what was going to be *Mountain*, and he helped me the next year to get some exposure from *Harper's*. He was sixteen years older than me. I liked him very much; unconsciously I think I turned him into my father, not the father I knew, though this is hindsight. I realized in Paris how much I loved him, perhaps because it was in the context of Paris. I was not impressed by the existentialist movement. I was not impressed by Sartre, by Beauvoir at that moment of my life. Anyway, I hadn't come to Paris for that. And I thought that Richard was much better than those people, much more interesting, much more alive. And that was part of what the world calls battle. I have never thought of it exactly as that, because there wasn't for me any kind of venom in it. There was no real rage, I was kind of exasperated. I used to tease him about liking white folks and all that jazz. I just didn't like the French intellectuals. I didn't like their patronizing him, that's what it comes to. I repeat, I think he was better than them, I thought he was somebody. Anyway, it is all in "Everybody's Protest Novel". It never occurred to me—maybe I was just being very cunning to myself—but it never occurred to myself that it could be read as an attack on Richard. I thought I was being a bright honoris student. I thought we could have a discussion about that. His reaction made me re-examine everything. I knew that whatever I had done I had not meant to do that.

Binder: What was his reproach to you?

Baldwin: That I had betrayed him.

Binder: Were you shocked by the figure of Bigger in *Native Son*? There were black critics who felt that he was a disgrace to the black community.

Baldwin: No, no, this is bullshit. I didn't think that at all. I knew a lot of Biggers. My objection to the novel had nothing to do with that. I felt really that what is wrong with the novel is the end, the whole Communist thing, Max's long speech in front of the jury. That is what I was really talking about in "Everybody's Protest Novel". Well, I didn't really talk about it, but I wish I had now. That was what bothered me most about the novel, that Bigger was going to be saved by serious abstractions, by turning him into some kind of Manichean symbol. The truth is that he is a black boy in Chicago, and there are no other niggers in the book. There aren't any black people in the book, really. We only have Richard Wright's word for Bessie, and the others don't exist at all. That was my objection to the book. And, you see, I am just a little bit too young to have gone through the thing with the Communist Party. But at one point that was the only way in

America for a black writer to get published. I am maybe two or three years too young to have to go through what everybody else had to go through. I suspect, and that is part of my battle with Richard, that part of it was due to the Algerian crisis, and part of it were Richard's attempts to deal with it. In a way, he was hamstrung by his position in France. And it was not that he was unwilling, I could see that when it began to happen to me, that he couldn't quite see the position he held, nobody can. I have to write about it one of these days. He was trying not so much to catch as to reassess something. Those years that I saw him off and on were years of refusal, they were also the years of the war of independence of Indochina for the French, the Algerian revolution, the Nigerian revolution, the years of civil rights in America. It was very strong, it was a very swift time. Everything was happening all at once. Richard went to Spain, Richard shot *Native Son* in Argentina, he went to Africa, trying to get it all together. I went to Little Rock, for the same reason. So one cannot deal with it without dealing with that whole upheaval that was happening in the world all together and all at once. And nobody was ready for it, no matter what one thought one knew.

Subsequently, after Richard died, two books came out posthumously. I always say it to myself, that the end of *Native Son* had something to do with the whole climate of the time and the Communist Party in it. The great book which Richard has published posthumously is *Lawd Today*, which is, I think, just a fantastic book, not afflicted with any of the Stalinist garbage at all of *Native Son*. It is full of niggers! It is full of life! A beautiful book. And then there is *American Hunger*, which was written at the same time as *Black Boy*, which is a "mother". So the whole career of Richard appears to be much more complex than what one imagined then. But in some of my instincts of teasing him I was not entirely wrong, you know.

Binder: Is there any book of yours that you like particularly? Any child of pleasure and pain?

Baldwin: They all are. *Mountain* would have been that at one point, obviously, but not any more. *Mountain* took ten years to write, I started it when I was seventeen. That was the beginning. Without that I couldn't have written anything else. *Giovanni's Room* was that at one point, too, because it was such a dangerous thing for me, and

I paid for that, too. There were all the obvious condemnations. That's cool.

Binder: For moral reasons?

Baldwin: Yes, for moral reasons. That was a put-down, you know, but I survived. And again, that was a very important turning point, too, that I survived. I had to get that out of the way in order to get to work. But I think that is finally true for everything you do.

Binder: When you start writing, do you start from an anecdote, or is it all collected and pent up in your mind? Do you have notes with situations or characters?

Baldwin: It is funny, but that's a very hard question to answer. One is bothered by something, you don't know what it is. It's a kind of irritation, and you are very reluctant to consider at first. Then you start scribbling something, you start playing with titles and names. Eventually, people, situations start to hit you. Sometimes it turns out to be nothing, very often it's a rehearsal for something that you are going to do much later. That's the weirdest thing of all. *Just Above My Head* has been with me for so long. I didn't do any rehearsals for it at all, except—this is hindsight—the central situation, the situation of the two brothers, is in an old short story, "Sonnny's Blues", and the metaphor is music, and to some extent but in a very different way in "Tell Me How Long the Train's Been Gone". But I really connect this in my head with "Sonny's Blues". The beginning is almost impossible to discuss, and when it's over you don't remember it. I remember some details of *Giovanni's Room.*

Binder: Is that book fairly close to autobiography?

Baldwin: No, it is more a study of what might have been or what I feel might have been. I mean, for example, some of the people I met. We all met in a bar, there was a blond French guy sitting at a table, he bought us drinks. And two or three days later I saw his face in the headlines of a Paris paper. He had been arrested and was later guillotined. That stuck in my mind, and the great question would be why would that stick in my mind. What curious connections one makes! And where every theory is suspect, where one's own memory is suspect. Had I never seen that man again, I would not have thought about him. It was just the fact that I had seen him two nights before, and he was on his way to the guillotine then. I saw him in the headlines, which reminded me that I was already working on him without knowing it. That is lurid! The rest is fable. It is not so much about homosexuality, it is what happens if you are so afraid that you finally cannot love anybody. That's what the book is about.

Binder: How do you relate to *Another Country*?

Baldwin: Well, I like *Another Country*. The reception of it was a scandal. That was something to get through.

Binder: Do reviews get to you?

Baldwin: Those did! I was bewildered, simply and completely bewildered. People either loved the book or hated it. There was nothing in between. The book itself is distant for me today, the situation is not. I was eighteen years younger, that was a revelation to me. O Lord, I would not like to go through that again!

Binder: It is one of your books that is still very much in demand.

Baldwin: I know, I am very glad about that, too. But in some quarters they didn't dig that at all. It was banned in all kind of weird places. I can't keep up with it, but I think it was banned in Cleveland. I know Chicago. It was taken out of the bookshelves, it never went to court, so it was never officially banned.

Binder: The same thing happened to Piri Thomas's *Down These Mean Streets*.

Baldwin: Yes, that's right. Of course, the effect that that had was simply to make the book sell even more. It was completely insane. I never knew what the fuck they were talking about.

Binder: What are you working on right now?

Baldwin: I am beginning a triple biography of Medgar W. Evers, Malcolm X and Martin Luther King. I worked with them.

Binder: Could you explain how you met Evers?

Baldwin: Medgar was the Field Secretary of the NAACP in Jackson, Mississippi. And in 1963 he was murdered. Ole Miss was under surveillance, it was protected by the FBI. I met Meredith at the end of the Christmas holidays, and so I met Medgar. Though I did not know him very long, we became very good friends. I took a field trip to the university, and so I saw him and Meredith. I was working on *Blues for Mr. Charlie*, and he was helpful with that. Then I was on the road and was going to come back to Mississippi to see him, and then he was murdered. I met Malcolm before that and Martin many years before that.

Binder: What do you think of the "Black Aesthetic" movement, do you find it well-defined, is it feasible?

Baldwin: I perhaps don't know enough about it. I can't speak with authority about, for example, Don Lee, whom I like very much. My hesitation is not about the concept of "Black Aesthetics". I don't want to be impertinent, and for one thing I am much older than the people who are involved in "Black Aesthetics". I think that it is very necessary. I don't want to use the term movement, because it has so many political connotations.

Binder: "Black Aesthetics" does have political implications, doesn't it?

Baldwin: Of course it does, but it gets beneath the word political. It really gets to the place where the political and the artistic responsibilities meet. And in that sense it is of enormous value. It is also not domestic, it is not confined to the continental limits of the United States. And it is not really confined to black people, you know. If one says that it involves all non-white people, then we are talking about the globe. It is an enormous affirmation of a sense of life, a sense of reality, which demolishes our western idea of reality. And in that sense it is part of the shape of future.

Binder: What are some of the writers you like to read or find promising?

Baldwin: They are not all young. One is Sterling Brown, and then there are Gwendolyn Brooks and Toni Morrison.

Binder: Do you like *Cane* by Jean Toomer?

Baldwin: Oh yes, oh yes. I am addicted to Gwendolyn Brooks in a way. Then I like Leroi Jones, Gayl Jones, Ed Bullins. Bullins is uneven, everyone is young, you know.

Binder: Are you the Richard Wright, the father figure, for younger writers?

Baldwin: I don't see myself in that role, no. I am lucky, I think, that we are connected, that we haven't lost each other. If they don't always like me, that's perfectly right and natural. But there is something organic, it has nothing to do with my talent or their talent. It has to do with a common apprehension, a contribution to our lives. I don't feel, as I might very well, that we are lost for each other. Maybe I have been very lucky, because I'm not thirty any more. I also have the feeling that I am much freer now than when I was thirty.

Now something, as I said before, can begin. I am lucky, because I could have died by now. You can die when you are fifty-two, and I can see why. It's enough to kill a team of horses.

Binder: Ralph Ellison was charged by many younger blacks to be too intellectual, too refined, too white, even. What is your reaction to that statement? He seemed to be a figure very much apart.

Baldwin: Well, there is nothing wrong with that. I can hardly talk about Ralph. I can talk about him as a writer. In his work he is incontestably a writer, and whatever his official aesthetic position may be, which I have deliberately not pursued, I would hazard that his aesthetic assessment, probably like my own, is of less relevance than the work itself. And in a short story like "The King of the Bingo Game" he is not too white. Or his *Invisible Man*, which is like all novels, a flawed novel, is a very, very, very, very important novel. And nothing what the kids can say, nothing that Ralph can say, can take away from that. For the rest, I have heard the various assessments that you report, and that is why I have deliberately avoided some of the essays, because I did not want to get into what in this context would be a kind of shouting match between us. I think Ralph's importance is incontestable. And the rest doesn't matter.

Binder: How do you feel about the new African literature?

Baldwin: Well, I have been reading it lately and am fascinated by it. It has been a liberation for me. I think it has been a great liberation for any black writer, and not just the black writer. It changes everything, you can breathe. It has nothing to do with the mooring post which we in the west have been tied to. It is a whole other dimension, it is a whole mythology, a whole new frame of imagery—which is freedom.

Binder: Even though they write in the respective language of the colonizer?

Baldwin: Yes, but they transform that. Mahalia Jackson sang in English, too, and it had nothing to do with England. You bring your experience to the language, and that changes the language. Americans should know that best and know it least. Americans wouldn't be able to talk to each other at all, if they had not any niggers there! It's true. They would have nothing but Doris Days. People in America have not been able to accept the fact that their reality is entangled and almost defined by the black reality. And instead of asserting that black reality they try to avoid it. Everything Americans do to pretend I did not happen brings them closer and closer to the abyss, and who is pushing them there, not me!

In Dialogue to Define Aesthetics: James Baldwin and Chinua Achebe

Dorothy Randall-Tsuruta/1981

From *The Black Scholar* 12 (March-April 1981): 72-79. Reprinted by permission.

We are not simply receivers, we are makers of aesthetics.
—Chinua Achebe, 1980

It was Wednesday, April 9, 1980. The opening session which would launch the annual meeting of the African Literature Association was about to begin. The theme for the year, "Defining an African Aesthetic," had roused people from various parts of the United States, Africa, the Caribbean, and Europe. Equally so the thought of witnessing the keynote speakers, Chinua Achebe and James Baldwin together in dialogue, had affected the rampage at airports around the globe. Many academicians, like myself, had left university teaching posts to attend—as our expense requisition forms intimated to our separate schools—a conference par excellence.

Dr. Mildred Lubin, conference co-convener, and professor of African Studies at the University of Florida at Gainesville, the hosting institution, made her way in leaping steps to the evening meeting. Stopping just outside the door to the auditorium, her contemplative glances swept once more behind her down the long corridor. Stepping inside the hall, she took note of the large gathering, then searching the room she peered anxiously into the eyes of her eager colleagues and equally earnest husband (Howard University Professor of Foreign Languages) before assuming center stage to set things in motion.

As conference co-convener it would be her unwanted role to bring down the high of the hour by announcing that the keynote speakers scheduled for evening appearances would be late arriving—that in fact, they would be rescheduled for the closing session (following the annual banquet), rather than the opening. She completed her kick-off address in fine form then introduced others responsible for organizing

210

the year's event. As the university president extended an official welcome to the campus, the room gradually, though not punctiliously, emptied of crestfallen enthusiasts who'd come out, presumably, only to hear Achebe and Baldwin.

But fate occasionally taxes the nerves temporarily and for good purpose: such was the case here. For we were all soon enough to experience a lively evening of conversation made all the more vital because two men who prior to the conference had known each other exclusively through the other's literary works, benefited additionally from time put to getting to know each other as friends.

Friday night, during his prelude to the dialogue with Baldwin on "Defining an African Aesthetic," Achebe alluded to the friendship which had a two part development: " . . . When I read *Go Tell It On The Mountain* in 1958, I knew here was a brother. And so I immediately proceeded to the American Information Service in the city where I lived to borrow some more books by Baldwin. Unfortunately, there were no other books by Baldwin, or anybody like him, in that library. And so I asked, "How come there are no books by Baldwin in this library?" I must say in fairness to the people concerned, they were moved and that situation was changed. Well that was 1958. A lot has happened in that time. And when I met him yesterday I nearly said, 'Mr. Baldwin, I presume.' "

Baldwin, in turn, also spoke of the historical coming together, adding instructively, " . . . I'll even say, of a somewhat unprecedented nature, my buddy whom I met yesterday, my brother whom I met yesterday—who I have not seen in 400 years, it was never intended that we should meet."

Then further into the evening, he returned to this theme saying, "When I read *Things Fall Apart* (Achebe's first novel) which is about an Ibo tribe in Nigeria, a tribe I never saw, a system—to put it that way—or a society, the rules of which were a mystery to me, I recognized everybody in it. And that book was about my father. How we got over I don't know, we did!"

The authors continued conversation through the evening with a warm regard for each other that invested the dialogue with a long-awaited international exchange between brothers.

Achebe arrived in Florida a matter of hours before Baldwin. But by Thursday noon, both men were registered in suites on the sixth floor of the student union building where off-campus visitors are lodged. Almost immediately upon checking in, they sequestered together in the company of longtime friends and steadfast scholars (Rico, Chinelo Achebe Harris, and doctors' Earnest Champion and Sondra O'Neale) in private dialogue and get-acquainted parties. I was fortunate to be present at these fortuitous first meetings which would add dimension to the authors' rescheduled public appearance together.

While much that went on behind the scenes was jocular in nature, the intervening time together allowed them serious pause for searching out each other's personality in a relaxed ambience. From my vantage point I could swear that those energy charged get-togethers promoted a warming of friendship that soared with the speed of microwave. By the time the two men reached for the microphones on Friday evening, they knew much of how the other responded on cue, under duress, on target, and according to personal dictate. Those loyal enthusiasts who had sulked noticeably from the auditorium on opening night, were treated closing night to a bonus that only fate could have arranged.

As the first speaker of the evening, Achebe announced that he considered dialogue a conversation. He outlined the format for the evening saying, "When I hear of 'dialogue' my mind goes to conversation not to two speeches." With that said, he explained that he and Baldwin would make opening statements and then they would involve the audience, taking questions, and "go from there." As soon as both speakers' opening statements were heard, it became clear that while their minds raced along parallel roads, they traveled in vehicles designed by the experiences they'd had in the country of their birth. Achebe spoke directly to African experiences that defined aesthetics, while Baldwin spoke of experiences that defined aesthetics as a result of the black American experience. In essence however, they spoke with one voice about black people and the black aesthetic. After references to Baldwin and his works, already recorded here, Achebe plunged into "Defining an African Aesthetic."

Achebe: The topic of African aesthetic is one of which I am very diffident about, because I didn't know if I could define aesthetic initially. And I am not sure, in fact, that we are operating on the same wave length, as they say. But if by aesthetic we mean those qualities of excellence which culture discerns from its works of art, then I will accept it. We do have an aesthetic. We had it and we have it! Now having said that, it's easier to say that than to tell you what it is. But I will try and single out one or two aspects of this. And it comes out, I've been talking with Jimmy Baldwin, it comes out again and again in what we said, so it must be true.

Now we can look at our aesthetic from our traditional culture. We can look at it from what has happened today. And I'd like to say right away that in my understanding, aesthetic cannot be fixed, immutable. It has to change as the occasion demands because in our understanding, art is made by man for man, and, therefore, according to the needs of man, his qualities of excellence. What he looks for in art will also change. So if somebody is thinking of aesthetics handed down like the logs to Moses, that is not the kind of thing we are talking about. We are talking about what our ancestors considered important in the stories they told, in their proverbs, in their legends, and their myths: why they repeated certain things over and over again. This is very important. This is what I understand. And I also understand that we are now in the twentieth century, and therefore we are not simply receivers of aesthetics . . . we are makers of aethetics. And we, especially the artists, are in a position to create, and society will endorse or not what they suggest. Therefore, aesthetics is not fixed, this is the first thing I want to say.

Now what are these aspects of it that I'd like to single out? The first I think I have already hinted at,—that art has a social purpose, that art belongs to people. It's not something that is hanging out there that has no connection with the needs of man. And art is unashamedly, unembarrassingly, if there is such a word, social. It is political; it is economic. The total life of man is reflected in his art. And so when people come to us and say, "Why are you . . . you artist so political?" I don't know what they are talking about. Because art is political. And further more I'd say this, that those who tell you "Do not put too much politics in your art," are not being honest. If you look very carefully you will see that they are the same people who are quite happy with the situation as it is.

And what they are saying is not don't introduce politics. What they are saying is don't upset the system. They are just as political as any of us. It's only that they are on the other side. Now in my enthusiasm, art cannot be on the side of the oppressor. When the Russian poet said that a poet cannot be a slave trader at the same time, he was absolutely right. A poet cannot be a slave trader. And he gave us a striking example of a French poet who became a slave trader. But he was honest enough to give up poetry. There are many slave traders who would like to be poets; they are entitled to be poets: but please, one job at a time. If you look at our aesthetics you will find this, that art is in the service of man. Art was not created to dominate and destroy man. Art is made by man for his own comfort.

The other thing I will single out is the holistic approach which people take to art. As someone said to me, "There are some dramatic elements in our own God." I said, "Oh yes, but Ibo people don't have the word drama in it." And someone else wrote [referring to *Things Fall Apart*], "this book is anthropological." Of course. It has to be. It is religious. Someone wrote to me and said, "this is religious anthropology." This is fine. It's that and more. So the definition of art is inclusive. It does not attempt to exclude. My ancestors, the Ibo people, had a very striking festival in which they celebrated the earth goddess. The striking thing about this festival (there are many striking things about it) is that nothing is left out. The whole of life of the community including the newly arrived white man, and the newly arrived district officer—with his bicycle—was incorporated in that art. You see if you leave anything hanging about loose in society it will harm you. What art tries to do is domesticate whatever is around and press it ito the service of man.

This brings me to the last point I will make because I hope I will come back. Our art is based on morality. Perhaps this sounds old fashioned to you,but it is not to us. The earth goddess among the Ibo people is the goddess of morality. An abomination is called an abomination against the arts. So you see in our aesthetic you cannot run away from morality. Morality is basic to the nature of art.

On this note Achebe concluded his opening statement, having projected his quiet melodious voice in enunciation characterized by grace and lucidity. With long-sighted contemplation, Baldwin took hold of the final point delineated in Achebe's discussion. He logged in with focus on "morality." He spoke decisively and with a toughness of manner not terribly underscored by a courteous intellect which coaxed the audience to bend forward in patient listening—that, all the better, to discern messages enclosed in his guttural asides.

Baldwin: I think when Chinua talks about aesthetic, beneath that word sleeps—think of it—the word morality. And beneath that word we are confronted with the way we treat each other. That is the key to any morality.

Now I want to suggest a difficult proposition to my innocent countrymen. I want you to think about this. This is 1980. The century has 20 years to go. I will still be here I assure you because I am stubborn,—until the year 2000. But I was here at the beginning of the century too—

At this point Baldwin was interrupted by what appeared to be technical problems with the recording equipment. By accident, a C.B. or short-wave radio operator's voice was picked up. Surprised, but in a merry mood, Badwin backed away from the microphone jesting, "Beg your pardon." When the static cleared seconds later he continued with his opening statement.

"We have seen, for example, in the 55 years I've been on earth tremendous cataclysms in the Western world, in the world: cataclysms that's seen changes. I'm back in Florida . . . after about, let's say, ten years. And we know, I hope we know (right?) that it's all been desegregated. It was being desegregated when I was here in 1957. Schools had been desegregated three years before that. I was in Boston a year ago, shortly after some patriots attempted to murder a black soldier, a veteran. They bayonetted him with the American flag.

Now I want to suggest an enormous proposition which I want you to think of very seriously. It is not an accident that we are here tonight. It is not an accident that my brother crossed so much water, and so many miles, and so many years to be here. It is not an accident that we both arrived here 400 years ago chained to each other because he spoke one tribal language and I spoke another. And had we been allowed to speak to each other, the institution of chattel slavery would have been doomed.

Do not forget it was not a thousand years ago that it was a crime to teach a slave to read or write. Do not forget either, in this country that calls itself a white country there are all the colors under heaven. To put it a little brutally—but as an old black lady said to me nearly thirty years ago in Alabama (and I'm quoting her), "White people don't hate black people. If they did we'd all be black."

Just as Baldwin completed the quote, another technical disturbance interrupted him. This time gruff white male voices came through Baldwin's microphone. Because static muzzled their words, only a growl registered their utterings as angry retorts. The audience, startled, but not yet alarmed, rose above the interference with a robust round of laughter. Baldwin examined the microphone in puzzled amusement, then undaunted, spoke on. "I don't quite know what that interference is but I guess the best thing to do is ignore. . . . " But he (as well as the laughter ringing in the room) was cut short again. This time a voice pushed through loud and clear with, "You gonna have to cut it out Mr. Baldwin. We can't stand for this kind of going on." The voice carried more angry words which were difficult to make out. A shocked audience drew a collective breath then fell to whispering and restless exclamations. A no longer patient Baldwin spoke forcefully into the mike: "Mr. Baldwin is nevertheless going to finish his statement. And I will tell you now, whoever you are, that if you assassinate me in the next two minues, I'm telling you this: it no longer matters what you think. The doctrine of white supremacy on which the Western world is based has had its hour—has had its day! It's over!"

The audience added to Baldwin's stand their own shouts of "right on" and more applause. As Baldwin sat down, the moderator, Ernest Champion (Professor of Ethnic Studies at Bowling Green in Ohio, formerly a native of Sri Lanka), rose to the speaker's place. He brought the audience to a standstill saying, "It is quite obvious that we are in the eye of the hurricane. But having this dialogue is quite important so all of us in this room will take it seriously." With that said he laid down the ground rules for submitting questions. He asked that no one make a personal statement, but instead get directly to the question.

While not all the questions and answers taken from the floor that evening will be recounted here, some are particularly worth *summarizing* in that they act as a lantern in triggering illumination on the topic for which all had come to listen or participate in dialogue. Champion, taking the permissible prerogative of his position as moderator, posed the first question which he directed to Achebe.

Question: In the context of what's happening in South Africa, in the context of what has happened in Rhodesia and Angola, can the African artist remove himself and take a neutral stand? That is, is there any question where lies his commitment? Is it to his art, his chosen art, or is it to his people?

Achebe: An artist is committed to art which is committed to people. So you can solve this problem quite nicely. May I repeat: the artist is committed to art which is committed to people. Therefore, in my view, there is no conflict.

The next question and the rest that were asked during the evening came from the audience. In most cases both authors articulated responses to the questions, but for purposes here the input *crucial* to a definition of aesthetics will be recorded.

Question: I'd like to ask Mr. Baldwin and Mr. Achebe if they liken this confrontation to the old battle royal where two blacks were pitted together and expected to tear each other apart?

Baldwin: The phrase 'battle royal' is a domestic American phrase, which may or may not apply in Nigeria: the principle certainly does. No. . . . "The poet is produced by the people because the people need him." He is not a clown and I am not a clown. We both know why we are here—you know why you are here too. I know the price an artist pays . . . I know the price a man pays. And I am here to try to say something which perhaps only a poet can attempt to say. I'm not here for Metro Goldwyn Mayer, I assure you. And this is not a battle royal. We are trying to make you see something. And maybe this moment we can only try to make you see it. But there ain't no money in it.

Achebe: Yes, we are not gladiators. But there is something we are committed to of fundamental importance, something everybody should be committed to. We are committed to the process of changing our position in the world. This is what our literature is about. There is a certain position assigned to me in the world, assigned to him [Baldwin] in the world, and we are saying we are not satisfied with that position. This is important to me—to everybody. I think you see it is important to me. You may not see that it is important to you but it is.

We want to create the new man. Mankind tries all kinds of ways, all kinds of solutions; some of them leading that far and no farther and it is wise that we try something else. We have followed your way and it seems there is a little problem at this point. And so we are offering a new aesthetic. There is nothing wrong with that. . . . Picasso did that. In 1904 he saw that Western art had run out of breath so he went to the Congo—the dispised Congo—and brought out a new art. Don't mind what he was saying before he died: that much is entirely his business. But he borrowed something which saved his art. And we are telling you what we think will save your art. We think we are right, but even if we are wrong it doesn't matter. It couldn't be worse than it is now.

Question: Mr. Baldwin what is your assessment of what's happening with black writers in America? And what kind of sentiment do you think they should be expressing given that this is the 1980's?

Baldwin: . . . We are in trouble. But there are two ways to be in trouble. One of them is to know you're in trouble. If you know you're in trouble you may be able to figure out the road.

This country is in trouble. Everybody is in trouble—not only the people who apparently know they are in trouble, not only the people who know they are not white. The white people in this country . . . *think* they are white: because "white is a state of mind." I'm quoting my friend Malcolm X. . . . white is a moral choice. Think back to Little Rock . . . Now for what black writers should do . . . I can write if you can live. And you can live if I can write. . . .

Question: (To Achebe) One of the Nigerian writers has said that there can be no great art without great prejudice and I'm just asking is it possible if this is true. And Michael O'Charro brings up as an example Joseph Conrad.

Achebe: Well there is an assumption there that Conrad's . . . *Heart of Darkness* is great art and I don't accept that. Great art flourishes on problems or anguish or prejudice. But the role of the writer must be very clear. The writer must not be on the side of oppression. In other words there must be no confusion. I write about prejudice; I write about wickedness; I write about murder; I write about rape: but I must not be caught on the side of murder or rape. It is as simple as that.

Baldwin, in responding to the same question, concentrated on the meaning of prejudice, elaborating on it as a state of mind as opposed to a color.

Baldwin: . . . You know what the black Muslim movement was all about. The only reason you talked to Martin is because you were afraid to talk to Malcolm. That's the *only* reason you talked to Martin. And then when both men (and this happened before your eyes), when both men arrived at the same point—that is to say when they connected,— then the great black disaster: the global disaster. At the point where Malcolm came back from Mecca and said, "White is a state of mind; white people are not devils. You are only as white as you want to be." And when Martin connected the plight of garbage men in Memphis with Korea and Viet Nam, then both men were killed.

The final three questions here recalled draw attention to African aesthetics and Marxist theory; aesthetics and Negritude; aesthetics and the African woman.

Question: You have both spoke in terms of the relation of the artist to his society, and morality underneath aesthetics. There is a strong literary tradition which also talks about the morality of art. And I'm speaking specifically about the Marxist tradition, not necessarily the Russian tradition. I'd like to know how you relate to that.

Achebe: Well . . . I was in East Africa two weeks ago and I was rather impressed by the level of radicalism which was manifest in that place. A number of very young people in Kenya have adopted the Marxist analysis of society. And I cannot quarrel with that. But I can't help feeling at the same time . . . that my own aesthetic definition, which I gave earlier on, would be a little uneasy about the narrowing of things to a point where we no longer accept the truth of the Ibo proverb that "Where something stands, something else will stand beside it," and that we become like the people we are talking about—the single-mindedness which leads to totalitarianism of all kinds, to fanaticism of all kinds. And I can't help the feeling that somehow at the base, art and fanaticism are not loggerheads.

And so I don't dismiss the Marxist interpretation. I think it is valid in its way. But when somebody says "I am the way, the truth, and the light. . . . " Now my own religion, the religion of my people says something else. It says, "You may worship one god to perfection and another god will kill you." Wherever something is, something else also is. And I think it is important that whatever the regimes are saying—that the artist keeps himself ready to enter the other plea. Perhaps it's not tidy—perhaps we are contradicting ourselves. But one of your poets has said, "Do I contradict myself? Very well."

For just about the entire time questions were being taken from the audience, Achebe resounded in good humor minus any signs of being piqued. However, the following question rubbed him wrong. His clear understanding of the tyrannical cleverness inherent in an aspect of the question revealed his answer—his chastisement, if I may—say a lantern throwing light on his beliefs.

Question: We were reminded two days ago that "a tiger cannot proclaim its tigertude." Do you believe that black writers who espouse the Negritude idology are promoting a harmful cause?

Achebe: Yes, we heard that. It is a very clever quip. . . . What you have not heard is the profound response which Senghor made. He said, "A tiger does not talk." Now I'm quoting myself because I used this information not so long ago: "The Negro talks and talking is part of his humanity. So don't compare me with a tiger. A tiger has not been oppressed in the forest; I have." So it is clever in a very superficial way. Which is not to say that you cannot quarrel with the founders of Negritude and what they are doing today. That's another story. But don't say that because somebody is mismanaging certain affairs today that the poetry he wrote twenty years ago is bad.

This last question drew poignant romp and succinct rebuff from Baldwin. From Achebe it drew something akin to a plea of self-defense, and more.

Question: We are now meeting in a state which has not ratified . . . the Equal Rights Amendment. And I say this just before asking a question, and I ask this as a friend Chinua, OK? What do you feel presently is the place of the African woman in African writing and the African aesthetic? And what do you see that place being in the future?

Baldwin: Chinua, let me take that first.

Chinua: OK. We will have it. (Laughter) Go on Brother.

Baldwin: What about the case of Mrs. Ronald Reagan? What kind of question after all is that? The state of the African woman. . . there'd be no African man if there'd been no African woman . . . to put it very simply. And to go further, the aesthetic morality which you are talking about—the sense of life, the answer to that question in a way, but nobody is going to admit it, can be found in this country.

Black people don't have yet what my countryman called the nuclear family. When I was young, and until today, when I was young running the streets of Harlem every child belonged to every mother and to every father. And if somebody found *me*—you know doing what I was not supposed to be doing, they'd kick my ass and take me home and tell my mother and father, "I just beat the shit out of him." Then they'd beat me again. And that's how I grew up.

Chinua: I'll come to it from another angle. The women in our culture are the center of our lives. Now this is not to pretend that all is well with our condition. But the only thing you can judge us by are the values, the aesthetics, if you like, of our life—what we say about the women, not what we do to women. And we say the "woman, mother is supreme." This is a name, a common name given to a child. And we call her 'Mother is supreme.' There is no name, 'Father is supreme.' There are a few other concepts that share this kind of honor. God is one; the supreme God. God is supreme. So traditionally I would say at least in principle we understand the position of the woman. Now that's traditionally.

A lot has happened today. And it's risky for me to attempt to speak for our women, because they can speak for themselves. So if the worse excesses of the Anglo Saxon civilization is the idea that two people doing the same work can be paid different salaries, we've never had it—believe it or not—in Nigeria. So don't think that because we are behind you in technology, we are behind you in women affairs. Women, in fact, are able to deal with this. More and more are appearing in literature; they are writing. I mean, they accuse me of not portraying the problems. How could I? So my answer is, "There is some on my part; there will be more when more and more of them (women) are writing. Then that problem will be corrected."

The evening ended in high exhilaration. Achebe had offered a form of insight which gives meaning to the present idea of aesthetics by linking it with clues from the past and with proverbs from the Ibo people and their religion. Baldwin had lectured one moment and guyed the next while pleading inviolate the rights of the black American against the doctrine of "white" supremacy. While to an impatient ear his remarks may have seemed equivocal at times, what he said held together on a traceable thread of thought. In taking on "Defining an African Aesthetic," each speaker conveyed an attractive side of his own character through charismatic analytical wit.

Baldwin was whisked away from the banquet room immediately following the final answer to the final question, which was all about how the two authors had influenced each other long before they met in person. He was hurried off to a waiting car by the same party of close friends with whom he and Achebe had been sequestered in the day and a half prior to the banquet and dialogue. Achebe stayed behind for nearly an hour fraternizing with well wishers, some who stood in line to get a book autographed, a picture taken with him, or to share some personal insight grasped during the evening's dialogue.

James Baldwin—Reflections of a Maverick
Julius Lester/1984

From *The New York Times Book Review*, 27 May 1984, pp. 1, 22-24. Reprinted by permission of the interviewer.

The hair is almost white now, but that is the only indication that James Baldwin will be 60 years old in August. Thirty-one years have passed since the publication of his first book, the novel, "Go Tell It on the Mountain," and 21 years since "The Fire Next Time" made him an international celebrity.

The intensity and passion that characterize his writing are evident in conversation. His voice, though soft, is deep and resonant, and in its modulations and rhythms one hears echoes of the boy preacher he once was. He gestures with a fluidity reminiscent of a conductor, as if there is an unseen orchestra that must be brought into harmony. The face he has written of as ugly, with its protuberant eyes, flat nose and wide mouth, has, in reality, the ritual beauty of a Benin head. Baldwin looks as if he were sculpted in flesh rather than merely being born of it.

The following is the edited transcript of a three-hour conversation taped in my home in Amherst, Mass., on a Sunday afternoon in April. As writers, 15 years apart in age, we wanted to compare our generations. As it turned out, we embodied our generations more than I, at least, had anticipated. I began by saying to Baldwin:

Your literary beginnings were as a part of the New York intelligentsia. It was right after the end of World War II that you began publishing reviews and essays in publications like The New Leader, The Nation, Commentary and Partisan Review. What was it like for a young black man, 21 years old, to be around people like Randall Jarrell, Dwight Macdonald, Lionel Trilling, Delmore Schwartz, Irving Howe and William Barrett, to name a few.

For me, these people were kind of an Olympus. I mean, in one way I was very intimidated by them, and I don't know what in the world they thought of me. Dwight Macdonald told me that I was

222

"terribly smart." [*Laughs*] I certainly learned from them, though I could not tell you exactly what I learned. A certain confidence in myself, perhaps.

Did you ever approach Langston Hughes? He was living in Harlem.
I knew of Langston Hughes, but it never occurred to me. I was too shy. Later on I realized that I could have. He didn't live far away, but it wouldn't have occurred to me. You see, there were two Harlems. These were those who lived in Sugar Hill and there was the Hollow, where we lived. There was a great divide between the black people on the Hill and us. I was just a ragged, funky black shoeshine boy and was afraid of the people on the Hill, who, for their part, didn't want to have anything to do with me. Langston, in fact, did not live on the Hill, but in my mind, he was associated with those people. So I would never have dreamed of going and knocking on his door.

And yet, you went and knocked on Richard Wright's door.
I suppose I did that because I had to. I'd just read "Uncle Tom's Children" and "Native Son." I knew of Langston and Countee Cullen, they were the only other black writers whose work I knew at that time, but for some reason they did not attract me. I'm not putting them down, but the world they were describing had nothing to do with me, at that time in my life. Later on I realized something else, but then their work did not resound to me. The black middle class was essentially an abstraction to me. Richard was very different, though. The life he described was the life I lived. I recognized the tenements. I knew that rat in "Native Son." I knew that woman in the story "Bright and Morning Star." All of that was urgent for me. And it was through Richard that I came to read the black writers who had preceded me, like Jean Toomer, and came to know Langston and Countee Cullen in a new way. By the time I went to see Richard I was committed to the idea of being a writer, though I knew how impossible it was. Maybe I went to see Richard to see if he would laugh at me.

Did he?
No. He was very nice to me. I think he found me kind of amusing and I'm sure I was. He was very distant in a way—we never got to be

close friends. But he was very tender, very helpful and we saw each other from time to time. I was still very shy, but I was very proud of him and I think he was proud of me . . . for a while. He may have been always, in fact.

In the essay "Alas, Poor Richard" you write about Wright's feeling that in your earlier essays, "Many Thousands Gone" and "Everybody's Protest Novel," you were trying to kill him—
That I betrayed him.

—And, I think, then, about Eldridge Cleaver's essay "Notes on a Native Son" from "Soul on Ice," which is critical of you. Have younger black writers looked on you as the literary father who must be killed?
I've never bought that analogy. Eldridge's attack on me—quite apart from everything else—is preposterous. In any case, Eldridge cannot claim to know me in any way whatsoever. And he certainly didn't love me. I knew Richard and I loved him. And that's a very, very, very great difference. I was not attacking him; I was trying to clarify something for myself. The analogy does not hold. I reject it in toto.

It is clear that you were trying to clarify something in yourself, but you certainly were very critical of him. And I can certainly understand how he could've reacted as he did.
But what are the reasons for that? I thought—and I still think—that a lot of what happened to us in Paris occurred because Richard was much, much better than a lot of the company he kept. I mean, the French existentialists. I didn't think that Simone de Beauvoir or Jean-Paul Sartre—to say nothing of the American colony—had any right whatsover to patronize that man. It revolted me and made me furious. And it made me furious at Richard, too, because he was better than that. A lot of my tone [in the essay] comes out of that. . . . Alas, poor Richard.

Did he have a responsibility for you as a younger black writer, and do you have a responsibility for younger black writers?
No, no. I never felt that Richard had a responsibility for me, and if he had, he'd discharged it. What I was thinking about, though, was the early 1950's when the world of white supremacy was breaking

up. I'm talking about the revolutions all over the world. Specifically, since we were in Paris, those in Tunisia, Algeria, the ferment in Senegal, the French loss of their Indo-Chinese empire. A whole lot of people—darker people, for the most part—came from all kinds of places to Richard's door as they do now to my door. And in that sense, he had a responsibility that he didn't know—well, who can blame him?

This may be one of those generational differences, but I don't know that I understand this claim you say black people have on you.

I see what you're saying. But it's not only black people, if you like. There is something unjust in it, but it's an irreducible injustice, I think. I found no way around it. But you can't execute the responsibility in the way people want you to. You have to do your work. But, at the same time, you're out there. You asked for it. And no matter how you react to it, you cannot pretend that it is not happening.

Do you ever resent the claim?

It has given me some trying moments, but "It comes with the territory." It is not my fault and it is not their fault that the world thinks it's white. Therefore someone who is not white and attempts to be in some way responsible is going to be claimed by multitudes of black kids. Just or unjust is irrelevant.

Witness is a word I've heard you use often to describe yourself. It is not a word I would apply to myself as a writer, and I don't know if any black writers with whom I am contemporary would, or even could, use the word. What are you a witness to?

Witness to whence I came, where I am. Witness to what I've seen and the possibilities that I think I see. . . . But I can see what you're saying. I don't think I ever resented it, but it exhausted me. I didn't resent it because it was an obligation that was impossible to fulfill. *They* have made you, produced you—and they have done so precisely so they could claim you. They can treat you very badly sometimes, as has happened to me. Still, they produced you because they need you and, for me, there's no way around that. Now, in order for me to execute what I see as my responsibility, I may have to offend them all, but that also comes with the territory. I don't see how I can repudiate it. I'm not trying to suggest, by the way, that Richard tried to repudiate it, either.

You have been politically engaged, but you have never succumbed to ideology, which has devoured some of the best black writers of my generation.

Perhaps I did not succumb to ideology, as you put it, because I have never seen myself as a spokesman. I am a witness. In the church in which I was raised you were supposed to bear witness to the truth. Now, later on, you wonder what in the world the truth is, but you do know what a lie is.

What's the difference between a spokesman and a witness?

A spokesman assumes that he is speaking for others. I never assumed that—I never assumed that I could. Fannie Lou Hamer [the Mississippi civil rights organizer], for example, could speak very eloquently for herself. What I tried to do, or to interpret and make clear was that what the Republic was doing to that woman, it was also doing to itself. No society can smash the social contract and be exempt from the consequences, and the consequences are chaos for everybody in the society.

There's a confidence in your use of the word witness—a confidence about the way the world is and the way it should be. I wonder if it's possible for writers now, black or white, to have that confidence. I wonder if the world hasn't changed between the time you started and the time we started.

Well, it may have. In one way or another, one is very much a prisoner of his time. But I know what I've seen and what I've seen makes me know I have to say, *I know.* I won't say I believe, because I know that we can be better than we are. That's the sum total of my wisdom in all these years. We can also be infinitely worse, but I know that the world we live in now is not necessarily the best world we can make. I can't be entirely wrong. There're two things we have to do— love each other and raise our children. We have to do that! The alternative, for me, would be suicide.

That sounds romantic to me.

I don't think I'm romantic. If I am, I wouldn't know it, so it's kind of a fruitless question.

When you say that the two things we have to do are love each

other and raise our children, my response is to look at American
society and say we don't do either very well.
That's quite true. But the fact that American society doesn't do that
doesn't get us off the hook. In fact, black people have attempted to
do that.

Have they? The first thing I think of is the black men selling junk to
black children.
I know that very well. I think I know why in any case, and I'm not
claiming that black people are better than white people. We treat
each other just the way the rest of the human race treats itself.
Abominably. Well, what am I to do in the face of that? The black man
selling junk to kids, I'd like to kill him. I don't think I'm romantic
about that. But I do know, too, that some of the evils that we live with
are really produced by the society we live in, by the choices that
society offers. I'm not trying to get anybody off the hook when I say
that.

It sounds like it.
No, I don't think so. For example, going back to the years in
Greenwich Village, the years I was getting my head beaten when I
was walking the streets, that doesn't happen now. Or it happens
more rarely, or in a different way. This means that the choice that a
white person had to make when I was growing up—to be seen or not
be seen with me, to be on my side or not to be on my side—that
choice is a little less dangerous now. That infinitesimal change makes
things a little easier for everybody.

Are there any white writers you would describe as witnesses?
Dostoyevsky, Dickens, James, Proust.

What about of your generation?
Well, bearing in mind that this is for the *New York Times,* whatever
I say I'm in a trick bag. Whomever I name, there'll be a lot of people
I'll have left out. I won't have a friend left. The only way I can answer
the question would be to say that, generally, most white American
writers think of themselves as *white.* To be a white American is to
have a very peculiar inheritance. All white American writers came
from someplace else, even if they were born here. My past, after all,
stretches back to Africa by way of Europe. But most white American

writers seem to have cut off their heritage at Ellis Island. Their testimony, for me, does not include enough. Or, one could put it another way. One could say that they reveal their heritage in unconscious ways. I could say this about Norman Mailer, for example. I think, for example, of John Updike and John Cheever, whose subject matter is roughly the same. But Cheever brought something to that subject that engages me—while John Updike's people do not engage me.

What do you think Cheever brought to his work?

Perhaps a depth of anguish. Somehow those lost suburbanites in Cheever's fiction are very moving. He engages your compassion. His people are not remote. The work of so many white writers is remote for me. I'm not trying to put them down. It's simply that they are not relevant to my experience. My experience is larger, and my comment says more about me than them. I think, too, that the effort on the part of the Republic to avoid the presence of black people reflects itself in American literature fatally, to the detriment of that literature.

What about somebody like William Styron?

Bill? Bill is a kind of exception, if only in the effort. I'm thinking, of course, of his "Confessions of Nat Turner," which has been so violently attacked and so praised and over-praised. It's a book I admire very much. But, you see, I read that book as the "Confessions of Bill Styron"—and I'm not trying to put the book down when I say that. I respect the book very much. I respect him very much and I respect his attempt to grapple with something almost no one in his generation is prepared to even look at.

I was curious about that, because when the book came out, you were the only black writer, as I recall, who liked it, and I felt a large generational gap between you and me.

I think that I was right.

Well, I have to question that. Perhaps my profound dissatisfaction with "The Confessions of Nat Turner" comes from my sense of its inadequate execution, as well as my wish that he had written it from the point of view of a white person affected by the Turner uprising. If he'd done that I could agree with you that he was attempting to grapple with something.

I can understand the objection you're raising, but I think it's finally irrelevant. I think Bill wrote the book from that point of view because he couldn't find another one, he had to try to put himself in the skin of Nat Turner. Now that may have been a great error, but I can't condemn him for it. It's beyond my province, really. The book meant something to me because it was a white Southern writer's attempt to deal with something that was tormenting him and frightening him. I respect him very much for that. Now, as to his execution, what is one to say about it?

I'm still waiting for the white writer to write a novel about a lynching from the point of view of the lyncher.
Yes, I quite agree with you. I said before that America's effort to avoid the presence of black people constricts American literature. It creates a trap white writers find themselves in.

We were talking about white writers as witnesses and you alluded to Mailer. How do you see Mailer?
Well, Mailer is something I've been desperately trying to avoid. [*Laughs*] All I can say is that—well, one of the hazards of being an American writer, and I'm well placed to know it, is that eventually you have nothing to write about. A funny thing happens on the way to the typewriter. There is a decidedly grave danger of becoming a celebrity, of becoming a star, of becoming a personality. Again, I'm very well placed to know that. It's symptomatic of the society that doesn't have any real respect for the artist. You're either a success or a failure and there's nothing in between. And if you are a success, you run the risk that Norman has run and that I run, too, of becoming a kind of show business personality. Then the legend becomes far more important than the work. It's as though you're living in an echo chamber. You hear only your own voice. And, when you become a celebrity, that voice is magnified by multitudes and you begin to drown in this endless duplication of what looks like yourself. You have to be really very lucky, and very stubborn, not to let that happen to you. It's a difficult trap to avoid. And that's part of Norman's dilemma, I think. A writer is supposed to write. If he appears on television or as a public speaker, so much the better or so much the worse, but the public persona is one thing. On the public platform or on television, I have to sound as if I know what I'm talking about. It's antithetical to the effort you make at the typewriter, where you don't

know a damned thing. And you have to know you don't know it. The moment you carry the persona to the typewriter, you are finished. Does that answer your question?

No, but it's an eloquent evasion.
Is it? But I don't want to talk about Norman! Why should I talk about Norman? I'm very fond of him and have great respect for his gifts. Well, perhaps he's a perfect example of what it means to be a white writer in this century, a white American writer in this country. It affords too many opportunities to avoid reality. . . . And I know much more about Norman than I'm willing to say in print. After all, I care about him.

I respect that, but I'd like to pursue it from another angle.
I'll have another drink, then.

In "Alas, Poor Richard," you write that it's "not possible to overstate the price a Negro pays to climb out of obscurity." And you go on to write that "The higher he rises, the less is his journey worth." Thinking about what you've just said about Mailer, I couldn't help also thinking that you've risen higher than any black writer, even higher than Wright in terms of public acclaim, recognition and esteem. How much has the journey been worth?
What happened to me came as a great surprise. Obviously, in the essay, I'm speaking to some extent of a public journey, though the word public is not used. I don't feel bitter about the journey, and that may be indicative-of something. I don't feel bitter and I don't feel betrayed. I was a maverick, a maverick in the sense that I depended on neither the white world nor the black world. That was the only way I could've played it. I would've been broken otherwise. I had to say, "A curse on both your houses." The fact that I went to Europe so early is probably what saved me. It gave me another touchstone— myself. Then the idea of becoming an artist as distinguished from a celebrity was real. I never wanted to become a celebrity. Being a maverick saved my life. What club could I have joined? I had to make peace with a great many things, not the least of which was my intelligence. You don't realize that you're intelligent until it gets you into trouble.

Is the celebrity James Baldwin anyone that you know?

That's a very good question. Not really. Not really. It's almost a garment I wear. But the celebrity never sees himself. I have some idea what I'm doing on that stage; above all, I have some idea what sustains me on that stage. But the celebrity is not exactly Jimmy, though he comes out of Jimmy and Jimmy nourishes that, too. I can see now, with hindsight, that I would've had to become a celebrity in order to survive. A boy like me with all his handicaps, real and fancied, could not have survived in obscurity. I can say that it would have had to happen this way, though I could not see it coming.

One night you were talking semicoherently about facing the fact of having to find a new langage.

Where was I? Oh, yes! I was here—at least I wasn't on television. Anyway, a language is a frame of reference, isn't it? And I can only be semicoherent about it now because I'm in the process of experimenting. I say a new language. I might say a new morality, which, in my terms, comes to the same thing. And that's on all levels—the level of color, the level of identity, the level of sexual identity, what love means, especially in a consumer society, for example. Everything is in question, according to me. One has to forge a new language to deal with it. That's as coherent as I can be about it.

What do you see as the task facing black writers today, regardless of age or generation?

This may sound strange, but I would say to make the question of color obsolete.

And how would a black writer do that?

Well, you ask me a reckless question, I'll give you a reckless answer—by realizing first of all that the world is not white. And by realizing that the real terror that engulfs the white world now is a visceral terror. I can't prove this, but I know it. It's the terror of being described by those they've been describing for so long. And that will make the concept of color obsolete. Do you see what I mean?

I see what you mean, but some black writers of my generation might say that the responsibility of black writers is to write about black people.

That is not a contradiction. If our voices are heard, it makes the concept of color obsolete. That has to be its inevitable result.

The Art of Fiction LXXVIII: James Baldwin
Jordan Elgrably and George Plimpton/1984

From *The Paris Review*, 26 (Spring 1984), 49-82. Reprinted by permission.

This interview was conducted in the two places dearest to James Baldwin's struggle as a writer. We met first in Paris, where he spent the first nine years of a burgeoning career and wrote his first two novels, *Go Tell It on the Mountain* and *Giovanni's Room*, along with his best known collection of essays, *Notes of a Native Son*. It was in Paris, he says, that he was first able to come to grips with his explosive relationship with himself and America. Our second talks were held at Baldwin's *poutres* and stone villa in St. Paul, where he has made his home for the past ten years. We lunched on an August weekend, together with seasonal guests and his secretary. Saturday, a storm raged amid intolerable heat and humidity, causing Baldwin's minor case of arthritis to pain his writing hand (left) and wrist. Erratic power shortages caused by the storm interrupted the tape machine by our side. In between blackouts we would discuss subjects at random or wait in silence while sipping our drinks.

Returning Sunday at Baldwin's invitation, the sun was shining and we were able to lunch outdoors at a picnic table, shaded by a bower that opened onto property dotted with fruit trees and a spectacular view of the Mediterranean littoral. Baldwin's mood had brightened considerably since the previous day, and we entered the office and study he refers to as his "torture chamber."

Baldwin writes in longhand ("you achieve shorter declarative sentences") on the standard legal pad, although a large, old Adler electric sits on one end of his desk—a rectangular oak plank with rattan chairs on either side. It is piled with writing utensils and drafts of several works-in-progress: a novel, a play, a scenario, essays on the Atlanta child murders, these last compiled in *The Evidence of Things Not Seen*. His most recent work includes *The Devil*

232

Finds Work, an attack on racial bias and fear in the film industry, and a novel, *Just Above My Head,* which draws on his experiences as a civil rights activist in the 1960s.

Interviewer: Would you tell us how you came to leave the States?

Baldwin: I was broke. I got to Paris with forty dollars in my pocket, but I had to get out of New York. My reflexes were tormented by the plight of other people. Reading had taken me away for long periods at a time, yet I still had to deal with the streets and the authorities and the cold. I knew what it meant to be white and I knew what it meant to a nigger, and I knew what was going to happen to me. My luck was running out. I was going to go to jail, I was going to kill somebody or be killed. My best friend had committed suicide two years earlier, jumping off the George Washington Bridge.

When I arrived in Paris in 1948 I didn't know a word of French. I didn't know anyone and I didn't want to know anyone. Later, when I'd encountered other Americans, I began to avoid them because they had more money than I did and I didn't want to feel like a freeloader. The forty dollars I came with, I recall, lasted me two or three days. Borrowing money whenever I could—often at the last minute—I moved from one hotel to another, not knowing what was going to happen to me. Then I got sick. To my surprise I wasn't thrown out of the hotel. This Corsican family, for reasons I'll never understand, took care of me. An old, old lady, a great old matriarch, nursed me back to health after three months; she used old folk remedies. And she had to climb five flights of stairs every morning to make sure I was kept alive. I went through this period where I was very much alone, and wanted to be. I wasn't part of any community until I later became the Angry Young Man in New York.

Interviewer: Why did you choose France?

Baldwin: It wasn't so much a matter of choosing France—it was a matter of getting out of America. I didn't know what was going to happen to me in France but I knew what was going to happen to me in New York. If I had stayed there, I would have gone under, like my friend on the George Washington Bridge.

Interviewer: You say the city beat him to death. You mean that metaphorically.

Baldwin: Not so metaphorically. Looking for a place to live. Looking for a job. You begin to doubt your judgment, you begin to doubt everything. You become imprecise. And that's when you're beginning to go under. You've been beaten, and it's been deliberate. The whole society has decided to make you *nothing*. And they don't even know they're doing it.

Interviewer: Has writing been a type of salvation?

Baldwin: I'm not so sure! I'm not sure I've escaped anything. One still lives with it, in many ways. It's happening all around us, every day. It's not happening to me in the same way, because I'm James Baldwin; I'm not riding the subways and I'm not looking for a place to live. But it's still happening. So salvation is a difficult word to use in such a context. I've been compelled in some ways by describing my circumstances to learn to live with them. It's not the same thing as accepting them.

Interviewer: Was there an instant you knew you were going to write, to be a writer rather than anything else?

Baldwin: Yes. The death of my father. Until my father died I thought I could do something else. I had wanted to be a musician, thought of being a painter, thought of being an actor. This was all before I was nineteen. Given the conditions in this country to be a black writer was impossible. When I was young, people thought you were not so much wicked as sick, they gave up on you. My father didn't think it was possible—he thought I'd get killed, get murdered. He said I was contesting the white man's definitions, which was quite right. But I had also learned from my father what he thought of the white man's definitions. He was a pious, very religious and in some ways a very beautiful man, and in some ways a terrible man. He died when his last child was born and I realized I had to make a jump—a leap. I'd been a preacher for three years, from age fourteen to seventeen. Those were three years which probably turned me to writing.

Interviewer: Were the sermons you delivered from the pulpit very carefully prepared, or were they absolutely off the top of your head?

Baldwin: I would improvise from the texts, like a jazz musician improvises from a theme. I never wrote a sermon—I studied the texts. I've never written a speech. I can't *read* a speech. It's kind of give and take. You have to sense the people you're talking to. You have to respond to what they hear.

Interviewer: Do you have a reader in your mind when you write?

Baldwin: No, you can't have that.

Interviewer: So it's quite unlike preaching?

Baldwin: Entirely. The two roles are completely unattached. When you are standing in the pulpit, you must sound as though you know what you're talking about. When you're writing, you're trying to find out something which you don't know. The whole language of writing for me is finding out what you don't want to know, what you don't want to find out. But something forces you to anyway.

Interviewer: Is that one of the reasons you decided to be a writer—to find out about yourself?

Baldwin: I'm not sure I decided. It was that or nothing, since in my own mind I was the father of my family, That's not quite the way *they* saw it, but still I was the oldest brother, and I took it very seriously, I had to set an example. I couldn't allow anything to happen to me because what then would happen to them? I could have become a junkie. On the roads I traveled and the streets I ran, anything could have happened to a boy like me—in New York. Sleeping on rooftops and in the subways. Until this day I'm terrified of the public toilet. In any case . . . my father died, and I sat down and figured out what I had to do.

Interviewer: When did you find time to write?

Baldwin: I was very young then. I could write *and* hold a few jobs. I was for a time a waiter . . . like George Orwell in *Down and Out in Paris and London*. I couldn't do it now. I worked on the Lower East Side and in what we now call Soho.

Interviewer: Was there anyone to guide you?

Baldwin: I remember standing on a street corner with the black painter Beauford Delaney down in the Village, waiting for the light to change, and he pointed down and said, "Look." I looked and all I saw was water. And he said, "Look again," which I did, and I saw oil on the water and the city reflected in the puddle. It was a great revelation to me. I can't explain it. He taught me how to see, and how to trust what I saw. Painters have often taught writers how to see. And once you've had that experience, you see differently.

Interviewer: Do you think painters would help a fledgling writer more than another writer might? Did you read a great deal?

Baldwin: I read everything. I read my way out of the two libraries in Harlem by the time I was thirteen. One does learn a great deal about writing this way. First of all, you learn how little you know. It is true that the more one learns the less one knows. I'm still learning how to write. I don't know what technique is. All I know is that you have to make the reader *see it.* This I learned from Dostoyevsky, from Balzac. I'm sure that my life in France would have been very different had I not met Balzac. Even though I hadn't experienced it yet, I understood something about the concierge, all the French institutions and personalities. The way that country and its society works. How to find my way around in it, not get lost in it, and not feel rejected by it. The French gave me what I could not get in America, which was a sense of "If I can do it, I may do it." I won't generalize, but in the years I grew up in the U.S., I could not do that. I'd already been defined.

Interviewer: Did what you wanted to write about come easily to you from the start?

Baldwin: I had to be released from a terrible shyness—an illusion that I could hide anything from anybody.

Interviewer: I would think that anyone who could time after time, and without notes, address a congregation would never be shy again.

Baldwin: I was scared then and I'm scared now. Communication is a two-way street, really, it's a matter of listening to one another. During the civil rights movement I was in the back of a church in Tallahassee and the pastor, who recognized me, called my name and asked me to say a few words. I was thirty-four and had left the pulpit seventeen years before. The moment in which I had to stand up and walk down the aisle and stand in that pulpit was the strangest moment in my life up to that time. I managed to get through it and when I walked down from the pulpit and back up the aisle, a little old black lady in the congregation said to a friend of hers, "He's little, but he's loud!"

Interviewer: What was the process whereby you were able to write?

Baldwin: I had to go through a time of isolation in order to come to terms with who and what I was, as distinguished from all the things

I'd been told I was. Right around 1950 I remember feeling that I'd come through *something*, shed a dying skin and was naked again. I wasn't, perhaps, but I certainly felt more at ease with myself. And then I was able to write. Throughout 1948 and 1949 I just tore up paper.

Interviewer: Those years were difficult, and yet you received four writing grants between 1945 and 1956. How much encouragement did they afford you?

Baldwin: Well, the first one was the most important in terms of morale—the Saxton Fellowship in 1945. I was twenty-one. I was launched into the publishing world, so to speak. And there was the novel, which became *Go Tell It on the Mountain* several years later.

Interviewer: The Saxton was intended to help you finish the novel you were working on?

Baldwin: It helped me finish the novel, it kept me *alive*. The novel didn't work, but I started doing book reviews for the *New Leader* at ten and twenty dollars a shot. I had to read everything and had to write all the time, and that's a great apprenticeship. The people I worked with were left-of-center Trotskyites, Socialist Trotskyites. I was a young Socialist. That was a very nice atmosphere for me; in a sense it saved me from despair. But most of the books I reviewed were Be Kind to Niggers, Be Kind to Jews, while America was going through one of its liberal convulsions. People suddenly discovered they had a Jewish problem, with books like *Gentleman's Agreement, Earth and High Heaven*, or they discovered they had niggers, with books like *King's Blood Royal* and *Pinky*.

Thousands of such tracts were published during those years and it seems to me I had to read every single one of them; the color of my skin made me an expert. And so, when I got to Paris, I had to discharge all that, which was really the reason for my essay, "Everybody's Protest Novel." I was convinced then—and I still am—that those sort of books do nothing but bolster up an image. All of this had quite a bit to do with the direction I took as a writer, because it seemed to me that if I took the role of a victim then I was simply reassuring the defenders of the status quo; as long as I was a victim they could pity me and add a few more pennies to my home relief check. Nothing would change in that way, I felt, and that essay was a beginning of my finding a new vocabulary and another point of view.

Interviewer: If you felt that it was a white man's world, what made you think that there was any point in writing? And why is writing a white man's world?

Baldwin: Because they own the business. Well, in retrospect, what it came down to was that I would not allow myself to be defined by other people, white or black. It was beneath me to blame anybody for what happened to me. What happened to me was *my* responsibility. I didn't want any pity. "Leave me alone, I'll figure it out." I was very wounded and I was very dangerous because you become what you hate. It's what happened to my father and I didn't want it to happen to me. His hatred was suppressed and turned against himself. He couldn't let it out—he could only let it out in the house with rage, and I found it happening to myself as well. And after my best friend jumped off the bridge, I knew that I was next. So—Paris. With forty dollars and a one-way ticket.

Interviewer: Once in Paris, you spent a lot of time upstairs at the Café de Flore. Is that where *Go Tell It on the Mountain* and *Giovanni's Room* were written?

Baldwin: A lot of *Go Tell It on the Mountain* had to be written there, between there and the Hotel Verneuil, where I stayed for a lot of the time I was in Paris. After ten years of carrying that book around, I finally finished it in Switzerland in three months. I remember playing Bessie Smith all the time while I was in the mountains, and playing her till I fell asleep. The book was very hard to write because I was too young when I started, seventeen; it was really about me and my father. There were things I couldn't deal with technically at first. Most of all, I couldn't deal with *me*. This is where reading Henry James helped me, with his whole idea about the center of consciousness and using a single intelligence to tell the story. He gave me the idea to make the novel happen on John's birthday.

Interviewer: Do you agree with Alberto Moravia, who said that one ought only to write in the first person, because the third projects a bourgeois point of view?

Baldwin: I don't know about that. The first person is the most terrifying view of all. I tend to be in accord with James, who hated the first person perspective, which the reader has no reason to trust—

why should you need this *I*? How is this person real by dint of that
bar blaring across the page?

Interviewer: When did you conceive of leaving black characters
out of *Giovanni's Room*?

Baldwin: I suppose the only honest answer to that is that *Giovanni's Room* came out of something I had to face. I don't quite
know when it came, though it broke off from what later turned into
Another Country. Giovanni was at a party and on his way to the
guillotine. He took all the light in the book, and then the book
stopped and nobody in the book would speak to me. I thought I
would seal Giovanni off into a short story, but it turned into *Giovanni's Room*. I certainly could not possibly have—not at that point in my
life—handled the other great weight, the "Negro problem." The
sexual-moral light was a hard thing to deal with. I could not handle
both propositions in the same book. There was no room for it. I
might do it differently today, but then, to have a black presence in the
book at that moment, and in Paris, would have been quite beyond
my powers.

Interviewer: Was it David who first appeared in *Giovanni's Room*?

Baldwin: It was, yes, but that novel has a curious history. I wrote
four novels before I published one, before I'd even left America. I
don't know what happened to them. When I came over they were in
a duffle bag, which I lost, and that's that. But the genesis of
Giovanni's Room is in America. David is the first person I thought of,
but that's due to a peculiar case involving a boy named Lucien Carr,
who murdered somebody. He was known to some of the people I
knew—I didn't know him personally. But I was fascinated by the trial,
which also involved a wealthy playboy and his wife in high-level
society. From this fascination came the first version of *Giovanni's
Room*, something called *Ignorant Armies*, a novel I never finished.
The bones of *Giovanni's Room* and *Another Country* were in that.

Interviewer: Wasn't it after your first two novels, which were in
many ways extremely personal, that you introduced more of the
political and sociological counterpoint (evident in your essays) into
Another Country?

Baldwin: From my point of view it does not quite work that way, making attempts to be merely personal or to bring in a larger scope. No one knows how he writes his book. Go *Tell It on the Mountain* was about my relationship to my father and to the church, which is the same thing really. It was an attempt to exorcise something, to find out what happened to my father, what happened to all of us, what had happened to me—to John—and how we were to move from one place to another. Of course it seems rather personal, but the book is not *about* John, the book is not *about* me.

Interviewer: "One writes out of one thing only—one's own experience," you've said.

Baldwin: Yes, and yet one's own experience is not necessarily one's twenty-four hour reality. Everything happens to you, which is what Whitman means when he says in his poem "Heroes," "I am the man/I suffered/I was there." It depends on what you mean by experience.

Interviewer: Nevertheless, it seems that your struggles with social injustices were kept apart as the material for your essays, while your fiction dealt predominantly with your own past.

Baldwin: If I wanted to survive as a writer I would eventually have had to write a book like *Another Country*. On the other hand, short stories like "Sonny's Blues" or "Previous Condition," which appeared before *Another Country*, were highly personal and yet went further than the immediate dilemmas of the young writer struggling in the Village or of Sonny in "Sonny's Blues."

Interviewer: Ralph Ellison said in his *Paris Review* interview that he writes "*primarily* not concerned with injustice, but with art," whereas one might almost find you a sort of spokesman for blacks.

Baldwin: I don't consider myself a spokesman—I have always thought it would be rather presumptuous.

Interviewer: Although you are aware of the fact that many people read and are moved by your essays, as well as your speeches and lectures . . .

Baldwin: Let's go back now. Those essays really date from the time I was in my early twenties, and were written for the *New Leader* and *The Nation* all those years ago. They were an attempt to get me beyond the chaos I mentioned earlier. I lived in Paris long enough to finish my first novel, which was very important for me (or I wouldn't be here at all). What held me in Paris later—from '55 to '57—was the fact that I was going through a kind of break-up in my private life, yet I knew I had to go back to America. And I went. Once I was in the civil rights milieu, once I'd met Martin Luther King, Jr. and Malcolm X and Medgar Evers and all those other people, the role I had to play was confirmed. I didn't think of myself as a public speaker, or as a spokesman, but I knew I could get a story past the editor's desk. And once you realize that you can do something, it would be difficult to live with yourself if you didn't do it.

Interviewer: When you were much younger, what distinctions did you make between art and protest?

Baldwin: I thought of them both as literature and still do. I don't see the contradiction which some people point out as inherent, though I can sense what Ralph, among others, means by that. The only way I could play it, once indeed I found myself on that road, was to assume that if I had the talent, and my talent was important, it would simply have to survive whatever life brought. I couldn't sit somewhere honing my talent to a fine edge after I had been to all those places in the South and seen those boys and girls, men and women, black and white, longing for change. It was impossible for me to drop them a visit and then leave.

Interviewer: You were in utter despair after the death of Martin Luther King, Jr. Did you find it difficult to write then, or do you work better out of anguish?

Baldwin: No one works better out of anguish at all; that's an incredible literary conceit. I didn't think I could write at all. I didn't see any point to it. I was hurt . . . I can't even talk about it. I didn't know how to continue, didn't see my way clear.

Interviewer: How did you eventually find your way out of the pain?

Baldwin: I really think through my brother, David. I was working on *No Name in the Street* but hadn't touched it after the assassination. He called me and I told him "I just can't finish this book. I don't know what to do with it." And he came across the ocean. I was here in St. Paul, living in Le Hameau across the road. I was sick, went to four or five hospitals. I was very lucky, because I could've gone mad. You see, I had left America after the funeral and gone to Istanbul. Worked—or tried to—there. Got sick in Istanbul, went to London, got sick in London, and I wanted to die. Collapsed.

I was shipped down here, out of the American Hospital in Paris. I'd been in the region in 1949, but I had never dreamt of coming to live in St. Paul. Once I was here, I stayed. I didn't really have any place else to go. Well, I could have gone back to America, and I did, to do a *Rap on Race*, which helped me significantly. But principally, David came and he read *No Name in the Street* and sent it on to New York.

Interviewer: In an *Esquire* essay, you once wrote that you've been "schooled in adversity and skilled in compromise." Does that perhaps reflect trying to get your work published?

Baldwin: No, though it has been such a stormy career. It's a terrible way to make a living. I find writing gets harder as time goes on. I'm speaking of the working process, which demands a certain amount of energy and courage (though I dislike using the word), and a certain amount of recklessness. I don't know, I doubt whether any-one—myself at least—knows how to *talk* about writing. Perhaps I'm afraid to.

Interviewer: Do you see it as conception, gestation, accouche-ment?

Baldwin: I don't think it that way, no. The whole process of con-ception—one talks about it after the fact, if one discusses it at all. But you really don't understand it. After the fact I may discuss a work, yet I'm uncertain that what I do say about it afterwards can be taken as gospel.

Interviewer: One critic suggested that James Baldwin's best work was yet to come and would be an autobiographical novel, which *Just Above My Head* was in part.

Baldwin: He may have a point there. I hope, certainly, that my best work is before me. It depends on what one means by "autobio-graphical." I certainly have not told my story yet. I know that, though I've revealed fragments.

Interviewer: Are you, or do you remain, very close to your characters?

Baldwin: I don't know if I feel close to them, now. After a time you find, however, that your characters are lost to you, making it quite impossible for you to judge them. When you've finished a novel it means, "The train stops here, you have to get off here." You never get the book you wanted, you settle for the book you get. I've always felt that when a book ended there was something I didn't see, and usually when I remark the discovery it's too late to do anything about it.

Interviewer: This occurs once it has already been published?

Baldwin: No, no, it happens when you are right here at the table. The publication date is something else again. It's out of your hands, then. What happens here is that you realize if you try to redo something, you may wreck everything else. But, if a book has brought you from one place to another, so that you see something you didn't see before, you've arrived at another point. This then is one's consolation, and you know that you must now proceed elsewhere.

Interviewer: Are there a lot of your characters walking around here?

Baldwin: No, they begin walking around before you put them on paper. And after you put them on paper you don't see them anymore. They may be wandering around here. *You* might see them.

Interviewer: So once you've captured a character in your work, it is no longer a phantom?

Baldwin: Actually, what has happened is that the character has tyrannized you for however long it took, and when the novel is over he or she says Ciao, thanks a lot. *Pointe finale.* Before *Another Country*, Ida talked to me for years. We get on very well now.

Interviewer: How soon after you concevied of Rufus, in *Another Country*, did you know he was going to commit suicide, or was he modeled after your adolescent friend who jumped off the George Washington Bridge in New York?

Baldwin: Oh, he was taken directly from that friend, yet, oddly enough, he was the last person to arrive in the novel. I'd written the book more than once and I'd felt I'd never get it right. Ida was important, but I wasn't sure I could cope with her. Ida and Vivaldo were the first people I was dealing with, but I couldn't find a way to make you understand Ida. Then Rufus came along and the entire action made sense.

Interviewer: And Richard, the rather idealistic writer?

Baldwin: This is all far beyond my memory. Well, there was Vivaldo, whose name I didn't know for sometime. He was called Daniel at first, and at one point was black. Ida, on the other hand, was always Ida. Richard and Cass were part of the decor. From my point of view, there was nothing in the least idealistic about Richard. He was modeled on several liberal American careerists from then and now. In any case, in order to make the reader see Ida, I had to give her a brother, who turned out to be Rufus. It's fascinating from the point of view of styles, and of accommodations to human pain, that it took me so long—from 1946 to 1960—to accept the fact that my friend was dead. From the moment Rufus was gone, I knew that if you knew what had happened to Ida, you'd equally understand Rufus, and you'd see why Ida throughout the book was so difficult with Vivaldo and everybody else—with herself above all, because she wasn't going to be able to live with the pain. The principal action in the book, for me, is the journey of Ida and Vivaldo toward some kind of coherence.

Interviewer: Is there a big shifting of gears between writing fiction and writing non-fiction?

Baldwin: Shifting gears, you ask. Every form is difficult, no one is easier than another. They all kick your ass. None of it comes easy.

Interviewer: How many pages do you write in a day?

Baldwin: I write at night. After the day is over, and supper is over, I begin, and work until about three or four A.M.

Interviewer: That's quite rare, isn't it, because most people write when they're fresh, in the morning.

Baldwin: I start working when everyone has gone to bed. I've had to do that ever since I was young—I had to wait until the kids were asleep. And then I was working at various jobs during the day. I've always had to write at night. But now that I'm established I do it because I'm alone at night.

Interviewer: When do you know something is the way you want it?

Baldwin: I do a lot of rewriting. It's very painful. You know it's finished when you can't do anything more to it, though it's never exactly the way you want it. In fact, the hardest thing I ever wrote was that suicide scene in *Another Country*. I always knew that Rufus had to commit suicide very early on, because that was the key to the book. But I kept putting it off. It had to do, of course, with reliving the suicide of my friend who jumped off the bridge. Also, it was very dangerous to do from the technical point of view because this central character dies in the first hundred pages, with a couple of hundred pages to go. The point up to the suicide is like a long prologue, and it is the only light on Ida. You never go into her mind, but I had to make you see what is happening to this girl by making you feel the blow of her brother's death—the key to her relationship with everybody. She tries to make everybody pay for it. You cannot do that, life is not like that, you only destroy yourself.

Interviewer: Is that the way a book starts for you, though? Something like that?

Baldwin: Probably that way for everybody: something that irritates you and won't let you go. That's the anguish of it. Do this book, or die. You have to go through that.

Interviewer: Does it purge you in any way?

Baldwin: I'm not so sure about *that*. For me it's like a journey, and the only thing you know is that if when the book is over, you are prepared to continue—you haven't cheated.

Interviewer: What would cheating be?

Baldwin: Avoiding. Lying.

Interviewer: So there is a compulsion to get it out?

Baldwin: Oh yes, to get it out and get it right. The word I'm using is compulsion. And it is true of the essay as well.

Interviewer: But the essay is a little bit simpler, isn't it, because you're angry about something which you can put your finger on . . .

Baldwin: An essay is not simpler, though it may seem so. An essay is essentially an argument. The writer's point of view in an essay is always absolutely clear. The writer is trying to make the readers see something, trying to convince them of something. In a novel or a play you're trying to *show* them something. The risks, in any case, are exactly the same.

Interviewer: What are your first drafts like?

Baldwin: They are overwritten. Most of the rewrite, then, is cleaning. Don't describe it, show it. That's what I try to teach all young writers—take it out! Don't describe a purple sunset, make me see that it is purple.

Interviewer: As your experience about writing accrues, what would you say increases with knowledge?

Baldwin: You learn how little you know. It becomes much more difficult because the hardest thing in the world is simplicity. And the most fearful thing, too. It becomes more difficult because you have to strip yourself of all your disguises, some of which you didn't know you had. You want to write a sentence as clean as a bone. That is the goal.

Interviewer: Do you mind what people say about your writing?

Baldwin: Ultimately not. I minded it when I was younger. You care about the people you care about, what they say. You care about the reviews so that somebody will read the book. So, those things are important, but not of ultimate importance.

Interviewer: The attitudes you found in America which made you go to France—are they still with us, are they exactly the same?

Baldwin: I always knew I would have to come back. If I were twenty-four now, I don't know if and where I would go. I don't know if I would go to France, I might go to Africa. You must remember when I was twenty-four there was really no Africa to go to, except Liberia. I thought of going to Israel, but I never did, and I was right about that. Now, though, a kid now . . . well, you see, something has happened which no one has really noticed, but it's very important: Europe is no longer a frame of reference, a standard bearer, the classic model for literature and for civilization. It's not the measuring stick. There are other standards in the world. It's a fascinating time to be living. There's a whole wide world which isn't now as it was when I was younger. When I was a kid the world was white, for all intents and purposes, and now it is struggling to *remain* white—a very different thing.

Interviewer: It's frequently been noted that you are a master of minor characters. How do you respond to that?

Baldwin: Well, minor characters are the subtext, illustrations of whatever it is you're trying to convey. I was always struck by the minor characters in Dostoyevsky and Dickens. The minor characters have a certain freedom which the major ones don't. They can make comments, they can move, yet they haven't got the same weight, or intensity.

Interviewer: You mean to say their actions are less accountable?

Baldwin: Oh no, if you fuck up a minor character you fuck up a major one. They are more a part of the decor—a kind of Greek chorus. They carry the tension in a much more explicit way than the majors.

Interviewer: Excuse me for asking, but might your mother be standing behind you while you're writing; is she perhaps behind many of your characters?

Baldwin: I wouldn't think so, but to tell you the truth, I wouldn't know. I've got five sisters. And in a funny way, there have been many women in my life, so it wouldn't be my mother.

Interviewer: Have you been through analysis?

Baldwin: God no, never got "adjusted."

Interviewer: Both you and William Styron (intentionally or not) write about victims and victimization. Styron has said he has never felt like a victim. Have you?

Baldwin: Well, I refuse to. Perhaps the turning point in one's life is realizing that to be treated like a victim is not necessarily to become one.

Interviewer: Do you believe in a community of writers? Is that of any interest to you?

Baldwin: No. I've never *seen* one in any case . . . and I don't think any writer ever has.

Interviewer: But weren't William Styron and Richard Wright, say, important to you in formulating your viewpoints?

Baldwin: Richard was very important to me. He was much older. He was very nice to me. He helped me with my first novel, really. That was 1944-45. I just knocked on his door out in Brooklyn! I introduced myself, and of course he'd no idea who I was. There were no essays then, no fiction—this was 1944. I adored him. I loved him. We were very unlike each other, as writers, probably as people too. And as I grew older, that became more and more apparent. And after that was Paris.

Interviewer: And Styron?

Baldwin: Well, as I was saying, Bill is a friend of mine who happens to be a writer.

Interviewer: Did you take a position on his book about Nat Turner?

Baldwin: I did. My position, though, is that I will not tell another writer what to write. If you don't like their alternative, write yours. I admired him for confronting it, and the result. It brought in the whole enormity of the issue of history versus fiction, fiction versus history, and which is which. . . . He writes out of reasons similar to mine: about something which hurt him and frightened him. When I was working on *Another Country* and Bill was working on *Nat Turner*, I stayed in his guest house for five months. His hours and mine are very different. I was going to bed at dawn, Bill was just coming up to his study to go to work; his hours going on as mine went off. We saw each other at suppertime.

Interviewer: What kind of conversations would you hold?

Baldwin: We never spoke about our work, or very rarely. It was a wonderful time in my life, but not at all literary. We sang songs, drank a little too much, and on occasion chatted with the people who were dropping in to see us. We had a certain common inheritance in terms of the music.

Interviewer: What sort of music are you hearing while in the immediate process of writing? Do you experience anything physical or emotional?

Baldwin: No. I'm very cold; cold probably isn't the word I want: *controlled*. Writing for me must be a very controlled exercise, formed by passions and hopes. That is the only reason you get through it, otherwise you may as well do something else. The act of writing itself is cold.

Interviewer: I'm going to presage my own question. Most of the novelists I've spoken to claim they read exceedingly fewer contemporary novels, but find themselves drawn to plays, history, memoirs, biographies, and poetry. I believe this is true for you as well.

Baldwin: In my case it is due to the fact that I'm always doing some kind of research. And yes, I read many plays and a lot of poetry as a kind of apprenticeship. You are fascinated, I am fascinated by a certain *optic*—a process of seeing things. Reading Emily Dickinson, for example, and others who are quite far removed from one's ostensible daily concerns, or obligations. They are freer, for that moment, than you are partly because they are dead. They may also be a source of strength. Contemporary novels are part of a universe in which you have a certain role and a certain responsibility. And, of course, an unavoidable curiosity.

Interviewer: You read contemporary novels out of a sense of responsibility?

Baldwin: In a way. At any rate, few novelists interest me—which has nothing to do with their values. I find most of them too remote for me. The world of John Updike, for instance, does not impinge on my world. On the other hand, the world of John Cheever *did* engage me. Obviously, I'm not making a very significant judgment about Updike. It's entirely subjective, what I'm saying. In the main, the concerns of most white Americans (to use *that* phrase) are boring, and terribly, terribly self-centered. In the worst sense. Everything is contingent, of course, on what you take yourself to be.

Interviewer: Are you suggesting they are less concerned, somehow, with social injustice?

Baldwin: No, no, you see, I don't want to make that kind of dichotomy. I'm not asking that anybody get on picket lines or take positions. That is entirely a private matter. What I'm saying has to do with the concept of the self, and the nature of self-indulgence which seems to me to be terribly strangling, and so limited it finally becomes sterile.

Interviewer: And yet in your own writing you deal with personal experiences quite often.

Baldwin: Yes, but—and here I'm in trouble with the language again—it depends upon how you conceive of yourself. It revolves, surely, around the multiplicity of your connections. Obviously you can only deal with your life and work from the vantage point of your self. There isn't any other vantage point, there is no other point of view. I can't say about any of my characters that they are utter fictions. I do have a sense of what nagged my attention where and when; even in the dimmest sense I know how a character impinged on me in reality, in what we call reality, the daily world. And then, of course, imagination has something to do with it. But it has got to be triggered by something, it cannot be triggered by itself.

Interviewer: What is it about Emily Dickinson that moves you?

Baldwin: Her use of language, certainly. Her solitude, as well, and the style of that solitude. There is something very moving and in the best sense funny. She isn't solemn. If you really want to know something about solitude, become famous. That is the turn of the screw. That solitude is practically insurmountable. Years ago I thought to be famous would be a kind of ten-day wonder, and then I could go right back to life as usual. But people treat you differently before you realize it. You see it in the wonder and the worry of your intimates. On the other side of that is a great responsibility.

Interviewer: Is one's past cluttered, as a celebrated writer?

Baldwin: There are many witnesses to my past, people who've disappeared, people who are dead, whom I loved. But I don't feel there are any ghosts, any regrets. I don't feel that kind of melancholy at all. No nostalgia. Everything is always around and before you. Novels that haven't worked, loves, struggles. And yet it all gives you something of immeasurable power.

Interviewer: This brings us to your concern with reality as being history, with seeing the present shaded by everything which occurred in a person's past. James Baldwin has always been bound by his past, and his future. At forty, you said you felt much older than that.

Baldwin: That is one of those things a person says at forty, at forty especially. It was a great shock to me, forty. And I did feel much older than that. Responding to history, I think a person is in sight of his or her death around the age of forty. You see it coming. You are not in sight of your death at thirty, less so at twenty-five. You are struck by the fact of your morality, that it is unlikely you'll live another forty years. So time alters you, actually becoming either an enemy or a friend.

Interviewer: You seem very troubled—but not by death?

Baldwin: Yes, true, but not at all by death. I'm troubled over getting my work done and over all the things I've not learned. It's useless to be troubled by death, because then, of course, you can't live at all.

Baldwin: "Essentially, America has not changed that much," you told the *New York Times* when *Just Above My Head* was being published. Have *you?*

Baldwin: In some ways I've changed precisely because America has not. I've been forced to change in some ways. I had a certain expectation for my country years ago, which I know I don't have now.

Interviewer: Yes, before 1968, you said, "I love America."

Baldwin: Long before then. I still do, though that feeling has changed in the face of it. I think that it is a spiritual disaster to pretend that one *doesn't* love one's country. You may disapprove of it, you may be forced to leave it, you may live your whole life as a battle, yet I don't think you can escape it. There isn't any other place to go— you don't pull up your roots and put them down someplace else. At least not in a single lifetime, or, if you do, you'll be aware of precisely what it means, knowing that your real roots are always elsewhere. If you try to pretend you don't see the immediate reality that formed you I think you'll go blind.

Interviewer: As a writer, are there any particular battles you feel you've won?

Baldwin: The battle of becoming a writer at all! "I'm going to be a great writer when I grow up," I used to tell my mother when I was a little boy. And I'm still going to be a great writer when I grow up.

Interviewer: What do you tell younger writers who come to you with the usual desperate question: How do I become a writer?

Baldwin: Write. Find a way to keep alive and write. There is nothing else to say. If you are going to be a writer there is nothing I can say to stop you; if you're not going to be a writer nothing I can say will help you. What you really need at the beginning is somebody to let you know that the effort is real.

Interviewer: Can you discern talent in someone?

Baldwin: Talent is insignificant. I know a lot of talented ruins. Beyond talent lie all the usual words: discipline, love, luck, but, most of all, endurance.

Interviewer: Would you suggest that a young writer from a minority consecrate himself to that minority, or is his first obligation his own self-realization as a writer?

Baldwin: Your self and your people are indistinguishable from each other, really, in spite of the quarrels you may have, and your people are all people.

Interviewer: Wasn't *Giovanni's Room* partially an attempt to break down these divisions, pointing out that David could be white, black, or yellow?

Baldwin: Certainly, for in terms of what happened to him, none of that mattered at all.

Interviewer: Yet, later on, notably in the case of Rufus and *Another Country*, one's race becomes essential to your story.

Baldwin: Important in that particular novel, yes, for *Another Country* is called that because it is trying to convey the reality of that country. The story would be different if it were in France, or even in England.

Interviewer: What is your present relationship with people like Ralph Ellison, Imamu Baraka (Leroi Jones) or Eldridge Cleaver?

Baldwin: I never had a relationship with Cleaver. I was in difficulties because of Cleaver, which I didn't want to talk about then, and don't wish to discuss now. My real difficulty with Cleaver, sadly, was visited on me by the kids who were following him, while he was calling me a faggot and the rest of it. I would come to a town to speak, Cleveland, let's say, and he would've been standing on the very same stage a couple of days earlier. I had to try to undo the damage I considered he was doing. I was handicapped with *Soul On Ice*, because what I might have said in those years about Eldridge would have been taken as an answer to his attack on me. So I never answered it, and I'm not answering it now. Cleaver reminded me of an old Baptist minister I used to work with when I was in the pulpit. I never trusted him at all. As for Baraka, he and I have had a stormy time too, but we're very good friends now.

Interviewer: Do you read each other's work?

Baldwin: Yes—at least I read his. And as for Ralph, I haven't seen him in many years.

Interviewer: You haven't corresponded at all?

Baldwin: No. I gather Ralph did not like what he considered I was doing to myself on the civil rights road. And so, we haven't seen each other.

Interviewer: If you were both to meet over lunch tomorrow, what might you talk about?

Baldwin: I'd love to meet him for lunch tomorrow, and share a bottle of bourbon, and probably talk about the last twenty years we haven't seen each other. I have nothing against him in any case. And I love his great book. We disagreed about tactics, I suppose. But I had to go through the civil rights movement and I don't regret it at all. And those people trusted me. There was something very beautiful about that period, something life-giving for me to be there, to march, to be a part of a sit-in, to see it through my own eyes.

Interviewer: Do you think that now blacks and whites can write about each other, honestly and convincingly?

Baldwin: Yes, though I have no overwhelming evidence in hand. But I think of the impact of spokespersons like Toni Morrison and other younger writers. I believe what one has to do as a Black American is to take white history, or history as written by whites, and claim it all—including Shakespeare.

Interviewer: "What other people write about me is irrelevant," you once wrote in *Essence*. Was that meant to go unqualified; do you not relate to criticism in any way?

Baldwin: It is never entirely true that you don't give a shit what others say about you, but you must throw it out of your mind. I went through a very trying period, after all, where on one side of town I was an Uncle Tom and on the other the Angry Young Man. It could make one's head spin, the number of labels that have been attached to me. And it was inevitably painful, and surprising, and indeed, bewildering. I *do* care what certain people think about me.

Interviewer: But not literary critics?

Baldwin: Literary critics cannot be one's concern. Ideally, however, what a critic can do is indicate where you've been excessive or unclear. As far as any sort of public opinion is a question, I would say that one cannot possibly react to any of it. Things may be said which hurt, and you don't like it, but what are you to do? Write a White Paper, or a Black Paper, defending yourself? You can't do that.

Interviewer: You have often left your home in St. Paul, returning to America and going on the road. Do you feel comfortable as a speaker?

Baldwin: I have never felt comfortable as a speaker, no.

Interviewer: You feel more at ease behind the typewriter?

Baldwin: Well, certainly, although I used to be a preacher, which helps on the road.

Interviewer: Can you talk a little more about your relationship to Richard Wright, under whose aegis you received your first writing grant?

Baldwin: As I said before, I just knocked on his door in New York. I was nineteen. And he was very nice. The only trouble was I didn't drink in those years. He drank bourbon. Now, I'm going to save you the trouble of asking me about writers and alcohol: I don't know any writers who don't drink. Everybody I've been close to drinks. But you don't drink while you're working. It's funny, because it is all a reflex, like lighting a cigarette. Your drink is made and then you go off to another place. When you finally get back to the drink it's mainly water. And the cigarette has gone out. Talking about Richard and our early hostile period, which I thought was ridiculously blown out of proportion, I should say that when I thought I was dealing with Richard, I was in fact thinking of Harriet Beecher Stowe and *Uncle*

Tom's Cabin. Richard's *Native Son* was the only contemporary representation there was of a black person in America. One of the reasons I wrote what I did about the book is a technical objection, which I uphold today. I could not accept the performance of the lawyer at the end of the book. I was very explicit about that. I think it was simply absurd to talk about this monster created by the American public, and then expect the public to save it! Altogether, I found it too simpleminded. Insofar as the American public creates a monster, they are not about to recognize it. You create a monster and destroy it. It is part of the American way of life, if you like. I reserve, in any case, the utmost respect for Richard, especially in light of his posthumous work, which I believe is his greatest novel, *Lawd Today.* Look it up.

Interviewer: Is there any resistance today to black writers in publishing houses?

Baldwin: There is an enormous resistance, though it differs from Wright's time. When I was young, the joke was "How many niggers you got at your plantation?" Or, more snidely, "How many niggers you got at your publishing house?" And some had one, most had none. That's not true now.

Interviewer: How does it strike you that in many circles James Baldwin is known as a prophetic writer?

Baldwin: I don't try to be prophetic, as I don't sit down to write literature. It is simply this: a writer has to take all the risks of putting down what he sees. No one can tell him about that. No one can control that reality. It reminds me of something Pablo Picasso was supposed to have said to Gertrude Stein while he was painting her portrait. Gertrude said, "I don't look like that." And Picasso replied, "You will." And he was right.

Blues for Mr. Baldwin

Angela Cobbina/1985

From *Concord Weekly*, 28 January 1985, pp. 31, 33. Reprinted by permission.

James Baldwin, novelist and essayist continues to be one of the most trenchant critics of the American way. Currently living in France, he makes the occasional journey to America. Angela Cobbina spoke to him about America and the West.

When James Baldwin read Chinua Achebe's *Things Fall Apart*, the story of Okonkwo and the arrival of the white man at the village of Umuofia immediately struck a chord with him.

"I loved the book. I did not know the village, I have never been to Nigeria, and I have only been to Africa once and that was 20 years ago, but I could identify with it: I recognised the situation. And Achebe has told me he felt the same about my book, *Go Tell It On The Mountain!*"

For Baldwin, *Things Fall Apart* confirmed for him once again the universality of the black experience, four hundred years out of Africa but infinitely linked by the oppressive bonds of slavery.

His novels and essays which have spoken with such sorrow and passion of that experience have turned him into one of America's foremost writers, a virtual guru among both blacks and whites.

Now at 60, after five years of publishing nothing, Baldwin is about to re-emerge with a series of essays and his sixth novel, *Petals for Mohammed*, due to be published in the spring.

But despite his stature, he remains an enormously approachable person, one who is eager to point out that he is struggling along just like the rest of us. I spoke to him during one of his brief visits to England. He had flown in especially to open an exhibition of photographs by the Trinidadian film director, Horace Ove, a close personal friend of his. He was staying at the home of another friend, a council flat in north London, and he appeared to be in jaunty spirits. The suffering he has absorbed, experienced and analysed over the years has etched itself eloquently on his face and in the resonant timbre of his voice. Both manage to convey the sensitive soul of a poet; even when he is not putting pen to paper Baldwin is a powerful figure.

But although he is treated reverentially in some quarters, in others he is pilloried. For his humanistic and often mystical approach to racism runs totally counter to the prevailing mood of black nationalism of the last few decades. And his success, both as a celebrity and as a writer in a white man's world, have raised doubts among some as to his integrity, doubts which are compounded by Baldwin's 36-year residence in France. He has been accused of "running away" from the struggle, of being out of touch, even trading off it, all of which he staunchly denies. He explained why he left the Harlem of his youth to journey to a country whose language he could not even speak.

"I left America much more than I went to live in France. I simply left. I got out of where I was because I was becoming a dangerous person to myself. And I also had a family. My father was dead, I was the eldest of nine children and I understood if I went under, they went under. In the world in which I moved, which was mainly a white world, what was in my eyes menaced me; what was on my tongue menaced me. It was only a matter of time before I would meet one cop too many, had one fight too many; that on some unlucky Tuesday, someone would say the wrong things at the wrong hour and one of us would die. That seemed to me a terrible waste".

When Baldwin left for France at the age of 28, he was emerging as a promising young writer. By the time he returned to the turmoil of the United States nine years later he was well on the road to international literary fame with his first novel, *Go Tell It On The Mountain*, a semiautobiographical story of a child evangelist growing up in Harlem. And he was poised to make a similar impact with *Giovanni's Room*, the novel in which he revealed his own homosexuality. He now describes himself as a "transatlantic commuter", living in France because of the solitude it offers him as a writer and returning to the States for long sojourns—one of his longest being during the momentous struggles of the civil rights era. Next month he will be back in the USA, "the sickest and most dangerous country in the world", he once wrote in his book, No Name In The Street. What has happened to the young men and women who followed Martin Luther King, Malcolm X and Megdar Evers? Have they all become sucked into the "American Dream"?

"Every black American is affected by the American dream in the same way as every black Englishman is affected by the notion of the British Empire. One has to deal with all that inside yourself, to find out what you are in what is essentially a white man's world, where you have a certain role to play—one that is defined by others from the most public to the most private".

But despite the set backs, despite the seeming ascendency of the 'Dream', the struggles of the Civil Rights era have not become petrified in time; they are continuing, he asserts, emphasising each word with a characteristically elegant gesture of the hands and change of pitch in his voice.

"Once you see a thing, you don't unsee it. The price you've got to pay for seeing it is not to turn tail. We are determined that the brothers should not have died in vain. The Civil Rights Movement has been betrayed by the American government and institutions, just as Martin Luther King predicted. But it is not dead, it is still there".

He added, failing to hide a note of slight annoyance: "Besides it was not a Civil Rights Movement. That's the American term for it. It was one of many slave insurrections. It's nonsense to call it a Civil Rights Movement. Martin knew this when he said: "Why are you fighting for your civil rights? If you're a citizen you have your civil rights".

Senator Jessie Jackson, Baldwin feels, reflects the constancy of struggle. He is a person Baldwin obviously deeply admires. Like 'Martin', like 'Malcolm', Jessie is a friend.

"Jessie's advent was really very important", Baldwin told me. "And this is for two reasons at least. One of them was that though he knew he could not possibly become president—which says a great deal about American society—he did get a great many people out to vote. This includes white people, not only those whites who voted against him, but those whites who voted for him". He pauses and smiles: "There is another America beneath Time Magazine. And he is also important because of his global presence. The American govern-

ment did not like at all what he did in Syria and they don't like what
he is doing in South Africa".

But equally for Baldwin, whose works are intensely preoccupied
with matters of morality and conscience, the struggle is also being
waged on a spiritual level as well.

"In this day and age it is impossible to conquer the state through a
bloody uprising. But we can do something else, something which we
are doing, which is to simply change things by our presence". He
jabs at the air with his fingers: "We're saying: 'I'm here; I was never
part of *Gone With the Wind*, I was never an intended slave, I was
never a happy darkie, I have a right to live on my terms, now get out
of my way!'"

It is this basic assertion of the 'truth' which Baldwin implicitly
believes has precipitated what he calls a "crisis of identity" or "panic"
in the western world—a world built entirely on lies, and as a result
spiritually and emotionally impoverished.

"Reagan is a symptom of the American panic just as Maggie
Thatcher is a symptom of the British panic. They want to thrust themselves, you and me, back into the past. Their identity is being
attacked because they told themselves nothing but lies about us. I can
now describe the people who described me. This involves a tremendous shift in the world. It is a dangerous time for us but a desperate
time for them". It was the theme Baldwin used in his speech to open
Ove's exhibition. And it is one no doubt that he has begun to explore
more explicitly in his latest works.

But rooted as he is in the bloody tumult of the Civil Rights Movement, Baldwin predicts there is more violent confrontation on the
way.

"People do not just give up things. The British didn't give up their
empire, but they could not hold on to it. The only question is what
chaos do people have to endure before there are any real changes.
So it's best to gird up the loins and take more vitamins". His fixedly
lugubrious face lights up with a fleeting smile.

The riots that erupted on the streets of major cities in Britain four
years ago were part of that chaos. "When I heard about them my first
thought was: 'I told you so. I hate to say that, but I told you so.' But
why were they called riots? They were not riots, they were insurrections. No one refers to the Polish situation as being a riot. It's only

a riot if black people do it. By its very definition the word is meant to make your action irrelevant. It's a mob rioting, nothing but a filthy mob. After every race riot in America, I've heard the same old song. White Americans say: 'What do they want?' They know damn well what we want and it's just a barometer of their cowardice".

Baldwin, then, has rejected anything that mildly approaches the orthodox definition of revolution. He sees the struggle of black people in apocalyptic, almost mystical terms, in which questions of ideology have no place. Baldwin's thinking is guided by simple commonsense notions of 'right is might', and 'truth will prevail'.

Equally he refuses to see black nationalism as the way forward, a stance he has made clear in all of his writing and earned him frequent accusations of "sell out". "I am not a black nationalist but some of my best friends are", he quipped. "Why aren't I a black nationalist? Because I don't believe it is enough to be black—one has to be human as well. We did not struggle for four hundred years just to become like the white man".

And he recalls the time when he was sitting with Malcolm X and his new baby. "I said: 'Malcolm are you trying to tell me if that child were white you would dash it to the floor because it's a devil's child?' Well, it was a difficult question and he couldn't answer it. Then he went to Mecca and when he returned I knew I didn't need to ask him that question anymore. It was then that American society began regarding him as dangerous".

Baldwin's vision of the world is a deeply humanistic one. He believes that the brotherhood of man, freed from the trap of colour, will eventually and inevitably prevail. Baldwin is first and foremost a thinker, an observer. The Atlanta killings, the subject of one of his latest essays, is an indication of the desperateness of American society today, he says. But despite this he confidently predicts, perhaps prophesies, that his vision will be a reality within the next half century.

"When the South African miner steps out of the mine, the party's over; now that's not going to take a thousand years," he says with steady conviction.

An Interview with Josephine Baker and James Baldwin

Henry Louis Gates, Jr./1985

From *The Southern Review*, 21 (July 1985), 594-602. Reprinted by permission of Brandt & Brandt Literary Agents, Inc.

In 1973, Henry Louis Gates, Jr., was in Paris interviewing black American expatriates. He sought to know why, after the "gains" of the sixties, so many black Americans still found it necessary to live abroad. In addition to interviewing Leroy Haynes, proprietor of a Parisian Soul Food restaurant, Beauford Delaney, painter, and Bob Reid, musician, Gates interviewed Josephine Baker and James Baldwin. Although some twelve years have passed since these interviews, the observations and comments of Baker and Baldwin offer us insights into the expatriate experience then, and America now.

The interview with Josephine Baker began in her home, "Villa Maryvonne," in Monte Carlo. Later, while she and Gates were dinner guests at James Baldwin's home in St. Paul-de-Vence in the south of France, Gates concluded his interview with Baker and interviewed Baldwin. Although all of the conversation over dinner that night was not preserved, Baker's and Baldwin's responses to Gates's questions were. The individual interviews I have edited to read as a single conversation so that the genial ambience of that evening in St. Paul could be captured. Gates speaks of that evening and the events that led up to it in his own introduction to this piece.—Anthony Barthelemy

So many questions that I should have asked that night, but did not! I was so captivated by the moment: under the widest star-filled evening sky that I can remember, in the backyard of Baldwin's villa at St. Paul, drunk on conversation, burgundy, and a peasant stew, drunk on the fact that James Baldwin and Josephine Baker were seated on my right and left. It was my twenty-second summer; a sublime awe, later that evening, led me to tears.

Those few days in the south of France probably had more to do with my subsequent career as a literary critic than any other single event. At the time, I was a correspondent at the London bureau of *Time* magazine, a training that is, probably, largely responsible for the quantity of my later critical writing, and for its anecdotal opening paragraphs. I had just graduated from Yale College in June, as a Scholar of the House in History. *Time*, to even my great surprise, had hired me to work as a correspondent during the six month collective vacations at the Univeristy of Cambridge. I figured that I would "read" philosophy or literature at Cambridge, take the M.A. degree, then join permanently the staff at *Time*.

So, I sailed to Southampton from New York on the *France* in June, 1973. After a week of pure fright and anxiety—after all, what *does* a *Time* correspondent *do*?, and *how?*—I decided to go for my fantasy. I proposed doing a story on "Black Expatriates," perhaps every young Afro-American would-be-intellectual's dream. To my astonishment, the story suggestion was approved. So, off we (Sharon Adams, to whom I am married, and I) went by boat, train, and automobile to Europe, in search of blackness and black people.

In the Paris bureau of *Time*—Paris was the only logical point of departure, after all—I dialed Jo Baker's phone number. (*Time* can get to virtually *anyone*.) She answered her own phone! Stumbling around, interrupting my tortured speech with loads of "uh's" and "um's," I asked her if she would allow me to interview her. On one condition, she responded: "Bring Jimmy Baldwin with you to Monte Carlo." Not missing a beat, I promised that I would bring him with me.

Baldwin agreed to see me, after I had begged one of his companions and told him that I was heading south anyway to see Jo Baker. Cecil Brown, the companion told me, was living there as well, so maybe I could interview him as well? Cecil Brown, I thought. Def-i-nite-ly! (*Jive-ass Nigger* had been a cult classic among us younger nationalists in the early seventies.) So, off we went.

Imagine sitting on a train, from Paris to Nice, on the hottest night of August, 1973, wondering how I could drag Baldwin from St. Paul to Monte Carlo, and scared to death of Baldwin in the first place. It was a thoroughly Maalox evening; to top everything else, our train broke down in a tunnel. We must have lost twenty pounds in that tunnel. Finally, just after dawn, we arrived at Nice, rented a car, then drove the short distance to St. Paul.

After the best midday meal that I had ever eaten, before or since, I trekked with great trepidation over to Baldwin's "house." "When I grow up . . . ," I remember thinking as I walked through the gate. I won't bore you with details; suffice it to say that if you ever get the chance to have dinner with Jimmy Baldwin at his house at St. Paul, then *do* it. "Maybe *I* could write *Notes of a Native Son* if I lived here," I thought.

I am about to confess something that literary critics should not confess: James Baldwin *was* literature for me, especially the essay. No doubt like everyone who is reading these pages, I started reading "black books" avidly, voraciously, at the age of thirteen or fourteen. I read *everything* written by black authors that could be ordered from Red Bowl's paper store in Piedmont, West Virginia. Le Roi Jones's *Home* and *Blues People*, Malcolm's *Autobiography*, and *Invisible Man* moved me beyond words—beyond my own experience, which is even a further piece, I would suppose. But nothing could surpass my love for the Complete Works of James Baldwin. In fact, I have never before written about Baldwin just because I cannot read his words outside of an extremely personal nexus of adolescent sensations and emotions. "Poignancy" only begins to describe those feelings. I learned to love written literature, of any sort, through the language of James Baldwin.

When Baldwin came into the garden to be interviewed, I was so excited that I could not blink back the tears. That probably explains why he suggested that we begin with wine. Well into that first (of several) bottles, I confessed to him my promise to Jo Baker. Not missing a beat, he told me to bring Jo *here*. Did he think that she would drive back from Monte Carlo with me? Just tell her that dinner is served at nine.

And she did, after a warm and loving lunch with her family (we met *eleven* of the legendary twelve children), at her favorite restaurant overlooking Cape Martin. She had recently returned from a pilgrimage to Israel, and was looking forward to her return to the stage, her marvelous comeback. She was tall, as gracious and as warm as she was elegant, sensuous at sixty-five. Pablo this; Robeson that; Salvador so and so: she had been friends with the Western tradition, and its modernists. Everywhere we drove, people waved from the sidewalks or ran over to the car. She was so very *thoughtful*, so intellectual, and so learned of the sort of experience that, perhaps, takes six decades or so to ferment. I cannot drink a glass of Cantenac Brown without recreating her in its bouquet.

How did all of this lead to my present career? *Time* would not print the story, because, they said, "Baldwin is passé, and Baker a memory of the thirties and forties." My narrative remains unpublished, but shall appear in a new essay collection called *With the Flow*. When I went "up" to Cambridge from *Time* and London in October, 1973, I was so angered by the idiocy of that decision that I threw myself into the B.A. curriculum for English Language and Literature. A year later, I was admitted into the Ph.D. program, and four years later, I was awarded my degree.

That evening was the very last time that my two heroes saw each other, and the last time that Jo Baker would be interviewed at her home. She would die, on the stage, too soon thereafter. One day I hope to be forced to write about my other hero, James Baldwin.— HLG

Gates: Mrs. Baker, why did you leave the United States?

Baker: I left in 1924, but the roots extend long before that. One of the first things I remember was the East St. Louis Race Riots (1906). I was hanging on to my mother's skirts, I was so little. All the sky was red with people's houses burning. On the bridge, there were running people with their tongues cut out. There was a woman who'd been pregnant with her insides cut out. That was the beginning of my feeling.

One day I realized I was living in a country where I was afraid to be black. It was only a country for white people, not black, so I left. I had been suffocating in the United States. I can't live anywhere that I can't breathe freedom. I must be free. Haven't I that right? I was created free. No chains did I wear when I came here. A lot of us left, not because we wanted to leave, but because we couldn't stand it anymore. Branded, banded, cut off. Canada Lee, Dr. Dubois, Paul Robeson, Marcus Garvey—all of us, forced to leave.

Gates: Did the French people offer you a respite from race prejudice?

Baker: The French adopted me immediately. They all went to the beaches to get dark like Josephine Baker. They had a contest to see who could be the darkest, like Josephine Baker, they said. The French got sick, trying to get black—café au lait—you weren't anything unless you were café au lait.

I felt liberated in Paris. People didn't stare at me. But when I heard an American accent in the streets of Paris, I became afraid. I would tremble in my stomach. I was afraid they'd humiliate me.

I was afraid to go into prominent restaurants in Paris. Once, I dined in a certain restaurant with friends. An American lady looked at our table and called the waiter. "Tell her to get out," the lady said. "In my country, she is belonging only in the kitchen." The French management asked the American lady to leave. To tell the truth, I was afraid of not being wanted.

Gates: Mr. Baldwin, when did you leave the United States and for what reasons?

Baldwin: It was November, 1948, Armistice Day as a matter of fact. I left because I was a writer. I had discovered writing and I had a family to save. I had only one weapon to save them, my writing. And I couldn't write in the United States.

Gates: But why did you flee to France?

Baldwin: I had to go somewhere where I could learn that it was possible for me to thrive as a writer. The French, you see, didn't see me; on the other hand, they watched me. Some people took care of me. Else I would have died. But the French left me alone.

Gates: Was it important for you to be left alone?

Baldwin: The only thing standing between my writing had to be me: it was I, it was me—I had to see that. Because the French left me alone, I was freed of crutches, the crutches of race. That's a scary thing.

Gates: Did you find any basic differences between Americans and Europeans, since you said that you could at least be left alone in Paris?

Baldwin: There was a difference, but now the difference is a superficial one. When I first came to Paris, it was poor—everybody was broke. Now, Europe thinks it has something again, that it has regained the material things it lost. So Europeans are becoming

Americans. The irony, of course, is that Europe began the trend even
before America was formed. The price of becoming "American" is
beating the hell out of everybody else.

Gates: Mrs. Baker, you said you felt "liberated" in France. Did the
freedom you found here in France sour you towards the United
States?

Baker: I love the country within which I was born. These people
are my people. I don't care what color they are—we are all Americans. We must have the application to stand up again.

Once I fought against the discriminatory laws in America but
America was strong then. Now, she is weak. I only want to extend my
fingers to pull it out of the quicksand, because that's where it is. I
have all the hope in the world, though. The storm will come; we can't
stop it. But that's all right. America will still be—but it will be the
America it was intended to be. We were a small train on the track.
We fell off. We'll get on again.

Gates: Where do you think the United States is heading, with
distrust in government so apparent, with Watergate attracting world-
wide attention?

Baker: America was the promised land. I just want to give them
my spirit; they've lost the path. That makes me suffer. I was so
unhappy in the United States; I saw my brothers and sisters so afraid.
The problem is deep—it has long roots. It is basic. The soil must be
purified, not only must the root be pruned. It makes me unhappy to
think that—I wouldn't be human if I weren't made unhappy by that.
Needlessly, people will suffer. They need someone who can give
them more than money. Someone to offer his hand, not just his
money.

Gates: Mr. Baldwin, do you think that Watergate is a new, a
significant departure in American history, or do you think it is the
logical extension of policies begun long before Nixon, before this
century even?

Baldwin: Simply stated, Watergate was a bunch of incompetent
hoods who got caught in the White House in the name of law and
order.

Gates: Do you think the public hearings, indictments, and possible
convictions could purge America, could allow it to change those
things which you do not like about it?

Baldwin: America is my country. Not only am I fond of it, I love it.

America would change itself if it could, if that change didn't hurt, but people rarely change. Take the German people, for example. The German experiment during the war was catastrophic. It was a horror not to be believed. But they haven't changed: the German nation is basically the same today as it was before the war.

In a different sense, it is easy to be a rebel at age eighteen; it is harder to be one at age twenty-five. A nation may change when it realizes it has to. But people don't give up things. They have things taken away from them. One does not give up a lover; you lose her.

Gates: What do you see as the significance of Vietnam to America?

Baker: I won't criticize America today. She is weak. I said all this years ago. It all came true. But it is never too late. It can be saved, but we Americans are so proud—false dignity, though. It's nothing to be ashamed about to acknowledge our mistakes; Vietnam was a mistake. All that money for no progress, that turned the whole world against America.

But actually, My Lai happened first with the Indians. We brought on our own enemies—nobody, no matter how powerful, needs enemies.

Gates: Did you ever regret that you had left the United States, or did you ever feel guilty, particularly during the Civil Rights Era, for not being there to participate?

Baker: Some of my own people called me an Uncle Tom; they said I was more French than the French. I've thought often about your question, about running away from the problem. At first, I wondered if it was cowardice, wondered whether I should have stayed to fight. But I couldn't have done anything. I would have been thwarted in ways in which I was free in France. I probably would have been killed.

But really, I belong to the world now. You know, America represented that: people coming from all over to make a nation. But America has forgotten that. I love all people at the same time. Our country is people of all countries. How else could there have been an America? And they made a beautiful nation. Each one depositing a little of his own beauty.

It's a sad thing to leave your country. How very often I've felt like the Wandering Jew with my twelve children on my arms. I've been able to bear it, though. It might be a mistake to love my country where brothers are humiliated, where they kill each other, but I do love it. We are a wealthy people, a cultivated people. I wish people there would love. They can't go on like that. There's going to be a horrible storm. It's going to be a disaster. They'll torture each other through hate. It's ironic: people ran from slavery in Europe to find freedom in America, and now. . . .

Gates: Why don't you return to live in America now; aren't things a lot better for blacks?

Baker: I don't think I could help America. I want to be useful, where I can help. America is desperate. In New York last year, I regretted for the first time not being young again. Young Americans need understanding and love. Children don't want to hear words; they want to see examples, not words—not blah, blah, blah—profound love, without malice, without hate.

Gates: When did you eventually return to the United States and why?

Baker: It was in 1963. I kept reading about the "March on Washington," about preparation for the march. I so much wanted to attend. But I was afraid they wouldn't let me.

You see, for years I was not allowed to enter the United States. They said I was a Communist, during President Eisenhower's administration. They would make a black soldier—to humiliate me—they would make a black soldier lead me from a plane to a private room. It was so terrible, so painful. But I survived.

Then, in 1963, we applied to President Kennedy for permission to go to the March on Washington. He issued me a permanent visa. I wore the uniform I went through the war with, with all its medals. Thank God for John Kennedy for helping me get into America.

They had humiliated me so much; but still, I love them as if nothing happened. They didn't know what they were doing—digging their own grave through their hate. Then came Vietnam.

Gates: So you were actually forbidden to return to the United States between 1924 and 1963?

Baker: Yes. They said I was a Communist because I dared love—thrown out for preferring freedom to riches, feelings to gold. I am not to be sold; no one can buy me. I lost America; I had nothing in my pockets, but I had my soul. I was so rich. For all this, they called me a

Communist. America drives some of its most sensitive people away. Take Jimmy Baldwin: he had to leave the States to say what he felt.

Gates: And what were your first impressions of life in "exile"?

Baldwin: I was no longer a captive nigger. I was the exotic attraction of the beast no longer in the cage. People paid attention. Of course you must realize that I am remembering the impression years later.

Gates: Did life abroad give you any particular insight into American society?

Baldwin: I realized that the truth of American history was not and had never been in the White House. The truth is what had happened to black people, since slavery.

Gates: What do you think characterized Europeans to make them more ready to accept you at a time when you felt uncomfortable living in America?

Baker: America has only been around for less than four hundred years; that's not a long time, really. Apparently it takes more than that to realize that a human being is a human being. Europeans are more basic. They see colors of the skin as colors of nature, like the flowers, for example.

Gates: Did you find any difference between the manner in which French men and women viewed you as a black man?

Baldwin: That's a very important question. Before the Algerian war, and that's crucial in this, the black man did not exist in the French imagination; neither did the Algerian. After Dien Bien Phu, and after the "Civil War" as the French persist in calling it, there began to be a discernible difference between the way women and police had treated you before and after the war.

Gates: But were black Americans treated like Algerians were during their quest for independence?

Baldwin: Of course I was removed, but you became a personal threat as a black American. You were a threat because you were visible. The French became conscious of your visibility because of the Algerians. You see, the French did not and don't know what a black man is. They'd like to put the blacks against the Algerians, to divide and rule, but the Arabs and black Americans were both slaves, one group was the slaves in Europe, the other back in America.

Gates: But surely you must believe that social change can come, that great men can effect change?

Baldwin: Change does come, but not when or in the ways we want it to come. George Jackson, Malcolm X—now people all over the world were changed by them. Because they told the secret; now, the secret was out.

Gates: And the secret?

Baldwin: Put it this way. In 1968, along with Lord Caradon (British Delegate to the United Nations then), I addressed an assembly of the World Council of Churches in Switzerland on "white racism or world community?" When Lord Caradon was asked why the West couldn't break relations with South Africa, he brought out charts and figures that showed that the West would be bankrupt if they did that: the prosperity of the West is standing on the back of the South African miner. When he stands up, the whole thing will be over.

Gates: How do you assess the results of the war in Vietnam on the American people?

Baldwin: Americans are terrified. For the first time they know that they are capable of genocide. History is built on genocide. But they can't face it. And it doesn't make any difference what Americans think that they think—they are terrified.

Gates: From your vantage point, where do you think not only America but Western Civilization is heading?

Baldwin: The old survivals of my generation will be wiped out. Western Civilization is heading for an apocalypse.

An Interview with James Baldwin
David C. Estes/1986

From *New Orleans Review* 13 (Fall 1986), 59-64. Reprinted by permission.

As essayist, James Baldwin has written about life in Harlem, Paris, Atlanta; about Martin Luther King, Malcolm X, Jimmie Carter; and about Richard Wright, Lorraine Hansberry, Norman Mailer. In examining contemporary culture he has turned his attention to politics, literature, the movies—and most importantly to his own self. To each subject he has brought the conviction, stated in the 1953 essay "Stranger in the Village," that "the interracial drama acted out on the American continent has not only created a new black man, it has created a new white man, too." Thus he has consistently chosen as his audience Americans, both black and white, and has offered them instruction about the failings and possibilities of their unique national society. Several of the essays in *Notes of a Native Son* (1955), published two years after his first novel, *Go Tell It on the Mountain*, are regarded as contemporary classics because of their polished style and timeless insights. *The Price of the Ticket: Collected Nonfiction 1948-1985* marks his long, productive career as essayist. It includes over forty shorter pieces as well as three book-length essays—*The Fire Next Time* (1963), *No Name in the Street* (1972), and *The Devil Finds Work* (1976). Baldwin's most recent book is *The Evidence of Things Not Seen* (1985), a meditation on the Atlanta child-murder case. It is his troubled and troubling personal re-encounter with "the terror of being destroyed" that dominates the inescapable memories of his own early life in America.

Why did you take on the project to write about Wayne Williams and the Atlanta child murders? What did you expect to find when you began the research for The Evidence of Things Not Seen?

It was thrown into my lap. I had not thought about doing it at all. My friend Walter Lowe of *Playboy* wrote me in the south of France to think about doing an essay concerning this case, about which I knew very little. There had not been very much in the French press. So I didn't quite know what was there, although it bugged me. I was a little afraid to do it, to go to Atlanta. Not because of Atlanta—I'd been there before—but because I was afraid to get involved in it and I wasn't sure I wanted to look any further.

It was an ongoing case. The boy was in jail and there were other developments in the city and among the parents and details which I've blotted out completely which drove me back to Atlanta several times to make sure I got the details right. The book is not a novel nor really an essay. It involves living, actual human beings. And there you get very frightened. You don't want to make inaccuracies. It was the first time I had ever used a tape recorder. I got hours of tape. At one moment I thought I was going crazy. I went to six, or seven, or eight places where the bodies had been found. After the seventh or the eighth, I realized I couldn't do that any more.

There is a sense in the book that you were trying to keep your distance, especially from the parents of both the victims and the murderer. In fact, you state at one point in it that you "never felt more of an interloper, a stranger" in all of your journeys than you did in Atlanta while researching this case.

It wasn't so much that I was trying to keep my distance, although that is certainly true. It was an eerie moment when you realize that you always ask "How are the kids?" I stopped asking. When I realized that, I realized I'm nuts. What are you going to say to the parents of a murdered child? You feel like an interloper when you walk in because no matter how gently you do it you are invading something. Grief, privacy, I don't know how to put that. I don't mean that they treated me that way. They were beautiful. But I felt that there was something sacred about it. One had to bury that feeling in order to do the project. It was deeper than an emotional reaction; I don't have any word for it.

It wasn't that I was keeping my distance from the parents. I was keeping a distance from my own pain. The murder of children is the most indefensible form of murder that there is. It was certainly for me the most unimaginable. I can imagine myself murdering you in a rage, or my lover, or my wife. I can understand that, but I don't understand how anyone can murder a child.

The carefully controlled structure of your earlier essays is absent from Evidence.

I had to risk that. What form or shape could I give it? It was not something that I was carrying in my imagination. It was something quite beyond my imagination. All I could really hope to do was write a fairly coherent report in which I raise important questions. But the reader is not going to believe a word I say, so I had to suggest far more than I could state. I had to raise some questions without seeming to raise them. Some questions are unavoidably forbidden.

Because you are an accomplished novelist, why didn't you use the approach of the New Journalism and tell the story of Wayne Williams by relying on the techniques of fiction?

It doesn't interest me, and I've read very little of it. Truman Capote's *In Cold Blood* is a very pretty performance, but in my mind it illustrates the ultimate pitfall of that particular approach. To put it another way, when I write a play or a novel, I write the ending and am responsible for it. Tolstoy has every right to throw Anna Karenina under the train. She begins in his imagination, and he has to take responsibility for her until the reader does. But the life of a living human being, no one writes it. You cannot deal with another human being as though he were a fictional creation.

I couldn't fictionalize the story of the Atlanta murders. It's beyond my province and would be very close to blasphemy. I might be able to fictionalize it years from now when something has happened to me and I can boil down the residue of the eyes of some of the parents and some of the children. I'm sure that will turn up finally in fiction because it left such a profound mark on me. But in dealing with it directly as an event that was occurring from day to day, it did not even occur to me to turn it into fiction, which would have been beyond my power. It was an event which had been written by a much greater author than I.

Reflecting on the writing of the New Journalists, I think the great difficulty or danger is not to make the event an occasion for the exhibition of your virtuosity. You must look to the event.

In other words, style can take away from the event itself.

In a way. I'm speaking only for myself, but I wouldn't want to use the occasion of the children as an occasion to show off. I don't think a writer ever should show off, anyway. Saul Bellow would say to me years and years ago, "Get that fancy footwork out of there." The hardest part of developing a style is that you have to learn to trust your voice. If I thought of my style I'd be crippled. Somebody else said to me a long time ago in France, "Find out what you can do, and then don't do it."

What has been the reaction to Evidence *in France where you are living?*

Because of some difficulty in arranging for the American publication, it appeared first there in a French version. They take it as an examination of a social crisis with racial implications, but a social crisis. The most honest of the critics are not afraid to compare it to the situation of the Algerian and African in Paris. In a way, it's not too much to say that some of them take it as a kind of warning. There is a great upsurge on the right in France, and a great many people are disturbed by that. So the book does not translate to them as a provincial, parochial American problem.

Were you conscious of the international implications of the case while you were writing?

I was thinking about it on one level, but for me to write the book was simply putting blinders on a horse. On either side was the trap of rage or the trap of sorrow. I had never run into this problem in writing a book before.

I was doing a long interview in Lausanne, and it suddenly happened that I could see one of those wide intervals. I was asked a question, and with no warning at all the face, body, and voice of one of the parents suddenly came back to me. I was suddenly back in that room, hearing that voice and seeing that face, and I had to stop the interview for a few minutes. Then I understood something.

What seem to be the European perceptions of contemporary American black writers in general?

A kind of uneasy bewilderment. Until very lately Europe never felt menaced by black people because they didn't see them. Now they are beginning to see them and are very uneasy. You have to realize that just after the war when the American black GI arrived he was a great, great wonder for Europe because he had nothing whatever to do with the Hollywood image of the Negro which was the only image they had. They were confronted with something they had not imagined. They didn't quite know where he came from. He came from America, of course, but America had come from Europe. Now that is beginning to be clear, and the reaction is a profound uneasiness. So the voice being heard from black writers also attacks the European notion of their identity. If I'm not what you thought I was, who are you?

Now that your collected non-fiction has appeared in The Price of the Ticket, *what reflections about your career as an essayist do you have as you look back over these pieces?*
   It actually was not my idea to do that book, but there was no point in refusing it either. But there was also something frightening about it. It's almost forty years, after all. On one level it marks a definitive end to my youth and the beginning of something else. No writer can judge his work. I don't think I've ever tried to judge mine. You just have to trust it. I've not been able to read the book, but I remember some of the moments when I wrote this or that. So in some ways it's a kind of melancholy inventory, not so much about myself as a writer (I'm not melancholy about that), but I think that what I found hard to decipher is to what extent or in what way my ostensible subject has changed. Nothing in the book could be written that way today.
   My career began when I was twenty-one or twenty-two in *The New Leader.* That was a very important time in my life. I had never intended to become an essayist. But it came about because of Saul Levitas who assigned me all these books to review. I will never know quite why he did that. I had to write a book review a week, and it was very good for me. You can always find turning points looking back, but there was one very long review of *Raintree County,* a novel about an America I had never seen. Between the time that I turned in the review and its publication, the author Ross Lockridge committed suicide. It was very shocking because it was such a sun-lit, optimistic book that had won every prize in sight. But he had blown his brains out. That marked me in a way. I didn't feel guilty about it since he hadn't read my review, but it struck me with great force. It was from

that point, in hindsight, that I began to be considered an essayist by other people.

Later, at *Commentary* I had a marvelous relationship with one of the editors—Robert Warshow, my first real editor. He asked me to do an essay about the Harlem ghetto. When I turned it in, Robert said, "Do it over." He didn't say anything more. So I did. And then he said, "You know more than that." I began to be aware of what he was doing. When he saw me come close to what I was afraid of, he circled it and said, "Tell me more about that." What I was afraid of was the relationship between Negroes and Jews in Harlem—afraid on many levels. I'd never consciously thought about it before, but then it began to hit me on a profound and private level because many of my friends were Jews, although they had nothing to do with the Jewish landlords and pawnbrokers in the ghetto. So I had been blotting it out. It was with Robert that I began to be able to talk about it, and that was a kind of liberation for me. I'm in his debt forever because after that I was clear in my own mind. I suddenly realized that perhaps I had been afraid to talk about it because I was a closet anti-Semite myself. One always has that terror. And then I realized that I wasn't. So something else was opened.

What major artistic problems have you had to confront in your non-fiction?

I was a black kid and was expected to write from that perspective. Yet I had to realize the black perspective was dictated by the white imagination. Since I wouldn't write from the perspective, essentially, of the victim, I had to find what my own perspective was and then use it. I couldn't talk about "them" and "us." So I had to use "we" and let the reader figure out who "we" is. That was the only possible choice of pronoun. It had to be "we." And we had to figure out who "we" was, or who "we" is. That was very liberating for me.

I was going through a whole lot of shit in New York because I was black, because I was always in the wrong neighborhood, because I was small. It was dangerous, and I was in a difficult position because I couldn't find a place to live. I was always being thrown out, fighting landlords. My best friend committed suicide when I was twenty-two, and I could see that I was with him on that road. I knew exactly what happened to him—everything that happened to me. The great battle

was not to interiorize the world's condemnation, not to see yourself as
the world saw you, and also not to depend on your skill. I was very
skillful—much more skillful than my friend, much more ruthless, too.
In my own mind I had my family to save. I could not go under; I
could not afford to. Yet I knew that I was going under. And at the
very same moment I was writing myself up to a wall. I knew I
couldn't continue. It was too confining. I wrote my first two short
stories, and then I split.

*You said earlier that you never intended to become an essayist.
Did you ever consider one or the other of the genres in which you
worked as being more important than another?*
No, as a matter of fact I didn't. I thought of myself as a writer. I
didn't want to get trapped in any particular form. I wanted to try
them all. That's why I say I remember having written myself into a
wall. Significantly enough, the first thing I wrote when I got to Paris
and got myself more or less together was the essay "Everybody's
Protest Novel"—a summation of all the years I was reviewing those
"be kind to niggers" and "be kind to Jews" books. There was a
mountain of them, and every one came across my desk. I had to get
out of that, and "Everybody's Protest Novel" was my declaration of
independence. Then I began to finish my first novel and did
Giovanni's Room, which was another declaration of independence.
And then I was in some sense, if not free, clear.

*A striking feature of your work is the great amount of autobio-
graphical material that finds its way into essays which are not
primarily autobiographical.*
Well, I had to use myself as an example.

When did you realize that you should use yourself in this way?
It was not so much that I realized that I should. It was that I realized
I couldn't avoid it. I was the only witness I had. I had the idea that
most people found me a hostile black boy; I was not that. I had to
find a way to make them know it, and the only way was to use
myself.

*Does it take some measure of audacity to write autobiography, to
expect readers to find your personal life of interest to them?*
It didn't occur to me to be audacious. It occurred to me, first of all,

to be very frightening. Rather than audacity, it involved a great deal of humility to use myself as a witness, which is different from an example, to the condition of others who are in your condition but cannot speak—or cannot be heard. Jimmie Baldwin himself as a subject is not very interesting. There's nothing special about my life in that way at all. Everybody suffers. Everybody has to make choices. It was only in my social situation that I had to use my personal dilemma to illuminate something. I repeat, I am not speaking from the point of view of the victim. I am speaking as a person who has a right to be here. That's where the humility comes in, for you're setting yourself up to be corrected.

Which works have given you more insight into yourself, your fiction or your autobiographical accounts?
The essay called "Notes of a Native Son" was risky trying to deal with the relationship between me and my father and to extrapolate that into a social question. That's risky. On the other hand, *Giovanni's Room* was risky, too, in a very different way. I wouldn't say in a more personal way, but I knew very well what I was setting myself for when I wrote the book. I knew that, too, when I wrote "Notes," but it was much more direct. It involved not only me and my father, but also my family. There was always that delicacy because you are revealing not only your own secrets but those of other people. You simply have to realize that is what you are doing and you don't quite know what the consequences will be.

As you have grown older, have you ever wanted to retell an incident in your life about which you have already written?
No. I couldn't anyway. Every writer has only one tale to tell, and he has to find a way of telling it until the meaning becomes clearer and clearer, until the story becomes at once more narrow and larger, more and more precise and more and more reverberating.

On numerous occasions you have written about your teenage years. Yet the focus always changes. For example, the most recent account in "Here Be Dragons" touches on homosexual experiences, a subject not mentioned in "Notes of a Native Son."
You begin to see more than you did before in the same event. It reveals itself—more. There's more to it. It's not a conscious decision

to refashion the anecdote. In time one of the things that happens is that you become less frightened because there's less to be frightened of—quite unconsciously. This is not something which is cerebral. I don't know whether you can hunt more and more of your own life or if more and more of your own life will hunt you, but it comes back to you during points in your life in another light. One's relationship to the past changes. Yet that boy, the boy I was, still controls the man I am. If I didn't know as much as I think I do know about that boy, I would still be his prisoner. This happens to many people who are effectively stopped between the ages of seventeen and twenty and when they are fifty or sixty are still imprisoned by the boy or girl they have been. Perhaps what I'm saying is that all the action is to understand enough to be liberated from first of all one's terror and then one's self-image, to keep moving into a larger space.

In the preface to Evidence *you state that "no one wishes to be plunged, head down, into the torrent of what he does not remember and does not wish to remember." Am I correct that this suggests your reluctance to write autobiographical accounts?*

Certainly not so very long ago I was reluctant—terrified. Well, I'm still terrified. But I think that in time terror begins to be a kind of luxury; you can't do anything with it, but it can do a lot with you. You have to learn how to ride it. When I was writing *Just Above My Head*, I'd never been more frightened in my life either as a man or as a writer. Yet I knew it had to be done. That book is not directly autobiographical at all, but it is autobiographical on a much deeper level. There are elements which you can place in my life. My brother was once a member of a quartet in the Deep South, for example. Yet there are no direct, one-on-one relationships between my life and the lives of the people in that book. It truly is a composite. A novel or anything I write begins with an incoherent disturbance, and you can't run away from it. You have to sit and wait and see what it is. It may be the things I've forgotten or think I've forgotten that suddenly begin to stir.

What do you think readers hope to find in autobiographies?

Somebody said to me once that it's not so much what happens as who it happens to. The sound of the voice is the key; without that it's false.

In No Name in the Street *you say that "no one knows how identities are forged, but it is safe to say identities are not invented." What do you feel is the relationship between writing an autobiography and the forging of an identity?*

You have to be aware of the temptation to invent, which is the same thing as the temptation to evade. You have to be aware that you would not like to violate your self-image, and on the other hand at the very same moment, you have to be aware that your self-image is entirely false. You have to discard your self-image. You don't have to be corrected by your public; you can be corrected by your friends or your lovers. They see you quite beyond your self-image in a way you don't see yourself. And without that you couldn't live at all. I'm writing for the people who would know if I were lying. They can call me on it. Otherwise, I'd be locked into my own fantasy.

The stormy reception of William Styron's Confessions of Nat Turner, *although fictional, seems to illustrate what you are saying about how the image an autobiography presents can be challenged. What are your reactions now to that controversy and your defense of Styron at the time?*

Looking back, I feel I would do the same thing. I happen to like the novel. I was working at Bill's house when he was doing *Nat Turner*, and we used to talk about it—or around it—from time to time. Bill comes from Virginia where the insurrection occurred. So it seemed to me that it was part of my inheritance and was also part of his. I didn't read the book so much as a confession of Nat Turner but as a confession of Bill Styron, and I don't mean that as a "put-down." He had taken an historical event which belongs to everybody and especially to the man it torments the most, and he tried to make some kind of peace with it, to tell the truth—very much like Faulkner, although I didn't always agree with Faulkner, especially as he got older. It's one of those books which proves what I'm always saying, that history is not the past, but the present. In any case, I thought Bill's book was a very honest, very honorable job, and when he was attacked, I didn't think it was fair at all. My position was if you don't like his Nat Turner, write yours.

What is your vision of the America to which you must respond as a writer?

This is a curiously and dangerously fragmented society while, perhaps unlike any society in the past, it has all the stirrings of well-being. It has at its back the resonance of the American Dream and the history of conquest. But it is also based on a lie, the lie of Manifest Destiny. So it's a country immobilized, with a past it cannot explain away. That's why everyone's so cheerful, and the Americans who are crying have to be cheerful. Everyone is friendly, and nobody is friends. Everybody has something to hide, and when you have to hide, you have to cry for despair. Despair is the American crime. So one is trapped in a kind of Sunday purgatory, and the only way out of that is to confront what you are afraid of. The American image of the black face contains everything America most wants and everything that terrifies it. It also contains the castrations, the lynchings, the burnings, the continual daily and hourly debasements of life, and you cannot do those things without doing something to yourself.

Do you feel that artists in such a nation as ours can find an audience willing to listen to them?

The artist cannot attempt to answer that question because if he does he'll go mad. The public is going to assume you are a success or a failure, the book was a hit or not. The publisher looks at the market. But if you depend on the market, you might as well become a traveling salesman. The artist has to assume that he creates his audience and that the audience won't be there until he starts to work. The artist is responsible for his audience, which may exist in his lifetime or may never exist until long after he is dead. The artist has to realize that commerce is only a detail. If you try to beat your last success, you stop writing. It's a high risk endeavor.

Last Testament: An Interview with James Baldwin

Quincy Troupe/1988

From *The Village Voice*, 12 January 1988, p. 36. Reprinted by permission.

On November 13 and 14, 1987, writer Quincy Troupe interviewed James Baldwin at his home in St. Paul de Vence, France. It was to be the last known public commentary from Baldwin the writer, a man who had been labeled a firebrand, a polemicist, a man in self-imposed exile—a man whom Amiri Baraka termed in his eulogy, "God's revolutionary mouth." The interview reveals, however, a man who struggled with imposed identities—as a young minister, as a writer, and as a man.

While many writers live with the fear and inspiration that what needs to be said has still not been said, Baldwin warns that "it's been said, and it's been said. It's been heard and not heard." The interview, too lengthy to print here in its entirety, has been excerpted. As it begins Troupe and Baldwin have been talking about Baldwin's friend trumpeter Miles Davis, which leads Baldwin into some thought on living with fame.

—Thulani Davis

James Baldwin: It's difficult to be a legend. It's hard for me to recognize *me*. You spend a lot of time trying to avoid it. It's really something, to be a legend, unbearable. The way the world treats you is unbearable, and especially if you're black. It's unbearable because time is passing and you are not your legend, but you're trapped in it. Nobody will let you out of it. Except other people who know what it is. But very few people have experienced it, know about it, and I think that can drive you mad; I know it can. I know it can.

You have to be lucky. You have to have friends. I think at bottom you have to be serious. No one can point it out to you; you have to

281

see it yourself. That's the only way you can act on it. And when it arrives it's a great shock.

Quincy Troupe: *To find out?*
It's a great shock to realize that you've been so divorced. So divorced from who you think you are—from who you really are. Who you think you are, you're not at all. . . . I don't know who I thought I was. I was a witness, I thought. I was a very despairing witness though, too. What I was actually doing was trying to avoid a certain estrangement perhaps, an estrangement between myself and my generation. It was virtually complete, the estrangement was, in terms of what I might have thought and expected—my theories. About what I might have hoped—I'm talking now in terms of one's function as an artist. And the country itself, being black and trying to deal with that.

Why do you think it occurred. That estrangement between your generation and the country?
Well, because I was right. That's a strange way to put it. I *was* right. I was right about what was happening in the country. What was about to happen to all of us really, one way or the another. And the choices people would have to make. And watching people make them and denying them at the same time. I began to feel more and more homeless in terms of the whole relationship between France and me, and America and *me* has always been a little painful, you know. Because my family's in America I will always go back. It couldn't have been a question in my mind. But in the meantime you keep the door open and the price of keeping the door open was to actually be, in a sense, victimized by my own legend.

You know, I was trying to tell the truth and it takes a long time to realize that you can't—that there's no point in going to the mat, so to speak, no point in going to Texas again. There's no point in saying this again. It's been said, and it's been said, and it's been said. It's been heard and not heard. You are a broken motor.

A broken motor?
Yes. You're a running motor and you're repeating, you're repeating, you're repeating and it causes a breakdown, lessening of will power. And sooner or later your will gives out—it has to. You're lucky

if it is a physical matter—most times it's spiritual. See, all this involves hiding from something else—not dealing with how lonely you are. And of course, at the very bottom it involves the terror of every artist confronted with what he or she has to do, you know, the next work. And everybody, in one way or another, and to some extent, tries to avoid it. And you avoid it more when you get older than you do when you're younger, still there's something terrifying about it, about doing the work.

O.K. Let's change the subject and talk about some writers. Amiri Baraka?

I remember the first time I met Amiri Baraka, who was then Leroi Jones. I was doing *The Amen Corner* and he was a student at Howard University. I liked him right away. He was a pop-eyed little boy poet. He showed me a couple of his poems. I liked them very much. And then he came to New York a couple of years later. He came to New York when I came back to New York from Paris. And by this time I knew the business. I'd been through the fucking business by that time. I was a survivor.

And I remember telling him that his agent wanted him to become the young James Baldwin. But I told him you're not the young James Baldwin. There's only one James Baldwin and you are Leroi Jones and there's only one Leroi Jones. Don't let them run this game on us, you know? You're Leroi Jones, I'm James Baldwin. And we're going to need each other. That's all I said. He didn't believe it then but time took care of that.

He believes it now?
Yes he knows it now.

What person has hurt you the most recently?
Ishmael Reed.

Why?
Because he is a great poet and it seemed to be beneath him. His anger and his contempt for me, which was both real, and not real. He ignored me for so long and then he called me a cock sucker, you know what I mean? It's boring. But I always did say he was a great poet, a great writer. But that does not mean I can put up with being insulted by him everytime I see him, which I won't.

What do you think about Toni Morrison?
Toni's my ally and it's really probably too complex to get into.
She's a black woman writer, which in the public domain makes it
more difficult to talk about.

What do you think are her gifts?
Her gift is in allegory. *Tar Baby* is an allegory. In fact all her novels
are. But they're hard to talk about in public. That's where you get in
trouble because her books and allegory are not always what they
seem to be about. I was too occupied with my recent illness to deal
with *Beloved*. But, in general, she's taken a myth, or she takes what
seems to be a myth, and turns it into something else. I don't know
how to put this—*Beloved* could be about the story of truth. She's
taken a whole lot of things and turned them upside down. Some of
them—you recognize the truth in it. I think that Toni's very painful to
read.

Why?
Because it's always, or most times, a horrifying allegory; but you
recognize that it works. But you don't really want to march through it.
Sometimes people have a lot against Toni, but she's got the most
believing story of everybody, this rather elegant matron, whose inten-
tions really are serious, and according to some people, lethal . . .

*We were talking once about the claustrophobia among writers. You
said you prefer actors and painters to writers.*
Yes. Well, first of all, when I was coming up there weren't any
writers that I knew. Langston Hughes was far away. The first writer I
met was Richard Wright and he was much older than me. And the
people I knew were people like Beauford Delaney and the women
who hung out with him; it was a whole world that was not literary.
That came later; then it wasn't literary. It came later in Paris, with
Sartre and others. But there was something else. And in Paris it had
nothing whatsoever to do with race for one thing. It was another kind
of freedom there altogether. It had nothing to do with literature. But
when I looked back on it years and years later, looked back at myself
on the American literary scene, I could see what almost happened to
me was an attempt to make myself fit in, so to speak, to wash myself
clean for the American literary academy.

You mean they wanted you scrubbed and squeaky clean?

Exactly. You have to be scrubbed and squeaky clean and then there's nothing left of you. Let me tell you a story.

When Ralph Ellison won the National Award in '52 for *Invisible Man*, I was up for it the next year, in 1953, for *Go Tell It on the Mountain*. But at the same time, I was far from scrubbed. I didn't win. Then, years later, someone who was on the jury told me that since Ralph won it the year before they couldn't give it to a Negro two years in a row. Now, isn't that something?

Once, after I published *Go Tell It on the Mountain* and *Giovanni's Room*, my publisher, Knopf, told me I was "a Negro writer" and that I reached "a certain audience." "So," they told me, "you cannot afford to alienate that audience. This new book will ruin your career because you're not writing about the same things and in the same manner as you were before and we won't publish this book as a favor to you."

As a favor to you?
So I told them, "Fuck you." My editor, whose name I won't mention here, is dead now, poor man. I told them that I needed a boat ticket. So I took a boat to England with my book and I sold it in England before I sold it in America. You see, whites want black writers to mostly deliver something as if it were an official version of the black experience. But the vocabulary won't hold it, simply. No true account really of black life can be held, can be contained, in the American vocabulary. As it is, the only way that you can deal with it is by doing great violence to the assumptions on which the vocabulary is based. But they won't let you do that.

And when you go along, you find yourself very quickly painted into a corner; you've written yourself into a corner—because you can't compromise as a writer. By the time I left America in 1948 I had written myself into a corner as I perceived it. The book reviews and the short essays had led me to a place where I.was on a collision course with the truth; it was the way I was operating. It was only a matter of time before I'd simply be destroyed by it. And no amount of manipulation of vocabulary or art would have spared me. It's like I think that Al Murray and Ralph Ellison are totally trapped. It's sad, because they're both trapped in the same way, and they're both very gifted writers.

But you can't do anything with America unless you are willing to dissect it. You certainly cannot hope to fit yourself into it; nothing fits into it, not your past, not your present. *The Invisible Man* is fine as far as it goes until you ask yourself who's invisible to whom? You know, what is this dichotomy supposed to do? Are we invisible before each other? And invisible why, and by what system can one hope to be invisible? I don't know how anything in American life is worthy of this sacrifice. And further, I don't see anything in American life—for myself—to aspire to. Nothing at all. It's all so very false, so shallow, so plastic, so morally and ethically corrupt.

James Baldwin, 1924-1987: A Tribute—
The Last Interview

Quincy Troupe/1988

From *Essence*, 18 (March 1988), 53, 114, 117, 119. Copyright © 1988 by *Essence* Communications, Inc. Reprinted by permission.

On November 13, 1987, I flew from Paris to Nice to visit the distinguished American writer James Baldwin. Jimmy was an old friend who quite generously and without fail had always been there with his encouragement and help throughout my writing career. He always extended an invitation to me to visit him whenever I had the time, and I wanted to interview him for the Miles Davis autobiography I am writing with Davis. I also had heard that Jimmy was quite ill, and I wanted an opportunity to see him again.

On that gray morning I thought of James Baldwin and of the writer Richard Wright, among others, who would never be honored in the United States, as they were abroad, simply because they were Black. On the flight down to Nice, this thought profoundly saddened and troubled me. But by the time I arrived at Nice's Cote d'Azur airport, my spirits had lifted considerably, no doubt due in large measure to the sun-splashed beauty of Nice, but also because David Baldwin, Jimmy's brother, was there at the airport to greet me.

After I had collected my bags, on the way out of the airport, David informed me quite matter-of-factly that Jimmy had cancer and that the prognosis was that it was terminal. "At the most," he said, "the doctor gives him about a month." I was stunned, knocked off balance by the finality of the news and also by David's casual manner. But he added that he and others close by had decided to have an upbeat attitude about everything so that Jimmy's last days could be as normal as possible. David also told me that Jimmy had not been told that his cancer was terminal, although he believed that Jimmy probably knew because of the rapid deterioration of his physical condition. He said he was telling me this to prepare me for the way

Jimmy looked. As he went on in more detail I could see the unspeakable grief etched in the mask that was now his face.

On the winding drive up the mountain to Vence, David asked me to conduct an in-depth interview with Jimmy. Because of Jimmy's rapidly deteriorating condition, David knew that this would be the last opportunity for Jimmy to air his final thoughts and observations. Although that was what I had hoped to do, I hadn't really expected the situation to be as grave as it was.

Just down the hill from the village of St. Paul de Vence, reached by negotiating a narrow twisting road, is the 300-year-old farmhouse of James Baldwin. The red and white St. Paul city-limits sign spots the front-gate entrance to his home. To reach the two-story, light-brown stone-and-stucco house, one must follow a narrow cobblestone path umbrellaed by trees. Entering this comfortable home one is immediately struck by the commanding panoramic view from the dining-room windows. The scene opens out onto the valley below, now dotted with expensive villas. Mountains ring this picturesque valley; it is a beautiful, serene setting.

When I was taken to see Jimmy, who had been moved from the ground-floor wing of the house where he slept and worked to another bedroom that was very dark, I was shocked by his frail and weakened condition. I quickly hugged him and kissed the top of his head. I held him close for a long moment partly because I loved this man and also because I didn't want him to notice the sadness that had welled up into my eyes. But remembering that David had admonished me to "act normally," I quickly pulled myself together and told Jimmy how happy I was to see him. He smiled that brilliant smile of his, his large eyes bright and inquisitive, like those of a child. He told me in a very weak voice that he was convalescing and tired, but would come out to greet me properly in about two or three hours. Then those bright luminous owl eyes burned deeply into mine, as if seeking some clue, some sign that would give him a hint as to the seriousness of his condition. They probed for a moment and then released me from their questioning fire.

I was relieved when David led me out of the darkened house. I will never forget that image of Jimmy weakly sitting there, the feel of his now-wispy hair scratching my face when I hugged him, the birdlike frailty of his ravaged body and the parting telescopic image of him dressed in a red and green plaid robe that all but swallowed him, his large head lolling from one side to the other as his longtime friend, painter Lucien Happersburger, lifted him to put him to bed. It was a profoundly sad and moving experience that is etched indelibly in my mind.

Many articles in the house caught my attention, most notably the many paintings and pieces of sculpture, among them the colorful paintings of the late African-American expatriate painter Beauford Delaney, who had been one of Jimmy's best friends. There were two other pieces that I believed said very much about the political commitment of the man. One, a black pen-and-ink drawing of Nelson Mandela against an orange background, accompanied by a poem, was framed and hung over the dining-room fireplace, the most prominent place in the house. The other was an assemblage created by Jimmy's brother David in his honor. The items in this work were each of distinct interest, but when viewed as a composite, their political statement was obvious and stunning. The centerpiece was the citation of the French Legion of Honor, presented to James Baldwin in January 1986 by President François Mitterand. Beneath the framed citation, on the fireplace mantle and placed on each side of it, was a sword and an old hunting rifle, both pointing toward the certificate. Framed by these two pieces and sitting on the mantle was a black-and-white photograph of Jimmy, an abstract steel sculpture of an Indian pointing a bow and arrow, two crystal inkwells, a figure resembling a guitar and an oversize ink pen pointed directly toward the Legion of Honor citation. Later, when I asked David about the significance of the assemblage, he said, "It was my homage to my brother."

I, too, will miss Jimmy—his profound, courageous and penetrating observations of America, his writings and his fully lived life, which was bountiful and always represented those things that were meaningful and right.

I conducted my interview with him over a period of two days, whenever his physical condition allowed, and our conversations ranged over a variety of literary and political topics. He could not finish our last session because of the pain that overwhelmed him.

One of the last things he said to me was that he hoped that I and other writers would continue to be witnesses of our time; that we must speak out against institutionalized and individual tyranny wherever we found it. Because if left unchecked, it threatens to engulf and subjugate us all—the fire this time. And, of course, he is right. He is right—about the racism, violence and cynical indifference that characterize modern society, and especially the contemporary values that are dominant here in America today.

The following brief excerpts from our interview are some of James Baldwin's last words for publication. Savor them, as I have, from this profoundly human spirit who altered the course of so many lives with his enormous talent, his deep commitment to justice and his abiding love for humanity. He will be deeply missed.

Troupe: You've said you've felt an estrangement between your generation and the country. Why do you think it occurred?

Baldwin: Well, because I was right. That's a strange way to put it, but I *was* right. I was right about what was happening in the country, about what was going to happen to all of us, really. Years ago I began to feel more and more homeless in terms of the whole relationship between France and me and America and me. It has always been a little painful, you know. Since my family's in America, I will always go back. But, in the meantime, I keep the door open, and the price of keeping the door open was to actually be, in a sense, victimized by my own legend. You know, I was trying to tell the truth, and it takes a long time to realize that you can't—that there's no point in going to the mat, so to speak.

Troupe: You've had some serious run-ins with your editors and publishers . . .

Baldwin: Yes. It's very important for white Americans to believe their version of the Black experience. Let me again explain further. Once, after I published *Go Tell It on the Mountain* and *Giovanni's Room*, my publisher, Knopf, told me I was a "Negro writer" and that I reached a certain audience. They told me I could not afford to alienate that audience, and my new book would ruin my career because I was not writing about the same things and in the same manner as I had before. They said they wouldn't publish the book as a favor to me. So I took a boat to England and I sold my book there before I sold it in America. You see whites want Black writers to mostly deliver something as it were an official version of the Black experience. But no true account of Black life can be held, can be contained in the American vocabulary.

Let me tell you another story. After Ralph Ellison won the National Book Award for fiction in 1952 for *Invisible Man*, I was up for it the next year, in 1953, for *Go Tell It on the Mountain*. I didn't win. Then, years later, someone who was on the jury told me that since Ralph won it the year before they couldn't give it to a "Negro" two years in a row. Now, isn't that something?

Troupe: You said something to me once about how people shouldn't be jealous of someone's success. Do you recall that?

Baldwin: Well, what I was really trying to say was that people don't know what it is sometimes to be very successful. I meant that you can't be jealous of somebody else's success because you have no idea what it means. It looks like success to you, but you're not the one who's paying for it.

Troupe: And there's a price?

Baldwin: Of course there's a price. It's rough. For most great Black writers, in general, white and Black Americans won't read us until they have nothing else to read.

Troupe: Why do you think that is?

Baldwin: Well, because of the entire way of American life, the marrow of the American bone. There's nothing to be done about it. The whole American reality is based on the necessity of keeping Black people out of it. We are nonexistent. Except according to their terms, and their terms are unacceptable.

Troupe: How do you think white Americans feel now that they're in this economic crisis?

Baldwin: They're not thinking about it. Americans don't think of such things. They hope they'll go away. Because it's like a bad dream for them. They don't know how they got into it or, worse, won't recognize how. They don't know how they got into the chaos of their cities, for example. But they did it—because they wanted their children to be safe, to be raised safely. So they set up their communities so that they wouldn't have to go to school with Black children, whom they fear. And that dictates the structure of their cities, the chaos of their cities and the danger in which they live. They did it, inch by inch, stone by stone, decree by decree. Now their kids are deeply lost, and they can't even blame it on Black people.

They're trapped. And nothing will spring the trap, nothing. the world is present, and the world is not white, and America is not the symbol of civilization. Neither is England. Neither is France. Something else is happening that will engulf them by and by. You, Quincy, will be here, but I'll be gone. It's the only hope the world has—that Western hegemony and civilization be contained.

Index

A

Achebe, Chinua, 210–21, 255; *Things Fall Apart*, 211, 214, 255
Africa, 7, 13, 16, 17, 34, 35, 40, 71, 85, 86, 113, 135, 149, 151, 176, 227, 246
African aesthetic, 212–14, 218–21
Agnew, Spiro T., 91, 94, 99, 127, 145
Albany, N.Y., 94
Algeria, 135, 164, 175, 225, 268
Andrews, Raymond, *Apalachee Red,* 175
Angelou, Maya, *I Know Why the Caged Bird Sings,* 198
Anti-Defamation League, 64
Arendt, Hannah, 75
Atlanta, Ga., 172, 187, 188, 195
Attica, 109

B

Bach, Johann Sebastian, 176
Baldwin, David (brother), 90, 160, 241, 242, 278
Baldwin, David (father), 47, 48, 78, 91, 122, 123, 142, 143, 151, 161, 201, 234, 235, 238, 240
Baldwin, Emma (mother), 77, 78, 151, 161, 162, 197, 199, 201, 246, 247
Baldwin, James, on apartheid, 62; on the artist vs celebrity, 230, 231; on artistic problems and pressures, 34, 103, 104, 109–11, 156, 162, 163, 200, 229, 230, 275; on audience, 110, 280, 285, 290; autobiographical influence on writing, 163, 190, 191, 205, 206, 242–44, 246, 247, 249, 276–79; Baldwin Prize for fiction, 175; on being a writer, 14, 15, 21, 234, 251, 273; on the black church, 4, 182; on the black family, 9, 157, 196, 220; on the black woman, 9, 10, 195–97; on the black man, 9, 10, 15, 40, 41, 196, 197; on black movies, 129; on black power, 60, 61; on

black pride, 91, 92; on black women writers, 197, 198; childhood, 5, 38–40, 46–48, 198, 199; on Civil Rights Movement, 35, 36, 38, 41–43, 60, 62, 63, 68–71, 93, 94, 102, 111, 112, 145, 146, 173, 174, 178–81, 257; on desegregation, 69, 70, 174, 175, 215; on the division of labor, 20, 21, 129, 178, 187, 200; on the education of youth, 15, 72; on the enslavement of blacks, 52, 61, 95, 116, 121, 122, 184, 215; family, 47, 77, 78, 89, 161, 162, 197–99, 201, 202, 234, 235, 256; formative influences, 102, 163, 198, 236, 247; on the future of America, 26, 27, 45, 81, 82, 102, 140, 172, 181–84, 195, 286, 291, 292; on the inter-dependence of black American and African artists, 168, 169; on intra-racial unity, 36, 45, 48, 50–52, 66, 96, 99, 128, 152, 173; on literary critics, 34, 103, 104, 165, 166, 206, 252, 253, 291; love of country, 33, 164, 250, 251, 265, 266, 282; major themes: coping with sexuality, 8, 9, 11, 34, 49, 54, 55, 72, 79, 80, 183, 184; excavating history, 14, 21, 26, 44, 45, 62, 73, 74, 90, 95, 100, 115, 116, 118, 120, 150, 151, 170, 188, 191–94, 250, 252, 280; discovering identity, 4–6, 16, 23, 26, 27, 39, 40, 47, 48, 50, 51, 73–76, 79, 147, 180, 181, 182; saving the children, 126, 158, 160, 173, 226, 227; on the necessity of writing, 31, 106, 110, 161, 166, 201, 245; on political vs artistic responsibilities, 199, 207; on the process of writing, 162, 163, 165, 205, 236, 239, 240, 242–46, 248, 249, 251; relationship between the poet and the people, 155, 156, 187, 217, 218; responsibilities of a writer: destroying myths, 26; disturbing the peace, 21, 154, 155, 171, 178; criticizing society, 155, 156, 162; fusing image and reality, 31, 208, 209; recognizing the possibilities of love, 7, 48, 49, 101, 177, 206, 236, 237; telling the truth, 20, 21, 23,

293

Index 297

Stein, Gertrude, 254
Stowe, Harriet Beecher, *Uncle Tom's Cabin*, 253
Strauss, Richard, 30
Streisand, Barbra, 193
Student Non-Violent Coordinating Committee (SNCC), 61
Styron, William, 228, 229, 247, 248, 279; *Confessions of Nat Turner*, 228, 247, 248, 279
Switzerland, 3, 4, 163, 238

T

Tallahassee, Fla., 19, 43, 70
Thatcher, Margaret, 192, 258
Thomas, Piri, *Down These Mean Streets*, 206
Till, Emmett, 165
Time, 257, 261, 263
Tokyo, Japan, 84, 90
Tolstoy, Leo, *Anna Karenina*, 272
Toomer, Jean, 223; *Caine*, 207
Tubman, Harriet, 9

U

Underground railway, 9
United Nations, 71
University of Florida, 210
Updike, John, 228, 248, 249

V

Van Peebles, Melvin, 129
Vietnam, 61, 90, 130, 134–36, 148, 149, 166, 218, 266, 267, 269

W

Wallace, George C., 92, 112
Waller, Fats, 163
Washington, Booker T., 147
Washington, D. C., 13, 60, 69, 94
Washington Post, 119
Watergate, 265
Wayne, John, 99
West Africa, 131
West Side Story, 86
Women's Liberation Movement, 197
Wonder, Stevie, 152
Worthy, William, 64
Wright, Richard, 10, 14, 53, 67, 164, 196, 202–04, 207, 223–25, 247, 253, 254, 284, 287; *American Hunger*, 204; *Black Boy*, 204; "Bright and Morning Star," 223; *Lawd Today*, 204, 254; "Man of All Work," 10, 196; *Native Son*, 203, 204, 223, 254; *Uncle Tom's Children*, 223

Y

Yale University, 261
Yugoslavia, 87